Theory of the Global S|
Globality as Unfinishec

This ambitious study rewrites   ｇ.ｖｖａ liza-
tion. Martin Shaw argues that t   ｊ ｕｕ. meaning of globality is the
growing sense of worldwide human commonality as a practical
social force, arising from political struggle not technological change.
The book focusses upon two new concepts: the unfinished global-
democratic revolution and the global-Western state. Shaw shows
how an internationalized, post-imperial Western state conglomerate,
symbiotically linked to global institutions, is increasingly consolidated amidst worldwide democratic upheavals against authoritarian,
quasi-imperial non-Western states. This study explores the radical
implications of these concepts for social, political and international
theory, through a fundamental critique of modern 'national-international' social thought and dominant economistic versions of global
theory. Required reading for sociology and politics as well as
international relations, *Theory of the Global State* offers a historical,
theoretical and political framework for understanding state and
society in the emerging global age.

MARTIN SHAW is Professor of International Relations and Politics at
the University of Sussex. His recent publications include *Civil Society
and Media in Global Crises* (1996), *Global Society and International
Relations* (1994), *Post-Military Society* (1991) and *Dialectics of War*
(1988). He is editor of www.theglobalsite.ac.uk.

CAMBRIDGE STUDIES IN INTERNATIONAL RELATIONS: 73

Theory of the Global State

CAMBRIDGE STUDIES IN INTERNATIONAL RELATIONS

Series list continues at the end of the book

Theory of the Global State

Globality as Unfinished Revolution

Martin Shaw

CAMBRIDGE
UNIVERSITY PRESS

PUBLISHED BY THE PRESS SYNDICATE OF THE UNIVERSITY OF CAMBRIDGE
The Pitt Building, Trumpington Street, Cambridge, United Kingdom

CAMBRIDGE UNIVERSITY PRESS
The Edinburgh Building, Cambridge CB2 2RU, UK
40 West 20th Street, New York, NY 10011–4211, USA
477 Williamstown Road, Port Melbourne, VIC 3207, Australia
Ruiz de Alarcón 13, 28014 Madrid, Spain
Dock House, The Waterfront, Cape Town 8001, South Africa

http://www.cambridge.org

First published 2000
Reprinted 2002

Printed in the United Kingdom at the University Press, Cambridge

Typeset in Palatino 10 /12.5pt   [CE]

A catalogue record for this book is available from the British Library

ISBN 0 521 59250 X hardback
ISBN 0 521 59730 7 paperback

12624594

Contents

Part IV   Conclusion

Preface

This book offers a theoretical and historical synthesis of the politics of globality. It reflects my deep dissatisfaction with the ways in which the social scientists have so far grasped the meaning of 'global' change. The book is ambitious in its range and, because it touches on a considerable variety of materials, may not always satisfy specialists. I can only hope that, even where its specific judgements need to be qualified, its critical thrust will provoke serious reflection on the ways in which we understand (and act in) the world of the twenty-first century.

The book reflects my own institutional movement in the social sciences, from a sociological to an international relations context. It has involved a deeper engagement with the international literature, yet this has not shaken me in my belief that the perspectives of a historically oriented sociology offer a breadth of understanding that international relationists do not always achieve. At the same time, I remain unhappy about the gulf that still exists between 'global' theorizing in sociology and the work of historical sociologists, much of which has underestimated the scope of contemporary historical change. The sense that there is still a fundamental critical task, to shift the ways in which we think about the global, is what has made this book return repeatedly to the level of concepts rather than turn fully to the empirical exploration of global state power.

This book introduces new categories, and there is always a danger that readers who do not engage with the text as a whole will take these out of context. The title headlines 'the global state': the text makes it clear that I do not believe that this has been or is likely to be achieved in any simple sense. The title could as easily (but less

catchily) have referred to 'the Western-global state', since what I place
at the centre of my analysis is the symbiotic relationship between the
consolidation of a single dominant Western centre of state power and
the development of a more all-encompassing and legitimate global
layer of power. It could also have referred to 'contradictions of the
global state', since I argue that a complex global state structure is
being formed through fundamental and often violent political struggles. I have settled for the simplest main title, bearing in mind that
books with obscure titles often languish in obscurity, but I hope that
readers will not mistake this character of the title for that of the
argument.

   This book has been written through a transition that has been
geographic and personal as well as disciplinary. I wish to thank my
international relations colleagues and students at Sussex for their
stimulating intellectual comradeship and criticism. This has helped
me to develop the ideas of this book from their simpler early forms (in
which they were inflicted on my erstwhile sociological colleagues at
Hull). Burdens of academic leadership undoubtedly slowed down the
writing, but in a curious way may have helped the ideas to mature. I
wish to thank the series editor, Steve Smith, and my editor at the
Press, John Haslam, for their almost infinite patience with the consequent delays. I wish to express my thanks to various conference and
symposium organizers and editors who have given space to earlier
versions of this argument. I particularly thank Meghnad Desai and
the Centre for the Study of Global Governance at LSE, who published
my paper (given at the 1993 British International Studies Association
conference) as *The Global State and the Politics of Intervention* as long
ago as 1994; Mary Kaldor, of Sussex and the LSE Centre, for many
opportunities to test my arguments against her own ideas on 'new
wars'; my colleague Ronen Palan and the other editors of the *Review of
International Political Economy,* in which the core of the present argument was further developed, in 'The state of globalization' (4(3) 1997:
497–513); the editors of *Millennium,* at whose twenty-fifth anniversary
conference in 1996 I presented 'The state of international relations',
which appears in the collection edited by Sarah Owen-Vandersluis,
State and Identity Construction in International Relations (London: Macmillan, 2000, pp. 7–30); as well as the University of Sussex, at which I
presented a belated inaugural lecture, 'The unfinished global revolution: intellectuals and the new politics of international relations', on 9
November 1999, the tenth anniversary of the fall of the Berlin Wall,

published at *The global site*, http://www.theglobalsite.ac.uk (this lecture contributes to chapter 9).

Above all, Annabel's love has helped me to find the calm and warmth in which I have thrived. Together with Tom and Isabel, Kate and Fred, she has sustained me in the writing of this book.

1 Introduction: globality in historical perspective

At the beginning of the twenty-first century, there is a sense of living in a period of great change, which goes far beyond the coincidence of the new millennium. As ever in the modern world, there is a sense of traditional cultures and institutions under challenge from remorseless technological change and commercial expansion. At the same time, there is a profound sense of a significant historical movement: that the processes of change in our time are different from those that, in earlier periods, have made modernity.

There is deep uncertainty, however, about the definition of change. It is not clear what kind of transition this is, what sort of world it is producing, or whether it is desirable. Although there is a widespread sense of transformation, the problem of understanding is exacerbated by the difficulty of applying previous concepts of change to the new situation. As in all big transitions, the nature of change is a part of the novelty of the change itself. To illustrate this point, I shall explain later why the concept of revolution is appropriate to the current transformation. But this is not just another revolution in the sense in which revolutions have been understood in the nineteenth and twentieth centuries. In the present transition, the nature and meaning of revolution are also changing.

The aim of this book is therefore no less than an answer to the question of defining the change that is taking place. In the first chapter I give a general outline of the historical and conceptual problems. In the following chapters, I first indicate the comprehensive nature of the theoretical challenge posed by the transition from a national-and-international to a global world. Second, I develop a historical account of the current transition, outlining the interactions between structural transformations of state power and popular movements. Third, I discuss the developing state structure of globality, together with the problems of its coherence, which are of profound importance to the future of human society. Finally, I address the politics of unfinished global revolution.

This book proposes, therefore, that we should understand our historical transformation through three major concepts: *globality*, the *global revolution* and the *global state*. In this chapter I attempt to explain the need for these concepts, by examining existing models of contemporary change. First, I discuss three narratives of transition that have been bequeathed to us from late twentieth-century debate: postmodernity, the end of the Cold War and globalization. By locating these three narratives historically, I attempt to show the limitations of their understandings of the transition. Second, I examine the concepts of change that are involved in these narratives: transformation, transition and process. I advance my concept of global revolution as a more inclusive concept that embraces all three aspects. Third, I discuss the meaning of globality itself.

Three narratives of transition

As the sense of transformation grew at the end of the twentieth century, three kinds of narrative achieved wide currency. The accounts overlapped, but they have been only partially related to each other. Although versions of the narratives coexist in contemporary literature, they appear to have risen to prominence in a particular sequence. Each has come to dominate both public and academic debate in a given phase of the late twentieth-century historical transition. Understanding the sequence of the three narratives helps us towards a deeper understanding of the character of the transition itself, of which each is only a partial reflection.

The first idea was that of *postmodernity*. Its core was the denial of the certainties of the modern world. From a postmodern point of view, the only certain thing was that the old forms should no longer be considered fixed reference points. In postmodern accounts, the flux was the thing. However, the process of change could not be encapsulated in a single concept, leading to a new consensus. Postmodernism challenged all traditional models of understanding, denying itself the status of a new 'meta-narrative' of change. Zygmunt Bauman, its foremost sociological exponent, articulated the intimate links of postmodernity to modernity by proposing that '[t]he postmodern condition can be . . . described, on the one hand, as modernity emancipated from false consciousness'. However, he is less convincing when he argues that it can be described 'on the other, as a new type . . . a self-reproducing, pragmatically self-sustainable and logically self-contained social condition defined by distinctive features of its own'.[1] For many, the idea that there is a definite postmodern 'social condition' is a contradiction in terms.

These built-in tensions of postmodernity mean that its theorists oscillate between the denial of certain meaning, an echo of earlier 'nihilist' philosophies, and the assertion of new meaning, which reconnects to the emancipatory tradition of modernity. Thus Bauman denies that it is a simple negation of modernity: 'A theory of postmodernity . . . cannot be a modified theory of modernity, a theory of modernity with a set of negative markers.'[2] However, he confirms its negativity with the striking claim that 'The theory of postmodernity must be free of the metaphor of progress that informed all competing theories of modern society.'[3]

The second idea was that of *a post-Cold War world*. This reflected the apparently dramatic significance of changes in international politics. At the centre of post-Cold War narratives was the idea that winding down political and military conflict between blocs would involve fundamental transformations of political – and hence perhaps social and cultural – relations in general. One strand of post-Cold War thought advanced shallow claims for the victory of a particular version of the modernity which postmodern theorists questioned. According to Francis Fukuyama, the 'Worldwide Liberal Revolution' left 'only one competitor standing in the ring as an ideology of potentially universal validity: liberal democracy, the doctrine of individual freedom and popular sovereignty'. Liberalism was defined 'simply' (Fukuyama acknowledged) as 'a rule of law that recognizes certain individual rights or freedoms from government control', democracy by 'a strictly formal definition' stressing procedurality.[4] However, most post-Cold War accounts were more open-ended. Thus the international relationist James N. Rosenau argued that the new stage was one of 'post-international' politics, characterized by a fundamental 'turbulence' as a variety of new actors entered the arena.[5] As with postmodern accounts, the indeterminacy of change

---

[1] Bauman (1992: 188).   [2] Bauman (1992: 187–8).
[3] Bauman (1992: 189).   [4] Fukuyama (1992: 44).   [5] Rosenau (1990).

was important to such articulations of the 'post-Cold War' idea. The literature expressed, but did not generally resolve, this tension between the realization of modernist goals such as democracy, and the novelty (sometimes even taking 'regressive' forms) of the politics of the new era.

The third idea was, of course, that of *globalization*. This emphasized technical, economic and cultural transformations that were 'undermining' the significance of boundaries between nation-states. This narrative was often presented as a new certainty. It reflected, its proponents suggested, powerful, indeed unstoppable social forces, which were weakening traditional forms. Globalization appears more determinate than the other two accounts. Whereas their names imply no more than going beyond existing forms – whether of modernity in general or of the Cold War in particular – globalization suggests a positive content, a quality of the 'global' which social relations are acquiring. However, the one thing that few globalization theorists define is the meaning of the global. The idea of globalization appears as a step towards determinacy, but at its heart is still a basic uncertainty about the meaning of change.

The difference between 'postmodern' and 'global' concepts is therefore often less than might appear. Many 'global' theorists embrace the indeterminacy of postmodernity; conversely, postmodernists, when pressed to give a name to the 'new' condition, cite globality. Thus Jacques Derrida agreed, in response to questioning, that the political phenomena to which he refers are what are conventionally called 'globalization'. He explained that he didn't use the name 'globalization',

> Because today it's a confused concept and it's the screen for a number of non-concepts and sometimes of political tricks and political strategies. Of course something like globalization is happening – not only today of course, it started a long time ago – but today there is an acceleration of this *mondialization*, but as you know, using this word, this key word, allows a number of political appropriations – in the name of the free market for instance. People try to have us swallow the idea that globalization means the free market, or that the concentration of tele-technological communications beyond the States are what makes globalization possible, and should be supported or simply accepted. So I have, and I'm not the only one, many, many, reservations about the use one makes of this word: but I agree . . . this is, if not the ground (because I don't think it is a ground), but this is the space in which these problems take their

4

shape. I agree . . . but I wouldn't simply rely upon the word 'globalization' in order to name this phenomenon.[6]

Postmodernity and globalization both began to emerge as serious concepts of change in the 1970s.[7] This was the decade of *détente*, the period in which Cold War rivalries appeared to have relaxed, yet the crisis of the post-war boom produced great global economic instability, and there was a widespread sense of the dissolution of traditional cultural and social relations. The idea of the post-Cold War became a part of discussion later, when at the beginning of the 1980s the final phase of the Cold War heightened the sense of needing to move beyond its dangerous and constricting environment.[8]

In the 1970s, however, although there was a widespread sense of crisis and dissolution after the relative stability of earlier post-war decades, there was not yet a strong feeling of *transition*. Indeed the Second Cold War of the early 1980s reinforced awareness of a definite world structure, after the loosening of the previous decade. It was only when this faded, in the middle of the 1980s, that the sense of transition came into its own. It is from this point onwards that we can trace the definite influence of narratives of change.

First, postmodernism came to dominate a wide area of cultural and social debate in the mid- to late 1980s. Postmodern ideas were influential first in aesthetic discourses, from literature to architecture, but later came to affect social and political debates. Second, post-Cold War discourse gained credence in the late 1980s and the beginning of the 1990s, as *perestroika* was followed by the east European revolutions, the fall of the Berlin Wall, the collapse of the Soviet Union and the Gulf and Yugoslav wars. Third, globalization became dominant in the mid- and late 1990s, as the realities of increasingly global markets

---

[6] Derrida (1997). This was part of his response to my question: 'You don't seem to be able to name the process through which [political transformations are] happening, and it seems to me that one could understand what you're talking about in terms of globalization, the formation of a common social space, a single world-meaning within which all these old structures which try to absolutize and fix differences are changed, but this, it also seems to me, is a ground on which to found a new form of democracy, and that ground has to be found in the concept of globality and in the concept of world unification.'

[7] Anderson (1998: 15–46) gives the best account to date of this process, but he goes on (1998: 47–76) to make the more contestable claim that the debate was subsequently 'captured' by Frederic Jameson (1998).

[8] Thompson (1981) was an important early statement of this idea.

and communications seemed to eclipse (at least partially) the significance of the residual divisions between states.

The sequence of influence of these three grand ideas of the late twentieth-century changes is suggestive of the relations between them. Postmodernism, the least determinate of the three narratives – the one which emphasized uncertainty, relativism and fragmentation even to the point of celebrating them – came to the fore in advance of political change. As often in periods of transition, the strongest early intimations of change appear in culture – before politics or economics – but these are also the least clear indicators of the eventual shape of the new order.

Post-Cold War discourse, which was more determinate in centring the transition in key political and military changes, dominated during and immediately after the major political upheavals. It reflected the moment in which the 'new world order' of President Bush appeared to promise the 'end of history' which Fukuyama rashly proclaimed.[9] During this period there was a general optimism, even if many commentators were not so certain that the content of a post-Cold War world could be encapsulated in the comfortable verities of traditional liberalism.

Globalization, in turn, became dominant once the political transition ceased to impress, and the most pervasive forms of change appeared to be located in the expansion of market relations, ubiquitous commodification and the communications revolution that mediated them. The global remained largely undefined, however, because the content of globalization seemed little more than a speeding-up of the marketization of the previous, neo-liberal decade. The global meant principally, it seemed, the negation of the national boundaries which had defined the old order; it did not have a core meaning of its own.

We can understand these three accounts of change, therefore, as partial narratives of the same large set of events and processes, the same world-historical transition. Each overlaps with the others, while emphasizing aspects which the others tend to downplay. All of them are suggestive but none is adequate as an overall account of the change that has marked the end of the twentieth century. What they suggest are the need for, first, an integrated historical account which links the postmodern, post-Cold War and global moments, and

[9] Fukuyama (1992).

second, a more careful investigation of the only positive meaning which the transition has thrown up, the idea of the global.

Conceptualizing change

The debates of the late twentieth century have left considerable uncertainty about the ways in which contemporary change should be conceptualized. Uncertainty exists not only about the direction and meaning of change, but also about how change itself should be represented. This is a fundamental issue: the means and forms through which change occurs are important as both determinants and indicators of the content of change.

The three narratives suggest different understandings of this issue. For postmodern theorists, change is above all *transformation*. The very forms of cultural, social and political life are altering in a plurality of directions that were not, and could not have been, previously conceived. The whole point of the postmodern conceptualization is the denial of a unified process, let alone a single transition. Postmodern accounts suggest the diffuse, fragmentary dissolution of previously fixed relations, institutions and traditions.

For post-Cold War theorists, at the heart of contemporary change there is a very definite *transition* – or a set of transitions – from Cold War to post-Cold War, from history to post-history, from nation-state to newly legitimate international institutions. Despite the commendable reluctance of some early post-Cold War thinkers to foreclose the nature of change, the idea of transition has become entrenched, particularly in debate in and about the post-Communist, market societies in the former Soviet bloc.

For globalization theorists, contemporary change often has the relentless aspect of a single *process* – or a closely related set of processes – through which the market system colonizes new social space. Globalization renders territorial boundaries irrelevant – or in the more cautious versions which have become increasingly prominent, less significant. It also nullifies the cultural, political and technical boundaries that defined distinct worlds, isolated some social relations from world markets, and inhibited communications.

The three accounts of change correspond to the social arenas that they specify as core. In postmodern narratives, cultural change tends to be central to political and social change, and cultural change appears naturally as relatively diffuse transformation. For post-Cold

War narratives, political and military changes are central to wider social and economic changes, and these changes appear more as defined transition. For globalization narratives, technical and economic changes are central to cultural and political changes, and these changes appear as process.

Each of these images corresponds to important aspects of change at the beginning of the twenty-first century. Each, by emphasizing certain major areas and qualities of change, makes a contribution to our understanding. But each, by de-emphasizing other major areas and qualities, places obstacles in the way of our understanding the change of our times in its entirety. We need a new concept of change that suggests its broad, inclusive but uneven character. I propose that the concept of *global revolution* can be developed to encompass all these demands on our understanding.

The concept of revolution is now loosely, and sometimes trivially, employed to suggest radical or fundamental change in any field. My proposal should not be seen as trying to legislate its broader usage, but as a serious attempt to encapsulate the breadth and depth of contemporary *social* change. The global revolution differs in important respects from national and international revolutions, as I shall explain later in this book. But my use of the term suggests that contemporary change can be understood through an expansion of this classic historical social and political concept.

In particular, I use the term revolution in order to suggest that the political-military transitions of the current period have a particular significance for the development of cultural, economic and technical processes and transformations. The rupture in recent world politics has a meaning for the broad, general processes of global change that has hardly been grasped. The global revolution involves a transformation of social relations in general, but at its heart are key upheavals in relations of political and military power. As in classic revolutions, it is the connections between wider social and more narrowly political processes that give the changes of our times their distinctive revolutionary character.

So far, I have used domain terms such as economic, social, cultural, political and military as if their meanings were clear and self-evident. I am aware that they are not: these meanings change, and changes in them are important to the character of the global revolution. In my argument, the global revolution is not constituted by changes in given political or state spheres that alternately reflect and influence given spheres of economic and cultural life. As Michael Mann has written, in important transitions, the very meanings of terms such as 'society' undergo transformation.[10] In this book I want to explain how both changing meanings of, and relations between, culture, economy, society and state are involved in the fundamental changes of our time.

The meaning of global

If we are to understand the global revolution, we must first extricate the idea of the global from simple concepts of the process of globalization.[11] As I have already suggested, the latter term logically implies an understanding of the former: globalization must be the way in which things are made global. Yet it is evident, as I have noted, that the meaning of the global is often uncertain in the literature. I will go further: where it is specified, it is often simple and impoverished. In order to define 'global', I will first examine what seem to be the common ways in which this term is used. I will then discuss how we might expand our understanding. In this way, the definition of the global will lead us to the concept of globality, the first main concept of this book.

We can identify three accounts of the meaning of global that are implicated in recent debates about globalization. In much social-scientific as well as everyday usage, global is used interchangeably with world and international simply to indicate *areas of social life beyond the national level*. This weak, vague usage clearly reflects thought which has hardly begun to grapple with the distinctiveness of global relations. In this way of thinking, the difference between global and international cannot really be indicated, and a 'global world' is a tautology. The use of the word global rather than the other terms is little more than homage to intellectual fashion.

Beyond this confusion, the first substantive meaning is connected to the literal meaning of the word, belonging to the globe. Here global means *connected with the natural habitat of humankind*, our global planet, Earth. The understanding of the world as round is a fundamental tenet of distinctively modern thought. In recent decades, however, images of the world from outer space have enabled us to visualize the

---

[10] Mann (1993: 9).
[11] In this sense, I agree with the comment of Derrida (1997), quoted above, on the function of the word 'globalization'.

planet's global aspect very concretely. This understanding has been powerfully reinforced by many new insights into relationships between human social activity and the natural environment as a whole. Thus the new environmental literature is paradigmatic of global social science, in its disregard for – or relegation to secondary status of – national boundaries.[12]

Even more widespread, and more directly connected to the technological, economic and communications mainstreams of globalization debate, is a concept of the global as *the quality involved in the worldwide stretching of social relations*. In this concept, global social relations are relations that spread easily across the world, again increasingly disregarding national boundaries. Whereas the environmental concept of the global stresses the connection between human activity and nature, this concept is defined by transformations of human relations themselves, in which the changing relation to the natural environment is only one part.

According to Giddens, for example, the transformation of time-space relations means that social linkages are not merely spread over long distances but also intensified – leading to instantaneous worldwide connections. For him, 'globalization can . . . be defined as the intensification of worldwide social relations which link distant localities in such a way that local happenings are shaped by events occurring many miles away and vice versa'.[13] For many, what is also involved is the spread of a supraterritorial dimension of social relations.[14]

Both the environmental and the time-spatial concepts of the global give it a content beyond the confused equation with world or international. The environmental concept indicates that an important dimension of common global consciousness is our recognition of the physical habitat that we share. However, in some versions of it, a primacy of nature is proposed: human activity is seen as a problem for the planet. This interpretation of the global can lead, then, to the subordination of human society to the physical environment.

Compared with this, the spatial, or time-space, concept is more sophisticated. Nature, in Giddens' account for example, is no longer raw and unmediated, but socially transformed. Our altered relations with this socialized nature are part of the general transformation of

---

[12] See for example Smith and Warr (1991).
[13] Giddens (1990: 64).   [14] Scholte (1999: 11–14).

our social relations. However, accounts which emphasize spatial stretching still have too little to say about the content of global relations. Global relations are essentially more instant, long-distance, versions of pre-global relations, with the new dimensions that speed and density bring to interconnection. In so far as changed qualities of relations are recognized, they are seen as consequences of these essentially technical changes in the mechanisms of social life.

The global quality of social relations, in both these accounts, is seen as the result of cumulative changes in people's relations with each other and their physical environment. In essence, society has been globalized not because human beings thought or acted globally, but because in pursuit of other ends – profit, power, communication – worldwide connectedness has developed.

Of course, there is a large measure of truth in such an account. Whatever it is, the global aspect of social relations has not developed simply or mainly because most people had very clearly defined, specifically global aims and intentions. If it had, we would understand it much more easily and we would hardly need to argue so much about its meaning. So we must accept that the environmental and spatial accounts indicate important dimensions of the meaning of global. But have they grasped its core?

Held and McGrew provide a suggestive amplification of the spatial concept when they write: 'Globalization refers to an historical process which transforms the spatial organization of social relations and transactions, generating transcontinental or inter-regional networks of interaction *and the exercise of power.*'[15] As my emphasis suggests, the novel aspect of their definition is not the specification of worldwide as 'transcontinental or inter-regional' – a formulation which amplifies the spatial conception into a specific hierarchy of nations, continents/ regions and world – but the introduction of power into the definition. However, once again the content of the global transformation of power is not defined except in spatial terms.

Although the meaning of global is embedded in the largely spatial relations described by these partial concepts, in the more developed usages of the term it is also more than them. By global, we mean not just transformed conceptions of time and space but the new social meaning that these have involved. I propose that we understand this as the development of *a common consciousness of human society on a*

---

[15] Held and McGrew (1998: 220), emphasis added.

world scale. We mean an increasing awareness of the totality of human social relations as the largest constitutive framework of all relations. We mean that society is increasingly constituted primarily by this inclusive human framework – rather than by distinct tribes, civilizations, nations or religious communities, although all of these remain in increasingly complex and overlapping ways within global society.

Social relations become global, therefore, when they are significantly and systematically informed by an awareness of the common framework of worldwide human society. Society becomes global when this becomes its dominant, constitutive framework. Awareness of a common framework in human society is not new, of course: this idea has been one of the driving forces of modernity. The distinction between global and pre-global is therefore that, with the development of global relations, the understanding of human relations in a common worldwide frame comes to *predominate* over other, more partial understandings.

It may be properly asked, of course, how far this in fact is the case? How far has a global society actually come into existence? How far does the global definition of society prevail over other definitions? When and how did this happen? These are questions that I shall examine in more detail later in this book. If we accept that the global has a distinctive social meaning, however, beyond its environmental and time-spatial senses, we will look for its origins and manifestations in different places from those examined by both globalization *and* anti-globalization thought.

Fallacies of the globalization debate

Both globalization thinkers and their critics have tended to make two central mistakes indicated by our discussion so far. First, they have tended to see the global in terms of an essentially linear process, or linear processes, of globalization. Second, they have tended to fail to define the global, and hence have adopted (often implicitly) one of the restricted meanings that we have discussed. Because both proponents and critics have misunderstood the significance of the global, they have exchanged false antinomies, in an increasingly sterile disagreement.[16]

Two further principal fallacies can be identified at the heart of this debate. The first concerns the relationships between technology,

[16] See Held et al. (1999: 2–14).

economy and culture on the one hand and politics on the other. According to some globalizers, some kinds of technology, market relations and standardized cultural forms have become so powerful that states – or even political actors generally – have been weakened and marginalized and borders have become, more or less, irrelevant.[17] According to some anti-globalizers, if it can be shown that states remain influential and borders significant, then the globalization thesis has been brought seriously into question, if not refuted.[18]

Both sides of the debate have mistakenly assumed that economic and cultural change could transform politics in the sense of cause and effect. The elementary mistake here is the idea that, in the modern world, there are highly autonomous spheres of economics, culture and politics. In reality, to the extent that we can identify these spheres they are mutually constituted to very large degrees. It is simply implausible that there could have been significant technical, commercial or cultural change without important political antecedents and concomitants, as well as effects.

If these propositions are accepted, it follows that both globalization and anti-globalization positions tend towards conceptual naïvety. It literally does not make sense to propose that economic or cultural globalization could by itself undermine the nation-state, without specifically political transformations actively influencing the process. Powerful institutions such as states do not keel over at the sight of a multinational corporation, a worldwide market or a new communications technology. The activities of corporations, the markets in which they and others operate, and the technologies which are developed, all pose challenges to state institutions. Conversely, of course, if we accept that there are important processes of technological, economic and cultural change, it is inconceivable that states would remain essentially unchanged, wielding power in virtually the same ways as before.

The second, related fallacy of the debate is the idea that *global and national-international categories are inherently opposed.* According to some globalizers, a global world is one in which the national organization of economies and cultures is rapidly diminished in significance. Internationally structured relations have been replaced by more fluid, global relations. According to some anti-globalizers, if it can be shown

---

[17] Ohmae (1990).   [18] Hirst and Thompson (1996).

that national and international forms and relations remain of great significance, then globalization in any strong sense cannot be true.

Let us take as an example the argument about whether world trade is more or less internationalized now than in previous periods. Globalizers argue that goods as well as money flow across boundaries more than in any previous period. Anti-globalizers claim that before 1914 there were levels of international integration and openness as high, or almost as high, as at the end of the twentieth century, so what is new?[19]

Let us look at what is being measured here. First, the meaning of international trade (i.e. across state boundaries) might be expected to be somewhat different in today's world of many, often small, nation-states compared with the much smaller number of states, the most important of which were world empires, that existed at the beginning of the twentieth century. Second and more fundamentally, if global really means something different from international, how can globalization possibly be measured by the balance of national and international commerce?

In reality, what this example shows us is the poverty of the understanding of the global in most globalization debates. Globalizers and anti-globalizers alike assume that trade within a national economy is non-global, while that across national state boundaries is global. We can make no such assumptions, however. The evidence produced demonstrates little about the global or non-global content of either intra- or international trade. Mostly what it shows is the unsurprising – and unenlightening – fact that trade is still measured in national and international terms.

Neither side of this argument grapples seriously with the ways in which, on the one hand, global change involves transformations of national and international relations, and on the other, changed national and international relations go to make up much of what constitutes the global. Just as the simple antinomy of economics-culture and politics is beside the point, so is that of national-international and global. Both are false oppositions in which neither side can win the argument, because neither has understood the nature of the changes in social relations in our time – or the meaning of globality.

---

[19] Hirst and Thompson (1996: 49). Held et al. (1999) provide a balanced survey of this and related issues, which disputes this contention.

Grasping the revolution

To describe the changes through which we are living as a global revolution involves a very different assessment of the starting point, character and direction of change from conventional accounts of globalization. It also involves a radically different concept of the relationships between economic and cultural change, on the one hand, and political and military change, on the other. Although the term revolution is increasingly used in a loose sense, to indicate any radical change, it has had more or less precise meanings in the social-scientific literature. The sense in which the term is used here takes these as a starting-point.

Three main theses have been widely agreed. First, social revolutions, in which there are far-reaching transformations of social relations, may be distinguished from political revolutions, in which states are transformed without correspondingly fundamental changes in society.[20] Second, while political revolutions may not entail deep social upheavals, social revolutions necessarily involve political change: 'Virtually everyone who writes about social revolutions recognizes that they begin with overtly political causes . . . . And it is recognized that they culminate in the consolidation of new state organizations.'[21] Or as Lenin wrote, 'The basic question of every revolution is that of state power.'[22] Third, although revolutions are widely interpreted as products of international trends, the form of revolution has been national: they take place in geopolitical contexts that clearly define 'internal' and 'external'.[23] The defining moments of revolutions are constitutive changes in national social and political structures.

The relationship between national and international aspects of revolutions is now better understood. Revolutions not only represent national manifestations of more general, loosely international, social contradictions, as Marxists believed. They are not merely parts of international waves, such as those of 1789–93, 1848, 1917–23, 1941–5 and 1989–91, which affect many national societies simultaneously. As political crises, revolutions are also rooted in international – especially interstate – relations, and they in turn necessarily have international

---

[20] Skocpol (1979: 4).   [21] Skocpol (1979: 25).
[22] Quoted by Skocpol (1979: 284).
[23] Skocpol (1979), citing Hintze (in Gilbert, 1975).

15

effects. As Skocpol showed, the international context of revolution is not a contingent factor, but one in which revolutions are structurally implicated.[24] Revolutions are closely linked to wars as both manifestations and causes of instability in interstate relations.

What has been less well understood is the nature of revolution as a process of state transformation beyond the national level. The international has not just been a context of revolution, but part of what revolutions have been about. The revolutionary waves of the past two centuries have been part of, and have helped to define, major upheavals in the interstate system. These transformations of interstate relations have, in turn, been part of key transformations of state–society relations. Thus the French revolution and the wars which it began were the defining events in the transition to the national-and-international world of the nineteenth century. The Russian revolution was part of the Great War upheaval of this order, accentuating its crisis. The Chinese revolution was part of the Second World War transition, which worldwide resulted in the bloc-system of the Cold War. Likewise, I shall argue that the eastern and central European revolutions of recent years were manifestly defining events of the transition to the (emerging but still contested) global interstate world.

These successive transformations of state relations have been simultaneously changes in what would be distinguished conventionally as interstate and state–society relations. Looking at them from the perspective of the worldwide development of society, we can see them as a series of far-reaching revolutions in the totality of the relations between state institutions and the market economy on a world scale. In this sense, the international waves of national revolutions have been part of larger transformations in what I call the state relations and forms of the developing world capitalist society.

By *state relations* I mean the social relations of state power, through which society constitutes state institutions and state forms constitute the framework of society.[25] State relations thus include both interstate and state–society relations. By *state forms* I mean the structures of state institutions themselves, and the relations between institutions within

---

[24] Skocpol (1979).
[25] Society here is understood in the sense of the ensemble of social relations, rather than of a definite system. A fuller discussion of this question will be found in chapter 6; see also Shaw (1994: chapters 1 and 3).

and across distinct states. State forms thus also include what are conventionally understood as distinctive kinds of institution, namely nation-states and international organizations.

The contemporary transition from what Hobsbawm calls the 'short twentieth century' of 1914–89[26] to the 'twenty-first century' involves an explicit shift to a fundamentally different pattern of both relations and forms of state power. While the revolutions of the past two centuries signalled new phases of national-international relations and forms, the global revolution portends (if it has not yet achieved) a decisive movement beyond this structure of world politics. Confusingly, perhaps, modified national and international *forms* remain important in the emergent global world. But the fundamental state relations of the new era are no longer national and international in the historic sense. There is a unification of core world state institutions, so that *the political structure of social relations on a world scale has fundamentally changed.*

The concept of global revolution rather than globalization is likely to be controversial. The meaning given to it here may seem to fly in the face of conventional wisdom. The global revolution appears – in terms of the traditional distinction – a political rather than a social revolution. But this distinction needs to be qualified. The global revolution is not a social revolution in traditional terms – a transition from one historical system of social relations to another (like that from capitalism to socialism, for example). It nevertheless involves profound transformations of many aspects of social relations – and the ways in which they are structured politically. Some traditional Marxists have sensed this – in descriptions of a change 'back' to capitalist market relations in former Communist states as a 'counter-revolution'. But this shift is inadequately characterized in these terms, and in any case is only one aspect of social change in the global revolution.

The idea of the global revolution rescues globality from the realm of unintended, mechanical change. It asserts the role of conscious human agency in global transformation. Globality is not the result of a global teleology or a global spirit. It is, however, the outcome of the conscious and intentional actions of many individual and collective human actors. The things we intend and desire come into existence, of course, often by means other than those we envisage. The effects of our

---

[26] Hobsbawm (1994).

actions are often unpredictable. Yet human consciousness has decisive roles in the cumulative processes of any large change. There is no single guiding force, such as a revolutionary party, but there are many actors whose conscious interactions shape the new era.

The global revolution is therefore a revolution in a new sense – not simply a political rather than a social revolution, or a national and international revolution, but a set of changes in which these terms are themselves recast. The global revolution involves new relations of politics, economics and society, as well as of the national and international aspects of all these relations. For these reasons, it also involves a radical redefinition of the idea of revolution.

Key problems in the theory of globality

Political and academic debates at the beginning of the twenty-first century have begun to move tentatively beyond the idea of a process of globalization. The idea that globalization involves more than the intensification of the ecologically global or spatially worldwide character of social relations is gaining currency. The global has begun to be seen as a new principle or structure of social relations, increasingly actual as well as potential.

In these circumstances the concept of globality has begun to emerge. In its simplest meaning, globality is the condition or state in which things are global. The idea of globality represents the global as something increasingly achieved, real and manifest. Globality represents not just certain trends within the modern world, but a new condition or age in which the latter is brought into question. Globality represents a sufficiently fundamental shift in the very principles on which modern social organization is built for us to question the continuation of modernity.[27]

Modernity has been questioned before, of course – notably in the discourse of postmodernity. But as we have already seen, in emphasizing the disintegration of modernity, postmodern thought has eschewed the idea of any new synthesis, let alone end-point. Globality, in contrast, points to a kind of solution. Globality does not just dissolve, but supplants the classic modern framework. Mainstream critics of postmodern ideas, such as Giddens, integrate their insights into a 'late modern' project, of which globalization is a major aspect.

[27] Albrow (1996).

18

Theorists of globality, such as Albrow, see this concept as transcending both terms. Globality is not merely a late – or disintegrative – form of modernity, but a new structure of society and thought.

Globality is therefore a new structure and concept of social relations. Its novelty leads to three main problems that arise in establishing its meaning. First, there is *the continuing relation between structure and process*. If globality is both fundamental and novel in its significance, we cannot expect it to become established simply or overnight. The development of globality has been, and will be, a long, complex process. Globalization debates may have sometimes missed the point of globality, I have suggested, but their contests indicate the inconclusive character of global change to date. If we understand globality to involve a more thoroughgoing change, the processes of change are likely to be even more complex and of longer-lasting significance. Globality is hardly an end-point or a finished condition.

Second, if globality involves a rupture with modernity – a global revolution as I have called it – *the relations between globality and modernity are nevertheless likely to remain constitutive for a lengthy period*. A fundamental change is always not only long and complex, but also uneven and even apparently incoherent. Precisely if we wish to insist upon the discontinuity of contemporary developments, we need to account for manifold and deeply significant continuities. If globality is a break with modernity, it will nevertheless include – by transforming – many of the key forms of the modern world. To demonstrate the relation between continuity and discontinuity is a central task of global thought.

Third, if globality is a fundamentally new structure of relations, but enmeshed or embedded in so many old forms, *it is essential to define precisely in what the structure of globality consists, and how it has come about*. I defined the global as a common consciousness of human society on a world scale: an increasing awareness of the totality of human social relations as the largest constitutive framework of all relations. I argued that society is now constituted by this inclusive human framework, rather than by distinct tribes, civilizations, nations or religious communities – although all of these remain as parts of global society. But how, in what relations and forms, is this distinctive framework manifest? How has it come into existence? Has it come into being behind people's backs – or can we trace its development in human activity?

Method, argument and structure

If we take the idea of globality seriously, the foregoing are the key questions for social and political theory today. In this book, I work out answers to them through a methodology that is at the same time critical, historical and empirical-analytical. These three dimensions of my method are represented in three main sections of the book. However, although one dimension is to the fore and constitutes the presentation in each of the sections, these are not three separate methods. The questions, arguments and conclusions of each section are informed by those of the others.

In Part I, I develop a *critique* of national-international thought. Like Karl Marx, I take the view that ideas can be grasped as the expression their time in thought. Thus the critique of ideas is not abstract intellectual criticism, but an exploration of the links between thought and history, by which both are illuminated, and the possibility of change is explored.[28] I investigate the dialectics of universal and particular in the social thought of the national-international era. I hope to demonstrate both that a great deal about this thought can be understood through these contradictions, and that from the latter we can begin to understand the transition to a global world.

In Part II, I give an outline *historical account* of the global revolution. A major historical change cannot be understood merely by grasping the contradictions of thought discussed in the first part. We need a more concrete, explicitly historical synthesis, to propose a schema of the actions and events that have created globality. In this section I present, therefore, not a history in the full and detailed sense but an outline reinterpretation of what is known, which offers a coherent account and explanation of the emergence of a global structure in social relations.

In Part III, I develop an *analytical account* of the developing structure of globality in state relations, together with its contradictions. I try to show the key characteristics of the new structure, the contradictions that arise from the ways in which old relations and forms remain and are changed within it, and the new contradictions of globality. I present the structure of globality as by no means completely formed – let alone stable, secure or safe for human beings who live in the globalizing world. In the sense that distinctively global state relations

---

[28] See Marx (1965).

and forms have not yet been fully consolidated, in ways that correspond to the demands of global consciousness in society, I present global change as an unfinished revolution.

In the concluding chapter, I discuss the politics of the global transition, exploring further the idea of the unfinished global revolution. I argue that the problems of globalization and globality cannot be addressed through a reassertion of pre-global ideas and programmes, but only through a new global politics.

Part I
Critique

2 Critique of national and international relations

The key theoretical issue is the *order* of question that globality represents in our understanding of society. The debate about modernity and globality, which we began to consider in the previous chapter, provides one possible avenue for answering this. Both the common understandings of globality – in terms of ecological unity and of intensified social relations due to transformations of time and space – underline its links with modernity. The continuities between previous phases of modernity and our current condition are certainly fundamental, as writers such as Giddens have emphasized.[1] Globality seems easily conceived of as late modernity, or as postmodernity in the sense that Bauman proposed.[2] When Albrow suggested that globality fundamentally transcends this most general condition of the social order of recent centuries,[3] he appeared to contradict a broad sociological consensus.

The extended concept of globality that I have proposed – centred on the developing social unity of humankind – largely supports this radical case. The argument here is that while some key modern features remain central, globality brings real challenges to our understanding of modernity as a whole. It is not, of course, that concepts of human commonality as such are novel. Clearly they pre-date not just globality but modernity as well. In a certain sense, moreover, they have been central to modernity. But the modern centrality of human commonality was always understood in terms of the built-in tension between commonality and division. While human society worldwide

---

[1] Giddens (1990, 1991).
[2] Bauman (1992); see chapter 1.   [3] Albrow (1996).

was understood as based on common features, it was also grasped as fundamentally fractured.

What is suggested by the extended definition of globality is that in some important sense this fracturing has begun to be overcome. If we are not to fall for a naïve vision of growing human solidarity, promising a simple and unrealistic world peace, it is important to be careful in specifying what has – and therefore what has not – changed. Human society today is hardly undivided, including by violence, nor is it likely to become so. The quality of fracturing as such is not disappearing. What have changed, however, are the balance and terms of the relationship between commonality and division. Globality, in its full sense, represents a very substantial enhancement of commonality. In this sense, the meaning of human division has changed.

Human society has been divided in a multitude of ways: by civilization, religion, empire, nation, class, race, gender and culture, to name but some of the most important. Divisions have been manifestly complex and overlapping. In the light of the universalizing tendency of modernity, each *could* be seen as relative to the others. But commonly this relativity has not been grasped; on the contrary, particular divisions have been made absolute, so that segments of humanity have seen themselves as self-sufficient moral and political communities.

In the epoch of modernity, this paradox of universality and division has been especially powerful. The universal vision has been articulated with unprecedented strength and in novel, secular terms; but at the same time it has been chronically and structurally compromised. Powerful new forms of particularity, centred on the nation, have been given absolute significance. This tension has been implicit in modern social and political development.

It is these relationships which globality transforms. Fractures in human society remain deep but they appear less determinate, as postmodernists have divined. Tensions reappear in novel terms, which are increasingly relativized by the greater consciousness of the global human whole. While many still absolutize their partial visions, communities and truths, there is a powerful new impetus behind those who demonstrate the mutuality of all these human viewpoints. Thus partiality is exposed, and particularist visions are forced to address commonality.

This chapter discusses how the tension of universality and particularity has been structurally embedded, as nationality-internationality, in modern thought. I explore how the contradictions of its theorization point the way to its radical supersession in global theory, which is discussed in the following chapter.

The problem of nationality and internationality

The many fractures of modern society have been superimposed upon each other not arbitrarily or randomly but in particular ways. Marx and his followers have argued that class relations organize the other divisions. Recently postmodern views have challenged the assumption of hierarchy, while sociological writers have emphasized the mutual constitution of different institutional clusters and forms of power.[4] Among these, the principle of nationality and internationality has constituted a major framework of social differentiation in the high-modern world.

There is no proposal here that we understand the relations of structure reductively, with nationality-internationality as the root. The various ordering principles noted above – civilization, religion, empire, class, race, gender, culture – all have their distinctive logics and histories, many of which have been more important than nationality-internationality in earlier periods. In the last two centuries, however, many of these orders have become more or less fused with the national-international.

The claim here is that the institutionally defined order of national-international relations has been a principal context in which all the other main forms of social division have been entrenched. The fixity of nation has become a standard for the absolutization of forms of social division in general. The idea of class, for example, became most thoroughly absolutized when it was entrenched in the ideology of the Soviet state. Race and culture have been made absolute in the ideologies of imperial nation-states.

Three implications of the argument need to be underlined. First, it is a national *and* international principle, or nationality-internationality, that is pervasive. Social relations are never simply national in form. Clearly, if the world is to be divided into national units, the possibility of relations between or beyond those units must be envisaged. The idea of internationality is *generally* entailed by that of nationality, and

---

[4] See Giddens (1985), Mann (1986, 1993).

is also part of the constitution of nationality. Each idea presumes and is constituted in relation to the other.

Internationality is therefore not, as sometimes supposed, the general opposite of nationality. The idea of internationality understands relations between and beyond nations in terms of the national principle. However, in a national-international world, antagonistic international relations reinforce separated nationalities. Cooperative international relations, in contrast, internationalize and partially transcend nationality. In a national-international order the tension between universal and particular can only be expressed in terms of internationality. In this sense, in some circumstances, internationality is opposed to nationality.

Second, to see nationality-internationality as a key constitutive principle of high modern order does not imply that each of the other principles is implicated with it in the same way. Clearly other dimensions have been more or less tightly tied into national and international relations and concepts. They have been more or less related to particular kinds of national and international identities and ideologies. Other dimensions have been implicated in the different ways in which nationality-internationality contains and expresses particularist-universalist contradictions. Class and gender, for example, have been both implicated within, and opposed to, nationality.

Third, to identify nationality-internationality as the central organizing principle of difference in modernity is to argue that social relations are defined to a considerable extent by state or political relations. This is not an attempt to counterpose on principle a political-military to, for example, the socio-economic explanations of Marxism or the more cultural approach of many postmodern theorists. It is rather an argument that the meaning of these categories shifts in changing historical circumstances. In the high modern period particular kinds of relations between 'economy', 'politics' and 'culture' have prevailed. The transformation of these relations has been a striking feature of the development of globality.

Nationality-internationality is therefore a historically specific structure of state–society relationships. There is powerful testimony to its reality in many areas of social life and social understanding. It has a taken-for-granted character in much social discourse. Its power is acknowledged even by theoretical approaches which in principle take opposed views of the character of society (thus Marxists, while regarding capitalism as a worldwide mode of production, also routinely designate it in national terms). And, on any account, it remains a very significant structure in the global transition, and will remain so in any conceivable global world.

In this part of the book, therefore, nationality-internationality is examined as the prime categoric framework of pre-global, modern social order. Given its historical character, it is important to understand the processes involved in its origins, development and transformation. This understanding cannot be generated, however, simply by examining historical facts. Many of the principal facts are well known and widely agreed upon; it is their meaning that remains contested and uncertain.

In order to understand the historical character of nationality-internationality, I shall first examine critically the categories, modes of understanding and theories that have been developed in the *social thought of the national-international era*. In the discussion that follows I shall be interested in three aspects of this structure of thought. First, by what is nationality-internationality constituted, and how does it relate to other dimensions of modernity? Second, in what ways has nationality-internationality shaped the social thought of the modern era? Third, what light does social thought throw on the tensions of nationality-internationality, its articulation with other modern contradictions, and the processes by which it has increasingly been overcome in the movement towards globality?

The ideas that I discuss are selected according to three criteria. First, I shall consider those in which the problem of nationality-internationality itself is either explicitly or implicitly constitutive. Second, I shall consider ideas that have been considered particularly important, and which can therefore be seen as representative thought of the national and international era. Third, I shall examine those that throw critical light on the problem of nationality-internationality. Some theories will be relevant according to all three criteria, others according to one or two of them. I shall not categorize theories explicitly according to these three dimensions of concern, but rather develop a fluid synthesis of national-international social thought in which I address each of these concerns.

It should be emphasized that in considering nationality-internationality as a single, structural dimension of modernity, I nevertheless understand it as a very broad cluster of social and political institutions, cultural and ideological forms. Within this, there are many differences and tensions – not only between nationality and internationality, but between various ways in which each of these structural principles is embedded in institutions and practices. The manifold contradictions of national and international relations have been at the centre of modern society, and they have also been central to the transition to a global world, as I shall explain later.

A further general implication of this critique should be explicit at the start. In defining modern social thought as the national-international era in thought, I am arguing for a revolution in social theory itself. Modern social science, in its intellectual categories, modes of explanation and disciplinary organization, has been pervaded by nationality-internationality. The critique of national and international thought must therefore include these institutional forms, and the ways in which they too are being transformed.

Sovereignty and universality

National-international thought grew in importance with capitalism and modernity. In the early modern period, the sixteenth and seventeenth centuries, the nation-state as we understand it was still in the early stages of development. Spain, Portugal, England and France had achieved some degree of coherence as states with recognizably modern boundaries. Some national consciousness had developed, but ruled by absolute monarchs these were not nations in the modern sense. Most states of this period were not modern nation-states: in the continental European patchwork there were both multi-ethnic empires and monarchical mini-states, whose limitations would have to be transcended before modern nations would be created.

It is a curiosity of modern political theory, therefore, that the Treaty of Westphalia (1648), signed between overwhelmingly monarchical, pre-national states, should be regarded today as the foundation of the *international* system of states. In reality it codified the connection between interstate norms, on the one hand, and the relations of rulers and subjects, on the other. With an agreement centred on the formula, *cuius regio, eius religio*, already formulated in the Peace of Augsburg (1555), Westphalia resolved the religious conflicts between rulers that had culminated in the Thirty Years War. It bequeathed to the modern European state-system the constitutive ideas of the state as sovereign in its own territory, and of non-intervention by one state in the affairs of the other. By accepting the plurality of religious affiliations within the state-system, it also gave limited legitimacy to the idea of religious freedom and the rights of subjects to move to a jurisdiction of their own persuasion.[5]

The Westphalian idea was, however, essentially pre-modern in that it saw sovereignty as belonging to the ruler rather than the people. That is why the American and especially the French revolutions were such challenges to the *ancien régime* throughout Europe – to established patterns of relations between, as well as within, states. Westphalia was largely a rulers' charter, but the revolutions of the late eighteenth century ushered in for the first time a genuinely national-international era of interstate relations. Although curiously Westphalia is seen as foundational, the 'age of revolution'[6] transformed its legacy and laid the real foundations of the modern state-system – and of modern thought.

We are accustomed to think of the content of these classic revolutions as universal. The American Declaration of Independence and the French Declaration of the Rights of Man were couched in universal human terms. They proclaimed the equality of human beings and enshrined the notion of citizenship, rather than subjecthood, in the constitution of the modern state. However, this abstractly universal content belied considerable real partiality and inequality.

The critique of the Enlightenment thought embodied in these constitutive modern ideas has taken its cue from Marx in stressing their social, and especially class, limitations. Early modern liberal thought was 'the political theory of possessive individualism'.[7] Built in were decisive presuppositions of property, and hence social inequality. Only the privileged few, even among men, were to be admitted to liberty and political rights. Feminists have hardly needed to point out that women's complete exclusion was largely taken for granted – although the first challenges to this, such as Wollstonecraft's,[8] also began to emerge in the revolutionary period.

This critique has come from the standpoints of democratic, socialist and latterly feminist modernity, rather than globality. What it has itself largely taken for granted is the national-international form in which the Enlightenment was cast, both as theory and as practice. The modern, or if you like bourgeois, revolution of the late eighteenth century gave us principles with universal meaning, which are still relevant to this day. The principles were embedded, however, in the

---

[5] See Hirst (1997).   [6] Hobsbawm (1968).
[7] Macpherson (1962).   [8] Wollstonecraft (1982).

emerging national-international world. They could only be applied, first and foremost in the national context, and second, by liberal, socialist and feminist universalists, through international action.

Grasping the embedded nationality-internationality of modern liberal-democratic thought is a *sine qua non* of understanding the contemporary world crisis.[9] The Enlightenment and the great revolutions were centred in emergent nationality. At its best, the construction of democratic nations went hand in hand with internationalism – as in the work of Thomas Paine, democratic revolutionary and patriot of more than one country.[10] However, the most democratic modern nations were based from their beginnings on empire, colonization, slavery and chauvinism. From Napoleon onwards, the understanding of internationalism as enlightened domination was never far from the surface.

The great revolutions did, however, make historic modern advances in the definition of nationality. For the first time, emergent nations were defined not by ethnic community but by the principles that constituted them politically, and their constitutional expressions. However imperfect the principles themselves and even more their implementation, the idea of the nation as the embodiment of freedom and composed of citizens was a fundamental change.

With these changes came of course a redefinition of sovereignty. The people, not the ruler, now embodied sovereign power. This change greatly reinforced, just as it altered, the Westphalian principles. On the one hand, sovereignty was all the more sacred and inviolable now that the nation embodied it, since any interference in the affairs of the state was an affront to people as well as rulers. On the other hand, the internal constellation of sovereignty altered. No longer was freedom of thought or association, for example, a matter between the ruler and individuals or groups of his or her subjects. Such matters now concerned the whole nation and those who claimed to represent it. Very early in the French revolution, it became apparent that this doctrine could be a source of new tyrannies within the nation as well as empire without.

In the age of revolution, the nation-state, an emergent reality under absolute monarchs, became a norm intimately linked to universal principles of modernity. We are accustomed, in the light of the

---

[9] See Held's extensive critique of the national context of democratic thinking (1995).
[10] See Keane's excellent biography (1995).

dominant liberal internationalism of the late twentieth century, to seeing nationality and liberty as often opposed, normally in tension. With the benefit of hindsight, this is an entirely justifiable perspective on the national-international era. It is nevertheless a very partial one. Nationality and liberty were complementary universals in the founding consensus of modernity. They remain linked even to this day in the minds of many, not least in regions of the world where both have been denied by imperial, authoritarian states.

Since sovereign nationality was embedded in the foundations of the modern era, the application of principles equally to all human beings was a fundamental problem. If liberal or democratic principles applied to individuals within the context of the nation – and as Marxist and feminist critiques emphasized, they applied even within that context in unequal and restricted fashions – how could they apply to individuals across national boundaries?

The simplest answer was that they did not. The political principles of the modern state were (and largely remain) precisely that – principles implemented distinctly by each sovereign state, and applying to individuals cross-nationally only to the extent that different states adopted similar principles. The idea of the individual subject's rights in an interstate order, which had been given some credence after Westphalia, if anything diminished in the era of sovereign nations. Moreover, the major nation-states were also empires, and inequality between the imperial nation and the colonized was (albeit in varying forms) a common structural principle of European empires. Even with the fullest realization of liberal principles in the metropolis, there was hardly universal application.

How then could *universal* principles be proclaimed, in a context of nation-states? Universal principles could only have cross-national significance in two senses. First, they could function as ethical rather than political norms – abstracted from practice. Immanuel Kant, perhaps the greatest philosopher of the age of revolution, made an absolute distinction between the ethical and the empirical worlds.[11] Universal or cosmopolitan values were categorical imperatives, not empirical possibilities. Not just discrepancies with but fundamental violations of these values were accepted as incontrovertible realities.

Second, universal values could become practical through international action. In the national-international world, the international

---

[11] Reiss (1990).

had two dimensions. The first reflected its simplest meaning – relations between nations – understood in a way that is neutral as to the content of those relations. In these terms, war was as much an international reality as peace. The second dimension of inter-nationality specified, however, a particular content. In this sense, international was what was agreed between nations. It was in this sense, clearly, that universal values could be implemented, in so far as their consequences could be internationally agreed.

The problem of universality in the national-international era re-volved around how far it was possible to move from an ethical to a practical meaning, and from the neutral to the positive meaning of internationality. For the most part, very limited versions of univers-ality and internationality prevailed. The nation-state functioned as a barrier to, more than a means of, internationality in the cooperative sense. International, or more precisely interstate, relations remained marked by antagonistic nationality. Full, cross-national universality could not be much more than an abstract ideal – although there were always some contexts in which it was indeed embedded in practice.

Capitalist modernity

The tension between nationality-internationality and universality played a critical but not always an explicit role in the defining thought of the modern era. Kant dealt with this contradiction partly by counterposing the universal truth of reason to the empirical world. Empirically, he accepted the fact of a fragmented state-system, and could envisage only world federation, not world government. Kant's 'cosmopolitanism' has been one of his most enduring legacies to political thought, but it remains a chronically abstract pole. Con-temporary Kantian thought often remains trapped in this dualism, although some have begun to take the opportunity which globality offers to transcend it.[12]

Kant's successor, Georg Wilhelm Friedrich Hegel, refused to accept his dualism, seeing history as a dialectical process, in which reason both was defined by and defined human action. For the younger Hegel, reason did not exist except dialectically, in history. Later, however, in further attempting to understand the relationship between thought and practice, Hegel made two fundamental compro-

---

[12] O'Neill (1991, 1992).

mises with this radical position. He identified reason with God, and he identified the state as the realm of universality in which reason and history were reconciled. Hegel's accommodation to religion and the state – in his case, the absolutist Prussian monarchy in pre-national Germany – was a prime starting-point for Marx's critique, and thus for a new theoretical tradition which has been of fundamental significance for modern social thought.[13]

Marx's critique of religion did not simply invert Hegel's idealism, as did that of his materialist contemporary Ludwig Feuerbach, whom Marx also criticized.[14] Marx saw religion as a product of society, but not in a passive, reflective sense – it was an active protest of the socially alienated. Marx extended this analysis in his critique of Hegel's view of the state. The claim of his fellow Jews to religious freedom in the state, Marx contended, was a claim that would only partially overcome their alienation. For the political freedom they sought was an abstract freedom, just as the state in which it was embedded was a sphere of purely abstract universality. This abstraction meant that the state, like religion, was a sphere of alienation, and not therefore one in which the real, social alienation of the Jews could be overcome.[15]

Whereas Hegel had seen the state as the realm in which alienation and the contradictions of society were overcome, Marx saw the state as a realm of alienation, which could only be resolved by grasping the contradictions of society. In his life's work, therefore, Marx explored these contradictions of what Hegel and other thinkers had called civil society (society outside the state, including the economy), which he came to further define as the capitalist mode of production. Marx saw the negation of political universality in the alienation and exploitation of the producers in capitalism. Where Kant saw universality in abstract reason, and Hegel finally located it in the state, Marx eventually concluded that it belonged to the proletariat (working class) as a class. The proletariat, he argued, were universally oppressed, and hence had the potentiality to achieve universal liberation.

For Marx, therefore, the relations that defined particularity were those of classes-in-production; the potential for universality lay in the emergence of a self-conscious universal class. Nationality was, to be

---

[13] The idea of social theory, as distinct from to philosophy, stems from this period. See Marcuse (1968).

[14] See Marx (1965).   [15] Marx (1963).

certain, part of the particular relations that had to be overcome. But nationality was contingent to the character of these relations, not defining of them. The development of a self-conscious universal proletariat would *ipso facto* negate nationality. The proletariat, Marx and Engels proclaimed, had no country.[16]

Nevertheless, as a matter of practical politics Marx recognized classes as organized on a national basis. In his historical writings, Marx analysed the bourgeoisie as a nationally structured class, the occasional references to the international bourgeoisie outweighed by analyses of the French, British and other national capitalist classes. In his political programme, the universality of the proletariat was to be achieved through internationality – the very idea of the 'international' has its origins, Halliday argues, in the workers' internationals.[17] As a party, the proletarian revolution was to be organized through an international federation. As it achieved its goals through an international wave of national revolutions, proletarian power would also be organized in an international federation of revolutionary states.

Even more than other aspects of Marx's political programme, the international organization of revolutionary power remained ill defined. Marx and Engels rejected utopian blueprints and saw the revolution as an immanent deconstruction of the state as an institution. In this context, the general national-international character of the revolution was taken for granted as an inevitable consequence of the political relations of capitalism. The internationalism of the revolution was, of course, something to be fought for, but its form would be worked out in practice rather than defined in advance.

In Marx's political writings, therefore, universality is implicitly and explicitly understood as internationalism. In this sense, Marx follows the tradition of modern thought, and in particular Kant. Where he departs from Kant is in the idea that internationalism is not merely an abstract ideal but something realized in the practice of a certain class. Like his predecessors, however, Marx treats nationality-internationality as a necessary aspect of modern social organization. By treating it only incidentally and at the level of class – which is manifestly not where nationality-internationality originates – he failed to analyse its roots in what I have called the state relations and state forms of modernity.

In treating the national and international character of society in this

---

[16] Marx and Engels (1998).   [17] Halliday (1999).

way, Marx set a fateful precedent for modern social understanding. He constructed, in *Capital*, a theoretical framework for understanding the world that started from the commodity form of modern social relations. Marx's critique of the fetishized character of this form resolved it into the social relations of labour power and capital in production.[18] For Marx, these were the core relations of the entire mode of production, and hence of society at large. His unfinished work reached the point at which he showed that these social relations corresponded to the class relations that he had hypothesized in his early work.[19] Marx introduced 'foreign' trade merely as a 'counteracting influence' to the tendency of the rate of profit to fall.[20] Although elsewhere capitalism was presented as a universal mode of production, here by implication the basic capitalist economy was national in form. This tension has been generally reproduced in Marxist analysis, for example in the presentation of Britain as a typical 'capitalist society' rather than a national sub-formation of a worldwide social system.

This underdevelopment of Marx's argument reinforced its main logic, which emphasized the primacy of the social relations of capitalist production in understanding modern society. It contributed to an even more one-sided appropriation of Marx's theory by many of his followers – and indeed by their critics. The metaphor of base (mode of production) and superstructure (state, ideology, etc.), deployed at times by Marx,[21] was interpreted more mechanically than in his own often flexible historical interpretations. As is well known, the interpretation of these positions became a matter of major political controversy as well as of academic debate.

In the subsequent history of Marxism, both state and national-international relations were theorized more explicitly than by Marx himself, but often in ways which took not only his starting-point but frequently also his more specific judgements as given. Most famously, Lenin published two definitive pamphlets during the First World War. In the first, he defined imperialism as the 'highest stage' of capitalism, a composite of the organizational forms of capital – 'monopoly' (or joint-stock) and 'finance' (bank-dominated) capital – and the political forms of 'colonialism' and inter-imperial 'wars of redivision'.[22]

---

[18] Marx (1962a), chapter 1.   [19] Marx (1962b), chapter 52.
[20] Marx (1962b), chapter 14, section 5.   [21] Most famously in Marx (1971).
[22] Lenin (1973).

While later writers have debated the extent and relationships of these trends, what was most significant – and influential – about Lenin's ideas was his mechanical concept of economic cause and political effect. The concept of discrete relations of production and state forms remained intact, as it did for the most part in other, more sophisticated Marxist analyses of the time.[23] The state was seen as curiously separate from the forms and relations of capital, and Lenin dealt with it in a separate pamphlet. Although recognizing that the world war had made states much more repressive, the state – he argued with extensive quotations from Marx – was the product of class antagonisms *within* the national context.[24]

Because international relations and war were not part of Marx's paradigm, Lenin could not assign them a major explanatory role. Because capitals and states were held to operate according to separate logics – the former determining the latter – Lenin could not explain the new statist war economy of his time. These flaws were built into an orthodoxy that was still influential in the Marxist revival half a century later.[25] The only major Marxist to overcome them was Lenin's contemporary, Nikolai Bukharin. He produced a radical account in which imperialism was constituted by rival predatory states, each of which mobilized its own 'national state capitalism' in a war economy, to compete militarily as well as commercially with other states.[26] This was developed later, in Bukharin's enthusiasm for 'war communism', into a pre-Orwellian vision of a completely militarized world. In this, class struggle was expressed only at the international level in the competition of capitalist and socialist states and war economies.[27]

Bukharin's account anticipated the totalitarian fusion of state and economy that issued from the world war (first in Russia itself, later in Nazi Germany). However, it overstated the generalizability of this model.[28] Like Lenin, Bukharin underestimated the resilience of Western democracy, and its renewal rather than extinction in the context of war. He failed to foresee that it would actually be the democratic, welfare-Keynesian capitalist state that would triumph at the conclusion of the period of world wars. What Bukharin did accomplish, albeit imperfectly, was twofold. First, he showed that the national-international form of the state was pivotal to the understand-

---

[23] Notably Hilferding (1981), Luxemburg (1963).   [24] Lenin (1967).
[25] See Shaw (1984) for a critique.   [26] Bukharin (1972).
[27] Bukharin (1972).   [28] Shaw (1972).

ing of modern capitalism, rather than something that could be treated as secondary. Second, he showed that the national-international form was embedded in relations of war and militarism.

The understanding of these issues in the Marxist tradition largely vanished as it was sucked, as Bukharin was personally, into the vortex of Stalinist totalitarianism. Stalin contributed a decisive adaptation of Marxism to the nation-state, with his doctrine of 'socialism in one country' and subordination of international revolution to Soviet nation-state interests. Despite occasional glimpses of a perspective on militarized national capitalisms,[29] the serious Marxist analysis of these issues re-emerged only in the debate about the Cold War 'arms economy'.[30] Here the national-international framework was already being replaced by one of competing blocs, and the main focus of attention was economic consequences rather than state relations and forms in general.

A distinctive 'Western' strand came to dominate serious Marxist thought after the decline of the revolutionary period and the development of Stalinism.[31] Western Marxism involved a dual displacement, of classic Marxist concerns and also of the emergent problematic of the national-international, military framework of capitalism. First, economic and political analysis gave way to cultural and psychological concerns. Second, the proletarian vision was discarded: the working class was no longer seen as the carrier of universal values. This was explained by the Stalinist distortion of the proletarian revolution on the one hand, and the incorporation of the Western working class into 'organized', consumer capitalism on the other. Universal values could only be maintained from a more utopian, idealist point of view, more loosely linked to marginal groups in Western society or to the so-called Third World.[32]

Uniquely, the ideas of Antonio Gramsci straddled classical and Western Marxism, old and new concerns, and simultaneously focussed the national-international issue. In his prison notebooks, Gramsci revised not only Marx and Lenin, but also Hegel and the Italian idealist, Benedetto Croce. For Gramsci, within the perspective of the universal proletarian revolution it was essential to problematize national tradition, centred on civil society as well as on the state. Although in the 1970s Gramsci became the icon of a new parlia-

---

[29] For example, Sweezy (1967).   [30] Kidron (1968), Mandel (1970).
[31] Anderson (1976).   [32] Marcuse (1964), Worsley (1967).

mentary-democratic adaptation of Marxism in western Europe, his own perspective – not surprisingly in the context of Fascist Italy in which he wrote – had remained revolutionary in a classic sense.

For Gramsci, civil society was not the entire framework of economy and society, which it had been for Hegel and Marx, and which could therefore be used to explain the form of the state.[33] In contrast, he regarded civil society as a sphere of representation: 'between the economic structure and the state with its legislation and coercion stands civil society'.[34] The state was a coercive fortress surrounded by more consensual, value-laden outer 'defences' in civil society. The national character of the state was developed by 'traditional' intellectual groups within civil society. New institutions were evolved by 'organic' intellectual groupings emerging from the development of the latest stage of world capitalism.

In Gramsci's perspective, civil society was on the one hand a sphere of universal values, but on the other profoundly national in form and content. His solution to this quandary was for the contemporary bearer of genuine universality, the proletarian party, to engage with and transform the national tradition in the direction of international communism. For Gramsci, the party was the modern equivalent of Niccolò Machiavelli's Prince, the 'modern Prince' whose culture and strategy Gramsci's work aimed to elucidate. The party was the collective 'organic intellectual' of the national and international proletariat.

The fact that the revolutionary party remained at the centre of Gramsci's thinking – as much as it was for his Hegelian Marxist contemporary Georg Lukács[35] – emphasizes the gulf between his world and that of his late twentieth-century followers. There was a different kind of gulf, however, between him and his contemporaries. Stalin imposed a monolithic, nation-state-centred pseudo-internationalism; his chief opponent, Leon Trotsky, proclaimed abstract class internationalism.[36] Gramsci, in contrast, defined an approach, both abstract and at the same time centred on the Italian case, which was genuinely both national and international. It is important to recognize this characteristic of his work: it was a rare explicit formulation of the central political tension of the national-international era.

---

[33] Rosenberg (1994) has recently continued this tradition: see discussion below.
[34] Gramsci in Hoare and Smith (1971: 208).
[35] Lukács (1971).   [36] Trotsky (1965b).

(This also underlines, however, the substantial adaptation involved in bringing Gramsci into the debate about globality.[37])

Gramsci's work represents nevertheless the high point of Marxist thought on this question. For much subsequent Marxism has theorized capitalism as a worldwide system, not explaining but adapting relatively uncritically its national-international framework. Much Marxist-inspired literature, for example, has seen Third World 'underdevelopment' as a problem of world capitalism, while embracing the solution of national development as an escape from the capitalist world market.

Marx's principal legacy, therefore, is a fundamental ambiguity over the relationships between capitalism, as an incipiently worldwide mode of production, and the national-international framework within which it has been organized. For Marx, and therefore for most of his followers, the latter has never been a central question of analysis. The capitalist mode of production has been regarded simultaneously as dynamic in its breaching of all borders *and* as easily categorized in national terms.

Rosenberg offers a rare explicit attempt to resolve this conundrum. He argues that 'international relations do not precede but follow organically fundamental social relations' (the social relations of capitalism). At the same time, he claims, 'the international' and 'the domestic' are two sides of these fundamental relations: 'this is not an ontological difference, but merely a different form of structural relationship.'[38] Thus internationality (separated from any definite concept of nationality, since its opposite is seen as 'domestic' society) is both secondary to 'fundamental social relations' *and* one of the structural forms of these relations.

The sovereignty of the state, he argues, depends 'on both a kind of abstraction from production and the reconstitution of the state-political sphere external to civil society'. Sovereignty is 'the social form of the state in a society where political power is divided between public and private spheres.'[39] It 'entails the parallel consolidation of private political power in production.'[40] Hence

> the last thing this portends is the end of empire. Rather it means that the exercise of imperial power, like domestic social power, will have two linked aspects: a public political aspect which concerns the

[37] See chapter 3.   [38] Rosenberg (1994: 54–5).
[39] Rosenberg (1994: 55).   [40] Rosenberg (1994: 128).

management of the states-system, and a private political aspect which effects the extraction and relaying of surpluses. It means the rise of a new kind of empire: the empire of civil society.[41]

Rosenberg's solution is elegant, because it respects the distinct *forms* of state and capitalist power. However, it is unsatisfactory, because it fails to recognize the distinctive social relations surrounding state power, seeing state forms only as aspects of capitalist social relations. A good illustration of this error is evident in his treatment of the Soviet state as 'an enormous geopolitical challenge to the social form of the modern states-system'.[42] However, even if in a certain sense the Soviet Union did represent a different *form* of state power, in other senses this argument is highly implausible. Communist states adapted comprehensively to both the national and international forms of the state-system. Even more, in its social relations of domination and of antagonism towards other state centres, the Soviet state can actually be seen as representative. It was an extreme case of general trends towards militarized, imperial nation-statism, in the states-system of the early to mid-twentieth century; it later became one pole of the bloc-state system of the late twentieth century.[43]

It is not possible, therefore, to resolve the contradiction between capitalism and the state, within the framework of the theory of capitalism. The ambiguities arise because of the difference between capitalist and national-international ordering principles. Capitalism is not definable in terms of nationality-internationality. But nationality-internationality is not definable in terms of capitalism. And yet the relationship between the two is clearly of critical importance to each; we require a broader-based sociological explanation.

---

[41] Rosenberg (1994: 131).

[42] The Soviet Union, he claims, 'was precisely not a sovereign state, in the sense that we have been discussing sovereignty'. Soviet-type states 'withdrew their societies from the world market, and hence from the reach of private Western power. This was ultimately the political content of the Cold War. With the best will in the world, it would be impossible to understand the Soviet presence in the international system in terms of states and markets. It was precisely an attempt to abolish both of them.' Rosenberg (1994: 134).

[43] Rosenberg's aim is to provide a 'critique of the realist theory of international relations'. However, by denying the reality of the similarities between Soviet and Western states, he offers no defence to the simple realist explanation of them. An effective critique must, rather, offer an alternative explanation of the commonalities.

State, geopolitics and industrial society

Two further major kinds of answer to the question of nationality-internationality are suggested within modern social theory. One defines the national and, by implication, the international in terms of the state. The other defines them in terms of culture. We shall look at these in turn, in order to examine how far the literatures answer these general questions.

The dominant understanding of the national-international relations and forms of the state owes most to Max Weber. Other writers of the late nineteenth-century German historical school also contributed: Otto Hintze, for example, developed the idea that military organization was the key to the shape of the state.[44] This idea shades into the classical geopolitical theory of Halford Mackinder, imperialist founder of modern geography.[45] Nevertheless it is Weber who provided two key elements of the theory of the modern nation-state, which have provided the foundation for recent synthetic accounts of the national and international order.

First, Weber defines the state in a way that goes beyond the Marxian idea of it being a product of class antagonisms. 'A compulsory political organization with continuous operations will be called a "state"', he argues, 'insofar as its administrative staff successfully upholds the claim to the monopoly of the legitimate use of physical force in the enforcement of its order', in a given territory.[46] The Weberian concept of the monopoly of legitimate violence has remained seminal to understanding the state throughout the twentieth century.

Second, Weber defined a mode of understanding modern state institutions in his characterization of bureaucracy.[47] Although bureaucracies existed outside the state, its institutions were paradigms of the rigid, formalistic, rule-bound, hierarchical command-structure that Weber saw as the typical institutional form of legal-rational modernity. Gramsci's later analysis of Fordism, as the typical form of industrial organization in modern capitalism, and Foucault's insights into the wider forms of surveillance both raise questions – reinforced by much organizational sociology – about the typicality of Weber's concept of bureaucracy.[48] These alternative models only emphasize,

---

[44] See Gilbert (1975).   [45] Parker (1982).
[46] Cited by Mann (1993: 55).   [47] Gerth and Mills (1978).
[48] Gramsci, in Hoare and Smith (1971), Foucault (1977).

therefore, the particular connection of classic bureaucratic organization with the state.

Weber's insights have laid the foundations for the two main syntheses of the question of national and international relations in recent sociology. Giddens' account of the nation-state is based on his account of four main institutional clusters in modernity: capitalism, industrialism, surveillance and warfare. He makes the key claim of what may be called post-Marxist sociology – a sociology which does not simply offer an alternative to Marxism, but incorporates some of its insights – that our understanding of modern society cannot be reduced to, or chiefly organized around, our understanding of capitalism.[49]

Giddens' starting-point contrasts with those of others, including Mann, in that it separates capitalism from industrialism, and surveillance from warfare, not only in principle, but as distinct institutional clusters.[50] His argument does not always sustain these separations: industrialism has existed chiefly in the context of capitalism, while surveillance and warfare are to a large extent two sides of the state.[51] Certainly, surveillance, as Foucault suggested, is a general feature of modern society and exists outside the state; but the state can be seen as its classic and central locus.

Giddens brings surveillance and warfare together in his analysis of the modern state as a 'bordered power container'. Following Weber, he sees the state as achieving – through extensive means of surveillance, including bureaucracy – increasingly homogeneous control of the population in its territory. Within the territorial basis of the state, society is pacified – violence is 'extruded' from social relations in general including the forms of control by the state. The loose boundaries of pre-modern states are replaced by precise borders, which are securely policed. There is a sharpening distinction between policing, within the borders, and military force, without.

The other side of the bordered state, therefore, is that relations beyond it are characterized by precisely the violence that is overcome within. In pre-modern times, internal and external war could not be so clearly distinguished – armies fought warlords, bandits and rebels as well as other recognizable centres of state power. In modern conditions, interstate borders are borders of violence. Borders demar-

---

[49] Giddens (1985).   [50] Giddens (1985).
[51] See the critiques by Jessop (1989) and Shaw (1989).

cate the ordered world inside the nation-state, including what Marx called the 'dull compulsion' of capitalist relations, from the anarchy without. The other side of pacification is therefore increased violence between industrially militarized states – culminating in the danger of nuclear war.

Giddens' account has the virtues and vices of a synthesis of the nation-state relations of modernity. Written in the last phase of major nuclear-arms-centred international conflict, the Second Cold War, on the cusp of the global revolution, it offers an ideal type of an order that is now passing. Looked at from the new era, it summates the past but does not offer a model for the future. The extension of surveillance to the international level and the re-emergence of warfare within and across states have radically repositioned the borders of violence in the world, while rendering many boundaries between nation-states closer to administrative conveniences. From the point of view of the international relations literature, Giddens' account, despite its more sophisticated sociological underpinning, appears to encapsulate the 'old' relations of a nation-state-divided world, and to approximate the conclusions (but not the method) of power-political 'realists'.

Giddens' anti-reductionist position is mirrored by Mann's claim that we can identify four principal kinds of power: economic, political, military and ideological.[52] Mann offers a more complex model of the world of states, nations and classes. His is a longer account, tracing the emergence of what he calls the 'multi-power-actor civilization' of the West.[53] In his discussion of modernity, he encapsulates the tension between universality and nationality in modern thought, pointing out that the meaning of 'society' has oscillated between this broader definition and the narrow national sense.[54] He has polemicized for a 'geopolitical' explanation of militarism, arguing that rivalries of nation-states, rather than the pacific tendencies of industrialism or the militaristic tendencies of capitalism, are dominant. Capitalism, he argues, has changed 'only' the scale and intensity of warfare, due to advancing military technology.[55]

His major work, however, defines the major states of the 'long nineteenth century' (1760–1915) as idiosyncratic institutional messes, considerably removed from the bureaucratic ideal type of Weber. He shows how, paradoxically from the point of view of Marxist theory,

---

[52] Mann (1986, 1993).   [53] Mann (1986).
[54] Mann (1993: 9).   [55] Mann (1984).

nations and classes developed simultaneously as major collective actors in the late nineteenth-century world. The variable forms of the nation-state, in their variable interactions with social forces within states, interacted in complex ways to produce a variety of warlike outcomes.[56] Mann stresses that relations between the same sets of state and other actors can manifest 'polymorphous crystallization' – they crystallize in different ways, both over time in various issue areas, and at specific moments.[57] He also gives a distinct role to civil society in generating wars – for example, the extermination of indigenous populations by settler societies.[58]

Despite his earlier geopolitical polemics, Mann's historical sociology confounds any simple generalization about the character of nationality-internationality. The nation-state emerges from his account not as the outcome of class divisions *à la* Marx and Engels, as the homogeneous monopolizer of power of Weber or even as the bordered power-container of Giddens – still less the standard unified actor of international theory.[59] Rather, nation-states are contingent products of the interactions of state institutions, capital, nation and class. Their power relations are products of the ensemble of such relations in complex power networks 'inside' as well as 'outside' the state.

Mann's account is an antidote to all simplified general accounts of the state, and when he revises Weber's definition, it is to offer a looser, more qualified version:

1 The state is a differentiated set of institutions and personnel
2 embodying centrality, in the sense that political relations radiate to and from a centre, to cover a
3 territorially demarcated area over which it exercises
4 some degree of authoritative, binding rule making, backed up by some organized political force.[60]

Precisely because of its qualified character, this definition does not in itself offer us a straightforward handle on nationality-internationality. State power, according to Mann, does not come in the simple bundles of the 'nation-state', and national-international relations are closely tied into the processes of state power but not in a one-dimensional manner. Nations, like classes and other collective actors, have to be

---

[56] Mann (1993).   [57] Mann (1993: 78–86).
[58] Mann (1996).
[59] International theory is discussed further below.
[60] Mann (1993: 55).

forged, in the context of uneven patterns of statehood and variable organization of state institutions, together with which they form power networks. Mann examines the formation of nations in the context of power relations; others, however, see them more as socio-cultural realities.

Culture, nationality and ethnicity

While the dominant sociological literature on nationality and inter-nationality locates it in the context of the state, it has never been seen wholly in this context. Indeed, as the nation-state has been problema-tized in recent decades, one solution with wide currency has been to emphasize the cultural dimension of nationality. While modernist writers, Marxist and Weberian, continue to see nations as politically contingent,[61] a literature has grown up which distinguishes national identity from nationalism.[62] In these terms, national identity is a cultural universal, compared with the more transient political form of nationalism.

This facet of recent theory – which now increasingly affects accounts of international as well as national relations[63] – is, however, only one aspect of the increasing centrality of debates about culture in late modern social thought. In early and high modernity, cultural ques-tions were hardly recognized as objects of analysis. Culture was not an explicit category of Enlightenment thought, however much we might argue that it contained cultural assumptions. In the work of Marx, for example, the concept is not significant. The nearest he came to recognizing it was the idea of tradition, seen mainly as an obstacle to the constant revolutionization of social relations by capital.[64]

Although Marx acknowledged the sense of loss that went with the disappearance of old forms, in general he saw their abolition as progress. The more traditions were uprooted, the fewer barriers there would be to proletarian revolution in the consciousness of the working class. Ideas that were handed down were a burden: 'Men make history: not in the manner of their own choosing, but under circumstances given from the past. The ideas of all dead generations weigh like a nightmare on the minds of the living.'[65] Although in

---

[61] See for example Hobsbawm (1990).
[62] For example, Smith (1991).
[63] Lapid and Krachtowil (1997).
[64] See Marx and Engels (1998).   [65] Marx (1967).

some cases 'bourgeois' nationalism might be progressive, in general Marx saw national and ethnic consciousness among workers as forms of particularism which would be broken down in the development of universal class consciousness and international revolutionary struggle.

By the time of Weber, writing in the era of high nationalism and war, the eulogy of progress was breaking down, but the dilemma of modernity and culture deepened. In his idea of the rationalization of the world, Weber counterposed the legal-rational orientation in modern social action to more value-laden traditional forms. For Weber, this kind of rational action was – even if it originated in religious orientations – increasingly a purely technical, instrumental mode of rationality. Arising from capitalist property relations and the market, it was becoming universal and irresistible – for example, through bureaucratization. In a similar way to Marx, Weber saw traditional and charismatic modes of action displaced by the new rationality. Unlike Marx, he expressed his 'disenchantment' with this process, and saw no solution in socialism, which he believed – having observed German social democracy in action – would simply reinforce rationalization and bureaucratization.[66]

For Weber, what is now seen as the cultural realm was recognized in two main forms. On the one hand, different cultural forms were seen as preconditions of modernization and obstacles to its development. His sociology of the world religions emphasized their different predispositions towards capitalism.[67] On the other hand, Weber recognized the role of national tradition in the development of the state, and himself embraced a version of democratic German nationalism.[68]

Lukács developed Weber's ambivalence towards the cultural dimension of modern capitalism, incorporating the concept of rationalization into a critical Marxist account.[69] For Lukács, culture was interpreted under the aegis of capitalism. Cultural forms were recognized as belonging to historic classes. Cultural traditions, such as romanticism, discussed in a literary-aesthetic context, were seen as class-specific responses to the historical problems of capitalist development.[70] Lukács saw classical bourgeois culture as the framework of universal values in contemporary civilization, which the proletariat

---

[66] Gerth and Mills (1978).   [67] Weber (1965).
[68] Giddens (1972).   [69] Lukács (1971).
[70] For a complementary development of this approach, see Goldmann (1968).

would bring to fruition – while nationalism was reactionary. Similarly Trotsky, who rejected the possibility of proletarian culture, saw the proletariat as mastering the bourgeois legacy only through a period of rule, by which time communism would have created a universal culture, which would be developed in common.[71]

The dominant problematics in modern social theory, Marxist and Weberian, have thus tended to admit culture in universal and class aspects. They largely relegated national and religious cultural specificities to the category of traditional and non-rational residues of pre-modernity. Where they did not, as with Weber's nationalist writings, they have tended to be neglected in the incorporation of Weber into the later sociological tradition. Even the modern sociological synthesis of Parsons, while using Weber to tease out the role of values in the construction of social action, hardly dwelt on the specificity of cultures.[72] In his later elaboration of American structural-functionalism, the national dimension of Parsons' social system concept was not elaborated theoretically.[73]

In the canons of modern thought, it was once again Gramsci – struggling in a Fascist prison while Parsons was writing up his researches in an American university – who posed the problem of culture both in general, and in the context of the nation. For Gramsci, universal Western culture had a necessarily national context. He developed Marxist ideas in relation to the Italian tradition. In contrast to other Marxists who saw national differences as secondary, or as products of nation-state and inter-imperialist rivalry, Gramsci saw them as constitutive. Tradition was not merely a pre-capitalist residue, but a structural determinant of civil society and the state. For Gramsci, new forms of hegemony – in his time, the Fascist project of the corporate state – combined, as we have seen, traditional and organic (new) forms. Civil society was a nationally specific institutional context.[74]

Although Gramsci recognized cultural specificity in a new way, no more than earlier Marxists and sociologists did he develop the *concept* of culture or a *theory* of particular cultures and their relations. The problem of culture in social theory, in these senses, is essentially late modern. Only in recent decades has cultural theory emerged as a distinctive form, even if its early proponents, such as Raymond

---

[71] Trotsky (1960).   [72] Parsons (1949).
[73] Parsons (1972).   [74] Gramsci, in Hoare and Smith (1971).

Williams, were able to construct a significant tradition from the romantic reaction to industrialism and capitalism, and even if there were strong parallels in sociological thought.[75] In part, this tardiness reflects the thorough embedding of national-cultural concepts. Few problematized them, because they were part of the taken-for-granted order.

The givenness of culture was doubled-edged. On the one hand it meant that the framework of distinct national cultures was omnipresent, but on the other it meant that culture was never seen as being very important compared with political, economic and ideological power. In recent times, however, a distinctive cultural theory has both asserted the significance of culture in general and relativized particular cultures, a process begun in the works of Frankfurt theorists such as Theodor Adorno and Walter Benjamin between the world wars, but widely influential only well into the post-war period.[76]

Thus Williams' texts were foundational.[77] They epitomize, however, the tension between general and particular concepts of culture. On the one hand, he argues that 'culture is open': it is not a closed body of symbols, beliefs or values, and it does not belong simply to particular groups. He further claims that there is a development towards a 'common culture', within which elite, artistic and mass, popular culture exist in creative tension. On the other hand, the common culture of which he writes is both implicitly and explicitly national, albeit with English, Welsh and British referents and wider international influences. In these beginnings of modern cultural studies, however, the national-international context was not questioned as a general framework.

Parallel with the development of a concept of national culture in social theory has been a new exploration of the cultural construction of the nation. The givenness of nationality has been questioned, starting with Benedict Anderson's depiction of nations as 'imagined communities'.[78] The sense that nations were simply there, part of the infrastructure of social life, was challenged by the argument that they were real only in the sense of the imagination, in so far as people saw themselves as part of a community and acted upon this belief.

Anderson argued that 'all communities larger than primordial villages of face-to-face contact (and perhaps even these) are imagined',

[75] Williams (1958), Nisbet (1967).   [76] Adorno (1984), Benjamin (1970).
[77] Williams (1958, 1961).   [78] Anderson (1983).

and 'communities are to be distinguished, not by their falsity/ genuineness, but by the style in which they are imagined'. Nations are distinctive because the concept emerged 'in an age in which Enlightenment and Revolution were destroying the legitimacy of the divinely-ordained hierarchical dynastic realm'. They are imagined as finite, bounded and in relationship to other nations: 'No nation imagines itself coterminous with mankind.' A nation is 'imagined as a community, because, regardless of the actual inequality and exploitation that may prevail in each, the nation is always conceived in a deep, horizontal comradeship'.[79]

This relativization of nationality has been limited, however, by the contention of Anthony Smith that, while nationalism is indeed a product of modern forms of political community, nations (and national identities) are outgrowths of historic 'ethnies'. These are communities formed by relations of real or presumed common ancestry, history and memory.[80] In this sense, ethnies are thoroughly real – in a sense that corresponds to the concept of 'tradition' employed by Marx and Weber. So nations are both traditional and modern. Smith deploys this argument to confront the dismissal of nationality in much contemporary literature. Since nations are based on long historical evolution, they will not easily be displaced as referents of political community by new identities (European or global, for example) which do not have the same historical significance.[81] But since nations are also modern political forms, and the foundations of international order, they equally cannot be dismissed as ancient survivals.

Smith's arguments indicate how recent developments of social theory, in grounding nationality in cultural contexts, are far from automatically bringing nationality into question. The cultural turn in late modern social thought, in identifying nationality as a key component of modernity, both relativizes and legitimates it at the same time.

Internationality and anarchy

In the national and international world, the priority has long lain with the national. Nations are implicitly and explicitly understood as the

---

[79] Anderson (1983: 16).
[80] Smith (1986, 1991: 143–78). [81] Smith (1990, 1995).

basic units of social life; internationality is by definition a derivative phenomenon. Internationality has been understood in two principal ways – as conflict and as cooperation – which rest on contrasting evaluations of the significance of nationality itself. In the former sense, nations are the social foundations of inevitable interstate rivalry. In the latter, they are signifiers of political and cultural difference within a common framework: through international cooperation, universal values can be realized.

Whereas the national character of social relations has generally been perceived as deeply embedded in the modern world, even natural or primordial, internationality has often been understood as something to be established or achieved. This contrast may have been deeply mistaken, since for nations to exist they had to be recognized not only by their own members, but also by other states through international or interstate relations. However, it is internationality which has been widely seen as in need of constitution. For this reason, the foundational acts of the modern state-system – such as the Treaty of Westphalia – have been seen as codifying interstate order, even though they also provided a way of codifying states themselves.[82] Correspondingly, the constitution of nations has been neglected. Britain, for example, has been understood unproblematically as a historic nation, although it did not exist before its political constitution in the 1707 Act of Union between England and Scotland. Only after that was it elaborated as a social and cultural collectivity.[83]

A conflictual understanding of relations between nations has often gone together with a taken-for-granted view of nationality itself. Even critics such as Marx and Engels, for whom capitalism was a potentially universal order, took its embeddedness for granted. The proletariat's universal claims implied a conscious internationality that could only be established through political struggle against national identity. The distinctiveness of internationalism, liberal-pacifist as well as socialist, was widely felt by its adherents. A definite internationalist point of view was a challenge, it was believed, to the very character of a world of nations. Even in the days of the Cold War, a principled internationalism implied opposition to the dominant order. The converse was that to many rulers, and certainly to nationalists, internationalism was suspect if not anathema.

These assumptions have been reinforced by the dominant mode of

[82] Hirst (1997).   [83] Colley (1992).

academic analysis of international relations. As a distinct field of study, international relations was motivated from the 1930s and especially the 1950s by a reaction to the liberal internationalism which briefly held sway after the First World War.[84] Claiming a tradition which encompassed Thucydides, Machiavelli and Hobbes – but rejected Kant while ignoring Hegel and Marx – 'realist' international relations saw the international arena as inevitably conflictual, defined by competition for power between nation-states. Neither long-term direct military cooperation within alliances and blocs, nor the secular rise of infrastructural international institutions,[85] was seen as altering the character of international relations. Overarching military rivalries continued to justify the belief that international order was naturally conflictual.

A more balanced view, that international relations were simultaneously conflictual and cooperative, found expression in the 'English School' of international relations.[86] Developed from the tradition of thinking about international law originated by Hugo Grotius, this approach emphasized that in the Westphalian order there were common principles that all states recognized. These laid the ground rules for states' interaction, and some vestiges of them remained even in the most violent rivalries.

For Bull, therefore, international 'society', a society of states, was a tendency – stronger in some periods than others – within the international 'system', the pattern of interactions between states as a whole. This subtler concept might have had little appeal in the era of world wars. It was considerably more relevant to the curious mixture of manifest conflict and latent cooperation of the Cold War world. It was even more relevant to cooperative relations among nation-states within the Western bloc. Within international relations, therefore, the phase of *détente* in the 1970s saw the growth of arguments emphasizing the economic interdependence of states.[87] The onset of the Second Cold War, on the other hand, saw a tighter 'neo-realist' redefinition of international relations as a fundamentally anarchic system becoming widely influential.[88] Both these approaches were limited in locating international relations, however, primarily at the levels of states and state-system.

---

[84] Carr (1939), Morgenthau and Thompson (1985).
[85] Murphy (1994).   [86] Bull (1977), Wight (1977).
[87] Keohane and Nye (1977).   [88] Waltz (1979).

From standpoints in the mainstream of social, rather than political, theory this was hardly an acceptable starting-point. In sociological terms, a state-system could not be self-sustaining and states could not form a society: they were shaped by and within, as well as forming, social relations.[89] The theorization of national and international depended, however, on an adequate understanding of state relations, in the broad sense proposed above, as the social relations surrounding state institutions. The simple counterposition of economic and social relations to the state was hardly a plausible foundation for theorizing internationality. And yet this appeared to be the main alternative which social theory offered.

This was particularly true, as we have seen, for Marxist theory. National and international relations were a structural lacuna in this approach. Nevertheless, Marxists accounted for world order, encompassing economic, social and political relations. As the tradition revived in the 1970s, Marxists were still struggling with the implications of the 'internalist', class-struggle explanation of states bequeathed by Marx, Engels and Lenin.

One irony was the convergence between Marxism and orthodox international relations theory on the concept of 'anarchy'. For both, the world order was anarchic, in that it lacked and was likely to continue to lack any central authority. For international realists, of course, anarchy was politically constituted; for Marxists, the fact that capitalism was a system of competitive capitals was crucial. In the high national and international era, there was, however, a convergence of analysis as well as of terminology. As we have seen, Bukharin expressed this neatly in his world-view defined by competing national state capitalisms.[90] Classic realists also converged with Marxism, by recognizing economic strength as the infrastructure of national military power. E.H. Carr was, of course, a historian who engaged extensively with Marxism in his monumental history of Soviet power.

Realists mostly drew the conclusion that anarchy was unchangeable: even as the world of states has altered dramatically in the last years of the twentieth century, they have tended to argue that *plus ça change, plus c'est la même chose*.[91] Marxists, on the other hand, believe that anarchy is an aspect of capitalist relations and can be abolished

---

[89] Shaw (1994), chapter 4.
[90] Bukharin (1972).   [91] Miersheimer (1991).

with them – but that no changes short of this event can overcome it. As Marxism has retreated from revolutionary practice into a purely critical theory increasingly embedded in academia, this possibility has become increasingly improbable and hypothetical. In these circumstances, anarchy as the inevitable content of world order has become an increasingly common meaning of these two approaches.

The significant remaining difference between these two concepts of internationality is that, while in realist writings the nation-state international system is explicitly central, in the Marxist tradition, it is only indirectly present and more divergently theorized. Transnational corporations compete and combine with nation-states as the bearers of the new forms of anarchy. Where Western nation-states are representatives of corporate capital, nation-states in the so-called Third World can be, it has been argued, centres of resistance.[92] (The wider influence of Marxist concepts of the 'international' can be seen, therefore, chiefly in development studies.)

In the late (Cold War) national and international era, interstate conflict declined, while the salience of the nation-state as the political framework of capital was increasingly brought into question. This has brought about a slow change in the understanding of internationality in realist thought. Internationality, like nationality itself, has been defined increasingly in cultural terms. There are two main variants of this development. On the one hand, international relations are increasingly seen by many as intercultural relations, relations between nations as well as states. The divergence between states and nations, always a potential problem for realists (who saw them as unproblematically fused in the nation-state), has begun to be recognized. Security has been redefined in 'societal' terms, where society is a national or religious cultural community.[93] In international ethics, cultural relativism has reappeared in a conservative 'communitarianism' tied to acceptance of discrete cultural communities. And the concept has its Marxist-influenced, Third-Worldist counterpart in the idea of 'cultural imperialism'.[94] This variant of the new national-international culturalism is not a purely theoretical shift, but one increasingly adopted by actors on all sides. Thus the radical Islamist redefinition of Western imperialism as a decadent culture has been

---

[92] See for example Rosenberg (1994: 134) and MacLean (1999: 192–3).
[93] See for example Wæver (1993), and critique in Shaw (1994).
[94] Tomlinson (1990).

matched by a new Western concept of a 'clash of civilizations' typified by the West's opposition to radical Islam.[95] These ideas cut with the grain of older national-international definitions in popular culture.

The problem of the cultural concept of the international (as of the nation) is that, despite recognizing the increasing fluidity of political boundaries, it often proposes to regard cultural boundaries as relatively fixed. Little reflection is needed to see the problems with this. Political borders are at least formally defined. Cultural boundaries are inherently indeterminate; they are transgressed every time people make changes in their lives – whether moving from one city to another across the globe, marrying someone from a different background, or just incorporating the literature or even the cuisine from an 'other' tradition into their own repertoire.

These problems of an intercultural conception of international relations are evident even in its most benign forms. Just as internationalism was an advance on nationalism, multiculturalism (or cultural pluralism) appears an advance on cultural antagonism and apartheid. Just as internationalism assumes the nation, however, so multiculturalism assumes discrete and relatively fixed cultures. It is at best a very partial escape from separatism; it can also reinforce the false closure of group relations on which separatism feeds.[96] Culture is therefore the last refuge of old thinking about internationality as well as nationality. The idea of international as intercultural relations – whether as a 'new' explanation for conflict or as a seed-bed of cooperation – brings us up against the limits of nationality and internationality as a framework of understanding in today's world.

No wonder, then, that Yosef Lapid argues that international theory needs to recognize that 'the core meanings of culture and identity have undergone in recent years a series of largely parallel redefinitions'. This renders 'both concepts more highly compatible with emerging pluralities and fluid instabilities that have rendered traditional understandings largely untenable . . . The current rethinking recasts culture from a reified singular concept into a more nuanced and finely tuned semantic field. It rejects "congruent cultural wholeness" superstitions.'[97]

On the other hand, internationality itself has begun to be seen as socially constructed, rather than simply given by the objective struc-

---

[95] Huntington (1996).
[96] Calhoun (1994).   [97] Lapid (1997: 1).

ture of the state-system. Alexander Wendt has advocated an 'idealist' or 'constuctivist' social theory of international politics, embodying the 'minimal' claim 'that the deep structure of society is constructed by ideas rather than material forces'.[98] However, Wendt continues to define internationality as based on the idea of sovereignty, 'in which states recognize each other as having exclusive political authority within separate territories'. Like Rosenberg, he still accepts the distinction between 'domestic' and 'international' as axiomatic: 'At home states are bound by a thick structure of rules that holds their power accountable to society. Abroad they are bound by a different set of rules, the logic or as I shall argue, logics, of anarchy.'[99]

The difference, then, between Wendt's 'moderate constructivism' and Waltz's structural realism is that the former wishes to 'isolate the "difference that ideas make" in social life'.[100] He appeals to a new late modern consensus in social theory: 'most modern social theory is idealist in this sense'. 'Few would deny', he argues, '. . . that the structure of the contemporary international system contains a lot of culture . . . they will disagree about how much international culture "matters".'[101] Anarchy is not given, but is 'what states make of it'. In new foreign policy discourse, therefore, 'moral' claims are no longer juxtaposed to, but may partially constitute, 'interests'.[102]

This cautious culturalism still sees the division of nationality and internationality as given by the structures of statehood and geopolitics, taking it almost as much for granted as the realist international tradition. As Inayatullah and Blaney have wondered, is it 'worth tinkering with putative leakages within the anarchy problematique (that is materialism and/or rationalism) if the entire construct is so inherently and irreversibly incapable of retaining any culture, identity, or meaning-related content?'[103] A culturalized, idea-permeated national-international conception of politics continues to absolutize this particular form of structural divide. It ignores the understanding which state theory has given us of the continuities between national and international in power networks, and makes it difficult to historically problematize the national-international structure of power.

---

[98] Wendt (1999: 25).   [99] Wendt (1999: 13).
[100] Wendt (1999: 117).   [101] Wendt (1999: 25, 190).
[102] Wendt (1992, 1999: 125).   [103] Inayatullah and Blaney (1997: 71).

War and society

A central paradox of social thought is that in the national-international era, the world has been riven by war as never before; but the dominant understandings of modernity have grasped war as an abnormal disruption of ongoing patterns of social relations. Even more curiously, we might think, nationality and internationality themselves have been understood largely outside the war context. Although 'anarchic' international relations have been mediated largely by war, the fundamental significance of the social relations of war for the national-international world has been little explored.

The intellectual roots of these failures lie deep in the mainstream of social thought. The 'founder' of modern sociology, Auguste Comte, developed Henri de Saint-Simon's idea of an industrial society ruled by science and technology in which common values assured the reign of harmony. Comte wrote in the 1830s when the revolutionary wars had been left behind; for him, militarism was a relic of the pre-scientific, pre-industrial social order. It would disappear, he argued, with the consolidation of industrial society. This fundamental error reflected the failure to understand the national-international framework within which industrial society developed.[104]

And yet Comte's error was foundational for a major current of social thought. Moreover, not all sociology was as free-floating from national interests as Comte's vision of a peaceful international industrial society. The classics of twentieth-century sociology were created in the late nineteenth-century heyday of nationalism. Emile Durkheim, for example, developed an organic view of society in which the nation was the implicit framework, but war was not a central problem.[105] In the mid-twentieth century, Talcott Parsons' theory defined the 'social system', the object of social thought, as the national society. Writing at the height of the Cold War, he saw America as a normal model of modern society, and military relations as part of the external relation of the social system to its environment.[106]

Marx's and Weber's ideas offered rather more adequate frameworks in which to understand the role of war, but neither of them placed war itself at the centre of their understanding. In general, late twentieth-century sociologists have operationalized Comte's notion of warless

---

[104] See Aron (1958, 1979).
[105] Durkheim (1962).   [106] Parsons (1972).

industrialism – generally without acknowledging it – by implicitly defining war as an exceptional occurrence. Even Marxist and Weberian writers have been concerned, moreover, with the *role* of war in capitalism and the nation-state, rather than the *nature* of war as a form of social action and its capacity to shape – as well as reflect – other social institutions.

In the same period in which Hegel and Comte were writing, and just before Marx's earliest work, Karl von Clausewitz wrote *On War*. Clausewitz's work has been the foundation of modern strategic theory, but its fundamental contribution to the general tradition of social theory has been ignored. (Had it been acknowledged, it could have radically transformed the ways in which intellectual histories were written and social science disciplines moulded.) Clausewitz's work held a rather different vision of the future from Comte's. On the surface, this was because it looked back to the wars of the Napoleonic era, which the latter had consigned to history. At the same time it failed to confront the implications of the industrial society which held such fascination for the new sociology. But the combination of warfare and industrial capitalism was to become a key force of modernity in the nineteenth century, and even more in the twentieth.

The combination of Clausewitz's insights with modern social understanding is therefore a key theoretical task of the social sciences, generally neglected in all traditions.[107] Clausewitz's work was a contribution to the understanding of the modern world, especially its national-international structure, on a par with Kant's or Hegel's. Clausewitz did not develop his ideas as fully as Marx (and like the latter, he died before completing his principal work). But it is salutary to confront his marginalized ideas, often appropriated in a one-sided manner.

Clausewitz is widely known only for his dictum that 'war is the continuation of political intercourse, by other means'.[108] This has endeared him not only to mainstream political and strategic thinkers, but also to revolutionaries such as Marx and Engels, for whom it confirmed that war was a reflection of underlying political and hence economic relations. Its real significance was, however, the opposite of this. While war continued politics, it did so *by other means*. Clause-

---

[107] See Shaw (1988), chapter 1; Howard (1980).
[108] Clausewitz (1976).

witz's contribution was to clarify the nature and implications of these means.

War, he reasoned, was an act of force to compel an enemy to submit to our will; there was no logical limit to force, until submission was obtained. So while war's origins and general framing were in the political objectives of states, the practice of war had its own dynamics. These, Clausewitz argued, were comparable to the laws of commerce. War was a distinctive set of social activities, in which all war preparation, logistical planning and military organization led to the defining moment of battle. The clash of arms was not merely a moment of conflict between two armies but the culmination of a whole social organization. Clausewitz made the comparison with economics when he wrote that 'battle is to war as exchange is to commerce'[109] – he meant that battle, like exchange, is the moment of *realization* of a larger social process and a whole complex of relations.

Mary Kaldor has suggested that we can draw from this the conclusion that there is a 'mode of warfare' comparable – but not reducible – to the mode of production hypothesized by Marx.[110] This concept is helpful for understanding the structure of relationships within warfare which Clausewitz proposes, and it suggests an autonomous role for warfare in wider social relationships. Giddens proposes something similar with his concept of warfare as a distinct 'institutional cluster' of modernity; but this suggests less of the dynamic character indicated by the term 'mode' of warfare.[111]

It is important to follow Clausewitz further on the dynamics of warfare. If there was no logical limit to force, then escalation was a law of modern war, and war would tend to become absolute. This tendency was rooted, however, not just in the general characteristics of warfare, but in a particular sociology of war in the emerging national-international period. Clausewitz's ideas were based on his observations of the Napoleonic wars in which he had fought. He outlined the general features of this sociology in his account of the 'trinity' of modern warfare. Policy belonged to governments and strategy to the generals, but the violence of modern war – the key to its absolute tendency – lay in the participation of the people-in-arms of the new mass armies. Thus was the nation critical to a new mode of war.

[109] Clausewitz (1976).
[110] Kaldor (1982).   [111] Giddens (1985).

In this sense, the Clausewitzian theory expressed another s[...] the same revolutionary processes of the early national-internatio[...] era that inspired the Enlightenment mainstream. Clausewitz explored[...] much more concretely than Hegel, the relation between revolution and the modern state, in its mobilization of the violence of the people for national ends. Clausewitz accounted for the material framework of war: the limits to the tendency towards absolute war he saw in the environment of warfare, rather than in the process of war itself. Politics was one source of limitation, but the other, on which he laid more stress, was the 'friction' of climate, terrain, supply, transportation, etc. In the first quarter of the nineteenth century these were still very considerable constraints, as Napoleon's forced retreat from Moscow had shown.

Where Marx and Engels tended to see war as a reflection of economy and politics, Clausewitz developed an understanding of warfare as a mode of social action: 'To paraphrase Marx's First Thesis on Feuerbach, the defect of most social theory of war and militarism is that it has sought to reduce war to rational, material interests: it has not considered war as practice, i.e. what people do in war. Hence again "the active side has been developed abstractly" – in this case by military theory.'[112]

If Clausewitz's theory provides a crucial corrective to the naïve idea of warless industrialism, and introduces the idea of war as an active determination, nevertheless it has three main limitations. First its sociology was rudimentary – really little more than suggestive. Second, it did not offer a serious account of the emerging nation-state context of warfare.

Third, and above all, Clausewitz failed to anticipate the imminent industrialization of war, the consequences of which were to be fundamental.[113] In this sense, modern war has moved beyond the main parameters of his thought.[114] But his insights remain the starting-point for analysing dynamics of organized violence that have been central to the history of modernity. These relationships of war, state and society are fundamental to understanding the development

---

[112] Shaw (1988: 135, n.1).

[113] See Howard (1980), Shaw (1988) for appraisals of Clausewitz in the light of twentieth-century experience; MacNeill (1982) for the industrialization of war.

[114] Van Crefeld (1991) and Kaldor (1999) argue that warfare is now 'post-Clausewitzian'. However, this begs the question of how far modern industrialized total war could ever be described in 'Clausewitzian' terms. See chapter 4.

ternational order, its crisis and hence the emergence
torical understanding of the nature and role of war
extra to the understanding of modernity, capitalism
ternationality that this chapter has explored. I will
nent in the second, historical part of this book.

Revolution and civil war

If social theory has tended to miss the normality of war, it has also
tended to minimize the importance of revolutions to modernity.
Although great upheavals in society and politics (such as the French
and Russian revolutions) have set many of the parameters of modern
thought, revolutionary change, like war, has tended to be seen as
abnormal and disruptive. Even the Marxist perspective, in which
revolution was originally defining, has tended more recently to be
operationalized in non-revolutionary ways: for most Marxists, the
point is no longer to change, but to understand.

In chapter 1, I discussed the relationships between the national and
international aspects of revolution. Here, I want to emphasize the
close links of revolution to war, not only as manifestation and cause of
instability in interstate relations, but as forms of social action. The
theory of revolution, like that of war, has centred on its roles in social
and political transformation, and latterly in international change,
rather than its character as a social process. The study of revolution
still awaits its Clausewitz: there is no single thinker whose ideas are
as emblematic in its study. But we can begin to define the question of
the nature of revolution, and further explore its links with war.

The nearest revolution has to a Clausewitzian figure is Leon
Trotsky, co-leader of the 1917 Russian revolution and author of its
greatest history, written in exile at a similar distance in time from its
events to that which Clausewitz had from the Napoleonic wars in
which he had participated.[115] Revolution according to him is a mass
uprising of the oppressed classes directed at the seizure of political
power. Like war for Clausewitz, revolution for Trotsky is a process in
which social forces are mobilized for political ends. Above all, revolution is about power, about imposing the will of the revolutionary
forces on society through the defeat of the old state machine.

War is by definition an act of violence, imposed by armed 'forces'.

[115] Trotsky (1965a).

In revolution, in contrast, political rather than military mobilization is the essential mode. Its typical institutions are representative (in the proletarian case, workers' councils) and leading (revolutionary parties). At the decisive moment of revolution (comparable to the moment of battle in Clausewitz's view of warfare), violence is inherently possible – if not likely – because revolution is a decisive challenge of new social power to old. According to Trotsky, however, violence is not in general necessary for revolution. He emphasizes the relatively tiny number of deaths in Petrograd (St Petersburg), the centre of the Bolshevik revolution of October 1917.

In revolutions, inequality of armament is the norm. Revolutionaries are normally unable to match established power in technical military terms; their essential strength must lie in social and political mobilization. Revolution may be armed initially only on a limited scale, and through forms of organization which reflect its social roots – democratic militia rather than centralized force. The extent of violence in revolution, Trotsky therefore believed, was largely dependent on the resistance of the old order. Large-scale, organized violence arose from counterrevolution, rather than from revolution itself, and counterrevolution was likely to lead to civil war.

In civil war, the revolutionary forces then had little choice but to organize themselves in a military fashion. In Soviet Russia, of course, Trotsky himself became the Commissar for War. According to his biographer Isaac Deutscher, he then 'worshipped what he had burned and burned what he had worshipped'.[116] He abandoned democratic militia for a centralized standing army. Instead of viewing military centralism as a deviation from revolutionary norms, he elevated it as a model of the new order.

During the period of 'war communism' (1918–21), Trotsky and Bukharin, the critics of capitalist militarism, eulogized a new revolutionary militarism. From a classic Marxist viewpoint, this was a deviation from revolutionary principles. It was recognized as such by Lenin's eventual abandonment of war communism for a 'new economic policy' based on greater market freedom. The experience raised sharply, however, three questions about the relationship between revolution and war. Was there indeed a necessary relationship, if only in the overwhelming probability of military resistance from the old order – both within the nation-state and internationally

---

[116] Deutscher (1967).

from other states – and therefore of civil and/or interstate war? Was this relationship likely to become internal to the revolution, as in war communism? And was there any way to avoid the cycle of revolution, counterrevolution, war and militarization that appeared to constitute the essence of revolution?

Subsequent experience confirmed the seriousness of these questions. First, the military centralization of revolutionary power in Russia proved not a temporary phase but a constitutive process. Militarization led directly to the formation of a new terroristic order. The consolidation of extreme dictatorship under Stalin involved – as Trotsky, by now its sternest critic, testified in his work throughout the 1920s and 1930s – massive forms of 'counterrevolutionary' violence. There were not only purges of the revolutionary elite but genocide[117] of the peasantry (through the infamous 'liquidation of the kulaks') and brutal repression of the workers.

Second, new 'fascist' forms of counterrevolution in Italy and Germany (in response to revolutionary movements there after 1917) glorified the militarism of the previous world war. Fascism led in turn to new wars, including the definitive genocide of modernity, the Nazis' systematic killing of the Jews and many others. In the Holocaust, key elements of modernity – nationalism, industrial technology, bureaucracy, war – combined to define its fundamentally ambivalent legacy.[118]

Third, despite the efforts of some critical Marxists to rescue an 'orthodox' theory of revolution deriving from Lenin and Trotsky, after these experiences war was internalized in the revolutionary mainstream. Trotsky's distinction between the minimalist violence of revolution, and the murderousness of counterrevolution and Fascism, hardly survived the generalization of the Stalinist model. The major revolutions of the mid-twentieth century were nearly all carried out by Communist parties which had internalized Stalinist military centralism. Guerrilla war, led by monolithic authoritarian parties, was the

---

[117] Although the international definition of genocide after 1945 confined it to the deliberate destruction (in whole or in part) of national, racial and religious groups (Guttman and Rieff 1999: 142), there is no good sociological reason to regard the phenomenon as restricted in this way. The exclusion of mass killing of social classes from the definition cannot be justified, and indeed at least one other case of this, in Cambodia in the late 1970s, has been widely accepted as genocide.

[118] Bauman (1990); however, Bauman does not directly consider the extent to which genocide was a product of the specific relations of modern war.

new mode of revolution, from China and Vietnam to Yugoslavia and Albania, during and immediately after the Second World War. Only Stalin's accommodation to the Western powers prevented its more widespread application in 1944–5. Adaptations of it, in the name of revolutionary nationalisms (influenced to lesser or greater degrees by Communism), were normal throughout the so-called Third World during the Cold War era and continue even to this day.

The possibility of an alternative idea of revolution, as distinct from war, was indicated by a number of disparate developments that reacted against this new mainstream. Theoretically, as we have seen, Gramsci's idea of hegemony had already indicated, in the 1930s, the possibility of creating the groundwork for political transformation in culture and society, rather than engaging in direct and necessarily violent confrontation with established power. Gramsci paid lip-service, however, to the pervasive militarization of revolutionary discourse: he designated these two strategies the 'war of manoeuvre' and the 'war of position'. Substantively, however, Gramsci's concept was used to suggest an alternative to the increasingly militarized revolutionary mainstream.

Practically and symbolically of much greater significance, Mahatma Gandhi's approach of passive resistance offered a new way of acting for oppressed groups, based on Hindu thought.[119] Gandhi refused the strategically derived conceptions of classical revolutionary politics, advocating non-violence as a principle, and hoping to achieve emancipatory goals through the moral effect of action rather than through a calculus of power centred on force. Unlike Gramsci, Gandhi did not concern himself abstractly with the mechanisms by which moral hegemony was translated into power. He refused the quandary of violence in which Trotsky had originally defined the problem of revolutionary power.

In the latter part of the Cold War era, this looser discourse of revolution was further refined. In the student-led movements of the late 1960s, especially in France in May 1968, many proclaimed a 'revolution in the revolution' in which cultural transformation, democratic participation and non-violence were key principles. This revolution's legacy was largely appropriated, in the short term, by sterile sectarian currents reasserting Marxist and Stalinist traditions. In the

---

[119] Mukherjee (1993), Parekh (1989).

longer term, though, 1968 can be seen as a moment in the liberation of revolutionary thought from its classical political-military dilemma.[120]

Even more important in making the leap to a new, more inclusive, democratic and peaceful transformation of the concept of revolution, however, were the uprisings and oppositional movements in east-central Europe during the Communist period (which I discuss more fully in the next chapter). In the history of these movements, there was a development of thought and action. The movements of 1953 in Germany and 1956 in Hungary and Poland were classic insurrections. The Prague Spring of 1968 was a social movement in response to reform within the state. Polish Solidarity in the 1980s was constructed as a labour movement within the framework of the state. The successful democratic revolutions of 1989 in Germany, Czechoslovakia and Romania responded to democratic transformation throughout the bloc.

In the later movements, there was an emphasis on avoiding direct confrontation over state power which was reminiscent of Gramsci, an essentially Gandhian moral propaganda and passive resistance, and a general embrace of non-violence. The 'anti-politics' leading to the 'tender revolution' of 1989 centred (like Gramsci's ideas) on the development of 'civil society'.[121] Class elements were still involved – notably in Polish Solidarity – but the aims of the revolution were essentially democratic. While antagonistic to the state form of the Soviet bloc, the movements were – while often critical – essentially congruent with the traditions of the globally dominant West. In this sense, revolution had itself become a form of critical reconciliation with, rather than simple opposition to, the world order.

This tendency was also evident in tensions within many movements of the 1980s. The African National Congress in South Africa, which had embraced classic ideas of revolutionary armed struggle, gradually abandoned them in favour of mass democratic politics and non-violent political transformation within the state institutions. Under much less favourable circumstances and with greater political ambiguity, the Palestine Liberation Organization abandoned terrorism for political compromise with Israel. These cases were further evidence of the transformation of ideas of revolution, away from the militarized forms of earlier in the twentieth century, as the national and international era drew to its close.

---

[120] In this sense 1968 paved the way for the 'velvet revolutions' of 1989; see chapter 4.
[121] Kavan (1999).

3   Intimations of globality: *Hamlet* without the Prince

The social sciences have long contained, in a double sense, the challenge of the global. The modern tradition of social theory and analysis has encapsulated the essentially political tension at the heart of globalization. On the one hand, the master ideas of social thought, developed from the late eighteenth to the early twentieth century, centred on concepts of universal, implicitly global significance – civil society, capitalism, industrialism, modernity. On the other hand, the twentieth-century institutionalization of the social sciences in academic disciplines, research and teaching practice have largely nationalized and internationalized these concepts. Theory and analysis have come to refer, implicitly if not always explicitly, to the national and international frameworks of state and society that dominated social relations in the mid-twentieth century heyday of the nation-state.

The new transparency of global relations has therefore brought with it a conceptual crisis in the social sciences. Since the very meanings of core concepts change in a period of transition, we need to redefine them for a global age. Globality challenges the disciplines to move beyond the ways of thinking which have predominated in their historic development. We need, too, to reimagine the interrelations between the different social science disciplines.

In this chapter, I examine, first, how the social sciences have been contained by pre-global thought, and second, the forms that the amplification of the global has taken. In the light of the argument of the first chapter, that globality has political roots, I especially explore the intimations of global politics in the literatures, in order to demonstrate the limitations in the ways in which state power and political transformation have been understood. I aim to show, first, that global theory has systematically underestimated the political, and second, that theories of political change have not seriously grappled with the global.

Social science as stamp collecting

It is not too far-fetched to liken the world-view on which a great deal of mainstream social science is based to that of the stamp collector. As a youthful philatelist in the mid-twentieth century, I sorted my stamps by political jurisdiction. I directed my attention to the national forms – technical and symbolic – through which both intranational and international communication took place. I was not so concerned with the manifold social relations – personal, commercial, professional, etc. – which these forms concealed, although these were much more important, almost certainly more interesting, and less constituted by the apparatus of statehood.

Much social science sorted social relations in the same way, simply assuming the coincidence of social boundaries with state boundaries and that social action occurred primarily within, and secondarily across, these divisions. Social relations were represented by the national societies that were assumed to frame them. Just as I collected the various ephemera of national postal systems, social scientists collected distinctive national social forms. Japanese industrial relations, German national character, the American constitution, the British class system – not to mention the more exotic institutions of tribal societies – were the currency of social research.

The core disciplines of the social sciences, whose intellectual traditions are reference points for each other and for other fields, were therefore *domesticated* – in the sense of being preoccupied not with Western and world civilization as wholes but with the 'domestic' forms of particular national societies. Jan Aart Scholte has called this tendency 'methodological nationalism' and 'territorialism'.[1] What it involved, above all, was a slippage from the general to the particular without bringing into the open the problematic abstraction involved in isolating the national case.

The particular was often assumed to be representative of the general. In sociology and political science, for example, American or British society, state and capitalism with all their idiosyncrasies were

[1] Scholte (1999).

often held to typify society, state or capitalism as such. This tendency was not confined to conservative theorists such as Talcott Parsons. C. Wright Mills' radical critique of the 'power elite'[2] was often presented as an alternative model of power in modern society without acknowledging the American specificity that he put at the heart of his account. Marxists could write about class in Britain as though it was a typical rather than a very peculiar case of a capitalist society.[3]

In the domesticated core social sciences, when the general pattern of social relations on a world scale came to be represented by more than a single case, it was not usually by global, transnational or even international relations but by the *comparative* method. Comparing different particular social forms came to substitute for understanding the relations between them and the general structures within which these comparisons might be explained. National and comparative sociology and politics increasingly dominated the core disciplines in practice.

International relations conformed to this pattern as the exception that proved the rule. In the early post-war decades, when international realism was codified, world order could only be conceived of in terms of the international. In a world of nation-states, internationality represented the relations between units and actors under this single, simple rubric. The international, of course, meant interstate, since states were mostly assumed, by definition, to represent 'their' nations. The relationship between state and nation was unproblematic, indeed symbiotic.

The division of labour, between the domesticated disciplines and international relations, reflected a central irony of the Cold War West. Although Western nation-states were casting off the military rivalries of centuries to create a common network of power, with an increasing number of bloc and world institutions, national forms remained dominant. Western integration was first of all cooperation between the nation-states and, reflecting them, national societies that had emerged from the era of total war. Commonality presented itself first as the *alliance* and *similarity* of what continued to be seen as distinct units.

No wonder, then, that the comparative method became so influential in Western social science and that instead of global knowledge, international research generated comparative studies. The genre has gained new life, indeed, at the end of the twentieth century with the

[2] Mills (1956).   [3] See for example Westergaard and Resler (1975).

increasing dependence of much European social research on European Union funding with its in-built balancing of national interests. The post-Cold War incorporation of central and east European nation-states within the Western social science orbit has only accentuated this trend. Increasingly, however, the comparative method seems anachronistic, as simultaneously not just the Western world and its European sub-unit, but world society as a whole, begin to see themselves as integrated wholes. Within these larger frameworks, relations between individuals, firms, social groups and cultures are not necessarily, simply, or even primarily mediated by nationality-internationality.

Crisis of *ancien régime* social science

The possibility of global knowledge released by the end of the Cold War involves the simultaneous transformation both of concepts of nationality and of the ways in which integrationary, internationalist tendencies have been understood. The removal of the border of violence between the bloc worlds has accelerated the tendency to see national borders, too, as partial and relative. The dissolution of the ideological worlds has simultaneously loosened still further the sense of discrete nation-state units that were the building blocks of the Cold War. For all the posturing of new nationalists, the nation-state is indeed constantly relativized. The links between people can no longer be squeezed into a national-international straitjacket, even if this is still very much one of the dimensions which define them. This is as true of social relations 'within' states as it as of those 'across' their borders.

Instead social relations are increasingly grasped in their genuine complexity, as interpersonal, familial, industrial, commercial, professional, local, regional, transnational, world-regional, global – as well as national and international. Most social relations still have some national-international aspect. For example, my e-mail address is 'm.shaw@sussex.ac.uk', but the national signifier is of fairly trivial importance, since neither the content nor the mechanism of my communications depends necessarily on their national character. This exemplifies the fact that often the national-international is a residual category of convenience in global relations.

In this variety of terms in which social relations are now understood, some are intrinsically spatial (local, regional, national, transnational, international, world-regional) while others (interpersonal, familial, commercial, professional, lifestyle, movement) do not assume a particular spatial content. Global has an obvious spatial reference but, as I argued in chapter 1, its significance goes far beyond this. The global is the largest and most inclusive spatial framework of social relations – and, interplanetary exploration apart, the maximum possible framework. Its development represents the partial over-coming of the major divisions of the world – cultural as well as territorial. Precisely for these reasons, globality includes both the spatially and non-spatially defined differentiations of the world.

It is not accidental, therefore, that global categories have emerged as the main forms of the new theoretical discourse of the social sciences, and that the global has a different significance from the other terms. Those who oppose regional or transnational to global change therefore underestimate the significance of current transformations and misunderstand the debate on the global. To talk of global transformations does not mean that all relations are of a spatially worldwide or transregional kind. Rather global transformation, involving fundamental changes in both the spatial and non-spatial dimensions of social relations, includes the regional, transnational, etc. – whereas none of these terms can include the global.

At the beginning of the twenty-first century, therefore, social theory is becoming conscious of a global revolution. This represents a deep crisis for the social sciences. It is leading to the most important transformations of the structures of social knowledge in recent times. At the centre of these transformations is the question of whether the core disciplinary subjects can reconstitute themselves in global terms. So far, the evidence is that the theoretically constitutive subjects of sociology, politics and economics have indeed been largely disabled by their inherited methodological nationalism. Despite important new shoots, the mainstreams have hardly been globalized.

Writing of the nineteenth century, Mann notes that 'Throughout this period the nation-state and a broader transnational Western civilization competed as basic membership units. Sociology's master-concept, "society", kept metamorphosing between the two.'[4] Later, sociology was organized around the twin concepts of industrial and capitalist society. Both of these clearly held a potential for global understanding, but in the mid-twentieth century they were overwhelmingly operationalized as national categories, with the

---

[4] Mann (1993: 9).

comparative sociology of national societies substituted for global knowledge.

Even the new Marxism of the 1970s – with exceptions such as 'world-systems' theory that had their own characteristic weaknesses[5] – largely adapted itself to the national contexts of existing social science. Since the Marxist revival petered out, there has been if anything a further domestication of sociology, pragmatically integrating it in national and sub-national contexts. The understanding of politics, the international and the global have been addressed by thinkers such as Mann and Giddens, but their work has impinged only slowly on the institutionalized intellectual context of the discipline.

Moreover, 'global' ideas have met resistance. Barry Smart, for example, explicitly opposes the idea of a 'global sociology', 'with its connotations of a universalising, indivisible discipline', preferring the notion of 'a sociology of globalisation, or better still, sociological analyses of processes of globalisation'. For him, the idea of a 'global sociology', implying that 'there already exists a worldwide culture', is mistaken. Elevating the notion of 'society' to a global level suggests that 'the peoples of the world' are incorporated 'into a single world society, global society', and this will not do.[6] Moreover, where 'global' sociology has developed, the global has been largely conceived in socio-cultural terms. Thus for Leslie Sklair, 'the global system' is based on 'transnational practices' rather than 'state-centric' relations.[7]

Political science is arguably even more afflicted. In political theory, certainly, the normative agenda of globalization has led to a new problematization of the division of international and domestic politics. What is at stake, as David Held argues, is nothing less than a fundamental recasting of political theory as it has developed *within* the liberal-democratic nation-state. Democracy and other political values have to be reconstituted in global – or in Held's word, cosmopolitan – terms.[8]

However, in empirical political science the standard demarcation of national and international remains especially disabling. Comparative politics suffers from much the same weaknesses as comparative sociology, but politics has the vices as well as the virtues of the more

---

[5] Wallerstein (1979); see also discussion of world systems in Scholte (1999).
[6] Smart (1993: 135). For similar caution, see Kilminster (1998).
[7] Sklair (1991: 6).   [8] Held (1995).

explicitly national focus involved in studying states and party systems. Political studies adapt by analysing politics as process, at the expense of grasping the transformation of content. Thus the European Union or the United Nations can be seen as offering new contexts in which to explore the mechanics of political life and institution building, rather than challenges of historical change.[9] Even in historically oriented political studies, writers such as Hirst and Thompson have emphasized the continuing role, rather than the transformation, of the nation-state, and have seen (limited) transformation in international as opposed to global terms.[10] These diverging responses in political theory and political science raise, therefore, the problem of the continuing coherence of politics as a field, and its increasingly uncertain relations with international relations.[11]

As to the third constitutive discipline, economics, its widespread failure to recognize itself as a qualitative social science has not helped it to open up to the global. There is a real paradox, in that economic relations are universally acknowledged to be central to globalization, but professional economists are hardly in the forefront of theorizing the phenomenon. It is symptomatic that the economic relations of globalization are picked up more substantially in geography, sociology and (especially) the burgeoning field of international political economy (or IPE) which is closer to, or within, international relations and geography rather than economics. IPE is an interesting case of a general trend, that global issues are often best addressed through interdisciplinary fields and in subjects that are less constitutive of the social sciences as a whole.[12]

The disciplines of anthropology, geography and international relations have shown greater openness to global understanding than economics, politics and sociology, the historically defining fields of social science. Interestingly, the former are all fields in which historically the national-international nexus was formerly not just a

---

[9] See for example the justification of political science by Taggart (1999).

[10] Hirst and Thompson (1996).

[11] I have discussed this further in the Introduction to Shaw (1999).

[12] Underhill (1994: 18) expresses a core contention of IPE as that 'Politics is the means by which economic structures, in particular the structures of the market, are established and in turn transformed . . . The principal focus of political conflict, at the domestic or international level, concerns who gets what, when, and how. That is what the institutions of the market and the agencies of the state between them determine, and of course asymmetries of power abound.' It will be noted that while this politicizes economics it simultaneously interprets politics economistically.

methodological bias, but more or less *explicitly* constitutive. The openness of both social anthropology and geography to globalization debates follows their abandonment of nineteenth- and early twentieth-century nationalist and imperialist constructions of their subjects. These subjects underwent theoretical and ideological transformations earlier in the post-war period, which have prepared the way for the recognition of globalization.

Thus the old colonial-inspired traditions of social anthropology disintegrated with the independence movements of the 1960s, which required new ways of conceiving spatially differentiated relations.[13] The discipline's bias towards the study of less formal social relations facilitated an interest in relations defined in non-territorial and non-national ways – within and across rather than limited by state borders. The subject was thus implicitly globalist before global debates seriously developed. In particular, anthropologists have explored the transformation of culture in plural and hybrid forms.[14]

In geography, similarly, the old geopolitical foundations of the subject have long since eroded, rendered anachronistic by the collapse of empire. In geography's case, however, space remains a master concept, and even before global debates became widespread, geographers mapped economic and social relations in post-national terms. Not only have geographers been in the forefront of analysing the economics of globalization,[15] but the concept of space has also been peculiarly problematized, and geographers have accommodated debates on time, space and modernity from social theory. The result, however, appears to have been the decline of a distinctive disciplinary sense, as the boundaries between geography, political economy, international relations and sociological thought have become more and more fluid.

Critical geographers have embraced this new fluidity and redefined the role for geography within it. Peter Taylor, for example, sees geography as 'marginalized' in the old 'state-centric orthodoxy' of the social sciences. 'The mainstream social science trilogy of sociology, economics, and political science', he argues, 'neglected questions of space and place because they failed to problematize the embedded statism in which they developed.' 'New spaces' are

---

[13] Asad (1971).
[14] For example, Fardon (1995), Friedman (1994), Hannerz (1996) and Kahn (1995).
[15] Dicken (1998).

opened up in theory, however, by the 'new heterodoxy consequent upon globalization', in which 'the new subtleties of social space are integral'. Thus Taylor sees geography as particularly equipped for a social science which is discarding 'embedded statism' (by which he means something similar to Scholte's 'methodological nationalism' and 'territorialism').[16]

Other geographers have made less of a disciplinary pitch: Simon Dalby, for example, calls for 'the transgression of boundaries, academic and geopolitical', and argues that 'the discursive difficulties of contemporary world politics suggest the need for multiple and overlapping maps'.[17] He especially advocates crossing 'boundaries between international relations and contemporary thinking in political geography'.[18] This tendency is reinforced by the development of a postmodern 'critical geopolitics', in which geopolitical boundaries are regarded as socially and culturally constructed.[19]

In such transformations of disciplinary relations, an increasingly important role is played by interdisciplinary fields – such as environmental, communications and cultural studies as well as IPE – which have often seen the most radical posing of global transformation. An early example, of course, was development studies: in the postcolonial era, this was a principal arena for issues of world political economy and world sociology. But development studies also embody some of the contradictions of a social science that is emerging from the national-international framework. Paradigms governed by national-international conceptions have dominated the field, from the simple Western-sponsored stages-of-development model, to the more radical promise of autonomous national development that issued from the critique of imperialism. Some development studies have, as a result, a curiously old-fashioned flavour at the beginning of the twenty-first century. When it makes the nation its premise, this field, too, is challenged by contemporary global change.

Other interdisciplinary fields have been more obviously congruent with emergent globalism, but have also exemplified its difficulties. Communications and media studies have had an empirical importance because of the centrality of communications developments to globalism. And yet the communications literature, in stressing the technological mechanisms of worldwide linkages, still leaves us with

[16] Taylor (1996: 1921), Scholte (1999).   [17] Dalby (1996: 33, 39).
[18] Dalby (1996: 34).   [19] O'Tuathail (1996).

the question of how to understand their content. Critical political economy approaches, which emphasize the dominance of Western media corporations,[20] are in danger of missing the novelty of contemporary global communications. Media roles crystallize in contrasting ways, in critical tension with as well as supportive of globally dominant interests.[21]

In cultural studies, issues of global content have been more explicitly addressed. The field has housed debates that have been influential in introducing globalization issues into sociology – and more recently international relations.[22] Nevertheless it is difficult, as I shall argue later in this book, to encapsulate globality primarily in terms of culture. Globality represents a fundamental transformation of social relations in general. A correspondingly broad-based conception of a renewed, global social science is necessary.

Limits of the international

International relations is the field that superficially most resembles an arena for globalized social science. Certainly the discipline of international relations, much more than the core social sciences, was a Cold War product: it represented the bifurcation of superpowers and blocs rather than the burgeoning global relations that underlay them. Nevertheless, the erosion of the historic statist core of the field can be traced at least to the period of *détente* in the 1970s. Rather as geography and social anthropology were transformed in the aftermath of empire, so the ending of the Cold War has led to an accelerated renewal of international relations, making disciplinary definitions of the subject increasingly problematic.

If only at the level of theoretical debate, and outside the United States, the dominant realism has imploded since 1989. The field of international relations is currently one of the most highly theoreticized of the social sciences, its intellectual ferment testifying to serious issues at stake. A wide range of critical approaches jostles for dominance with new versions of realism and neo-realism. This has opened up the subject (in some eyes at least) as an interdisciplinary

---

[20] For example, Herman and McChessney (1997).
[21] On the 'polymorphous crystallization' of media, see Shaw (1996, 2000a). For the original elaboration of the concept, see Mann (1993: 80).
[22] Featherstone (1990), King (1990).

field for specialized global studies: global political economy, global environmental politics, global gender studies, etc.

International relations has the unique advantage for the purposes of global debate that while it assumed the national, it was at least constituted above the national level. In the Cold War era of institutionalized internationalism, the international encapsulated the dominant form of the emergent global order. It was possible for international relations to theorize world-level problems, if only as matters of international cooperation. In doing so, however, international relationists gave little more attention than any other social scientists to the specificity of the global. Instead they often encouraged a seamless elision of global with international politics.

This transformation is, however, very problematic. The international and the global are not two ways of expressing more or less the same idea. Certainly, global relations depend in practice on international, including interstate, relations. This aspect, explored more fully later in this book, is a source of much confusion. But the two concepts are of fundamentally different kinds. There is a core contradiction between them. Globality involves the unification of the social world and the relativization of difference within it. The international represents the division of social relations by national (historically, state; now increasingly, cultural) boundaries and the definition of particular kinds of difference as constitutive. The global incorporates manifold spatial relations; the international defines certain relations as central.

Global understanding can explain the international (including its defining contradiction and confusion between inter*national* and inter*state*). International theory cannot understand the global, except in the limited sense of one spatial level of inter- or trans-state relations. More radically, international relations may see in globality its own negation – the undermining of states, interstate relations and the international. These ways of comprehending the global are, however, profoundly limited: first, because the global is much more than a spatial level, and second, because global transformations involve the reconstitution, rather than the simple undermining or overcoming, of state forms and interstate relations.

International studies offer both empirical space for many fields of global enquiry, and tantalizing prospects of theoretical reformation. Ultimately, however, the disciplinary definition of the international is as limiting as the nation-centred operationalization of universal categories in the core disciplines. Most of the attempts to resolve this problem in international theory have remained *ad hoc*: greater emphases on non-state actors, supplementing strategy with political economy, cultural theory, feminism, etc. As we shall see below, even the most tightly focussed global theory remains seriously limited.

As in any major theoretical transition, much attention has been focussed on 'metatheoretical' issues. For Steve Smith, the division between 'constitutive' and 'explanatory' theory – between a view of the social world as like the 'natural' world ('that is to say as something outside of our theories') and of the social world as what we make it – is the key difference. 'Radically different types of theory are needed', he argues, 'to deal with each of these cases and these theories are not combinable so as to form one overarching theory of the social world.'[23] Thus attempts to overcome the differences between these types of account, such as the scientific realism of Roy Bhaskar and the structuration theory of Giddens, are viewed as untenable.[24] There is 'a fundamental divide within social theory, one which gives space to attempts to ground theory via hermeneutics as well as by appeal to functional or structural notions'.[25]

This metatheoretical divide crosses, however, the major substantive division in contemporary theory between traditional international and new global theorists. Postmodernist and constructivist writers, who for Smith are the consistent 'constitutive' theorists, have often underestimated the character of global change. Alexander Wendt, for example, argues that

> since states are the immanent form of subjectivity in world politics, this means that they should be the primary unit of analysis for thinking about the global regulation of violence. In that sense states still are at the center of the international system, and as such it makes no more sense to criticize a theory of international politics as 'state-centric' than it does to criticize a theory of forests for being 'tree-centric' . . . In sum, for critical IR theorists to eschew state-centric theorizing is to concede much of international politics to Neorealism.[26]

Let us examine these claims. First, Wendt exhibits a slippage from 'world' to 'international' politics, wherein lies a fundamental difficulty. Naturally states are the prime collective actors in international

---

[23] Smith (1995: 37).   [24] Smith (1995: 37), Bhaskar (1978), Giddens (1981).
[25] Smith (1995: 27).   [26] Wendt (1999: 9, 11).

politics, understood as *interstate* politics, in the same tautological sense that trees are integral to forests. But by no means can we assume, thereby, that they are the prime sources of subjectivity in world politics. Nevertheless, it remains true that world politics as a whole are, in a sense which Wendt's formulae do not allow us to understand, 'state-centric'.[27]

This paradox arises precisely because state power is a structural formation, in the sense that the 'subjectivity' of states (both of states as collective actors and of individuals and other collectivities acting within the state as a 'place') helps to constitute *objective* structures that face all actors, state and 'non-state'. Moreover, when Wendt sees interstate politics as a field quite distinct from world politics, economy and society in the fuller sense, he takes certain kinds of state subjectivities (within which the autonomies of international politics are subscribed) at face value, instead of understanding them in their larger social context.

In so doing, Wendt's subjectivist social theory reveals unexplored structural assumptions, i.e. about what has already been constituted and hence is objectively important. By prioritizing state subjectivities ('anarchy is what *states* make it'[28]) he tends to write out others. 'Consider', he asks us, 'the debate about the causes of the recent Bosnian Civil War.'[29] To which debate is he referring? Clearly it is not the debate among the victims, most of whom are highly conscious of the roles of the Serbian and Croatian states in causing their misery. Nor is it the debate in the International War Crimes Tribunal, in which the war has been ruled an *international* conflict. The Bosnian war has rarely been described as 'civil' anywhere in Europe. One can only assume that Wendt is reflecting the less well-informed sectors of US opinion, and/or that he is articulating an old (structural) prejudice that a war that is not straightforwardly interstate must be a 'civil' war.[30]

What this case reveals is that because they lack an adequate sense of

---

[27] It will become clearer below why, although formally I agree with this contention of Wendt, I give it a different meaning.

[28] Wendt (1992).

[29] Wendt (1999: 163). He asks us to consider the matter in the context of the formation of a Serbian 'collective memory' of victimization, which may have been reactivated by 'proximate causes' such as manipulative politics.

[30] As Kaldor (1999) argues, like most contemporary wars the Bosnian war was neither interstate nor civil, but a 'new war' which includes elements of both.

structure, would-be constitutive theorists often miss the relations that genuinely constitute politics. Without theories of the structures of power, we cannot locate action, any more than without understanding actors we can grasp structures. There has been considerable debate on the formal solution of the agency-structure dilemma in international theory.[31] But what this discussion suggests is that reflection on historical dilemmas needs to be fed into metatheoretical discussion; moreover these relations cannot be resolved at the level of metatheory.[32]

This case also suggests that we should not mistake metatheoretical differences for the major divide in understanding contemporary world politics. On the contrary, the key differences are between those who recognize and understand the character of the broad historic changes of our times, and those writers whose theories reflect old structures and ways of thought. In international relations, as elsewhere, change is uneven and contradictory. As we saw in chapter 1, there is a widespread recognition of post-Cold War change; the idea that world politics is now 'postinternational' has been proposed;[33] and there is considerable influence of postmodern thought. But none of these amounts to an understanding of globality. The remainder of this chapter will look at the ways in which the global has been approached, particularly in international relations, and the extent to which new global relations and forms of politics have been illuminated.

Economism and sociologism in global theory

By the end of the twentieth century, although the acknowledgement of the global was widespread, there was not yet a coherent global theory. Global understanding was developing in the social sciences in two main forms. There were accounts of globalization as a process, and studies of various social phenomena at the global level – global political economy, culture, etc. In the first case, globalization is often discussed without defining the global. In the second, global is an adjective qualifying predefined social forms, but its particular meaning is often equally unclarified. The problem for the new, globalized elements of the social sciences in general is that while they have incorporated global issues, global theory is still in the early stages of development.

---

[31] Wendt (1987, 1992), Hollis and Smith (1991, 1994).
[32] MacLean (1999: 179).   [33] Rosenau (1990).

Neither globalization theory nor adjectival globalism answered the key questions: the nature of the global, the kind of change that it signified, or the transformations of social science concepts that are entailed. Underlying both approaches, there were often three related kinds of weakness to be overcome. First, there were tendencies to confuse the social and spatial aspects of globality, reducing global change to its spatial dimension. Second, there were tendencies to underestimate its political and specifically state dimensions. Third, there were tendencies to represent global relations as mechanical processes of connection, in which conscious human action was diminished.

The global has been grasped as primarily economic, social or cultural – the state seen as the passive receiver of the effects of globalization, politics understood as an epiphenomenon of these other kinds of transformation, agency largely absent. The strength of these tendencies is emphasized by the fact that they prevail in studies of global phenomena even in fields which have traditionally emphasized the state and politics. It has proved particularly difficult to conceptualize the political dimension of global relations.

Even international relations, which has been constituted as a discipline by interstate and political relations, has found it difficult to conceive of globality except as the negation of statehood and politics. Thus a new textbook defined globalization as 'an ongoing trend whereby the world has – in many respects and at a generally accelerating rate – become one relatively borderless social sphere . . . Global phenomena can extend across the world at the same time and can move between places in no time; they are in this sense supraterritorial.'[34]

An emphasis on the borderlessness and supraterritoriality of the global was common, but also symptomatic of a collapse of serious state theory in international relations. For radical international theorists, escaping from the disabling realism of more traditional theory, often simply fled from the notion of state as well (in this sense, Wendt's comment quoted above is apposite). The tendency to discuss globalization as though it were primarily a set of socio-economic processes linked to the market liberalization of recent decades, which undermine the state, has been given widespread credence. This in turn has opened up the argument to the easy rebuttal which shows how much of world trade, investment, etc., remains within national

---

[34] Baylis and Smith (1997: 15).

economies. The debate then becomes trapped in this stale dilemma of globalization *versus* the nation-state, to which I referred in chapter 1.

It is interesting to note how widely post-realist international relations has been influenced by this 'economism' (and to a lesser extent, as we shall see, a parallel 'sociologism') and has advanced over-economic (or narrowly social) interpretations of world politics and the changing roles of states. The over-reliance of critical theorists on broadly Marxist approaches is part of the explanation for these failings, but their scope is wider than these influences. From the earliest days of transnational, let alone global, theorizing, critics of realism have rejected two key notions: the centrality of the state to world affairs, and the centrality of military power to the state.

Thus the pioneers of transnationalism, Robert Keohane and Joseph Nye, in their argument about 'complex interdependence' – a theory of the 1970s epoch of *détente* – saw realism as characterized, in its emphasis on state and military power, by a false conception of the issue agenda. In contrast, they emphasized the 'absence of a hierarchy among issues' which meant that 'military security does not consistently dominate the agenda'.[35] Military force was no longer used, they underlined, by governments within the transatlantic region against each other. Both these assertions were (and are) empirically valid and important, but Keohane and Nye's pluralist methodology prevented them from seeing beyond the surface agenda of policy-makers to the dimensions of power which defined states as institutions. They therefore set a trend when they drew – despite some important qualifications – the false conclusion that military force now had a 'minor role' in international politics.[36]

Keohane and Nye's work helped push international relations towards what has since become known as 'political economy'. Their concept of 'complex interdependence' remains seminal. They failed however to explicitly refine, let alone redefine, the conception of the state which realism had left behind. The state for them was still the nation-state, and interdependence at the political level was only conceived in terms of 'international organization' and above all the variety of issue-based 'regimes'. Because they had no coherent conception of the state to set against realism, they also failed to define the continuing importance of military power.

---

[35] Keohane and Nye (1977: 24–5).
[36] Keohane and Nye (1977: 27–8).

These weaknesses were also to prove seminal. In subsequent international relations and international political economy, 'interdependence' was largely conceived in the limited terms that they had defined. The state itself was still conceived in terms of the national entity, while linkages were seen in terms of common adaptations to the world market and in terms of discrete regimes. The economic functions of states were separated from their political-military roles. No comprehensive account was developed of the inceasingly integrated Western state in its military-political *and* economic aspects, in its international organizations, bilateral relations and role in the world system as a whole. Accounts of the global were developed, but primarily in an economic sense, with the political-military framework of state power – and therefore also the political meaning of global change – missing.

Keohane and Nye eschewed grand theoretical alternatives to realism, and especially Marxist-derived ideas. However, elsewhere in the 1970s political economy approaches were developing, especially in European sociology and political science, often based on Marxism. Much further development of international political economy, even in North America, also followed this trend. However, both non-Marxist and Marxist-influenced international political economy followed Keohane and Nye in failing to offer a redefinition of the state, and presented similar accounts of 'interdependence'. Thus Kenneth Ohmae dramatically proclaimed the 'end of the nation-state' and its replacement by 'region states' in geographical units like northern Italy and Hong Kong.[37] Susan Strange, analysing the role of the state in the world economy, identified 'the retreat of the state', or 'a decline in the authority of the state within its territorial borders' – a theme echoed in Martin van Crefeld's account of the 'decline of the state'.[38]

Others noted changing functions of states, such as the rise of the 'trading state', devoted to managing the balance of payments, encouraging exports and keeping manufacturing enterprises competitive.[39] Philip Cerny argued that there was a more complex 'structuration of the state . . . in today's world marketplace'. For him, the structural changes which states and state actors are involved in today may lead to a significantly different configuration in the future. However, this did 'not mean that the state will be superseded', merely that it 'may

[37] Ohmae (1993).
[38] Strange (1996), van Crefeld (1999).   [39] Rosecrance (1984).

83

have to change more than ever in order to turn its capabilities to the problems which are increasingly faced in the world economy if it is to maintain some kind of virtuous circle of structuration'. The trend was the 'change from the welfare state to the competition state', devoted to success in the more open world economy.[40]

Thus these writers continued to identify the state with the national entity, but noted the changed circumstances in which such entities now operated. None of them seriously problematized the shift towards an economic determination of nation-states, in the context of either the weakening of classic military functions, or the transfer of military functions to transnational institutions of Western power. Neither were these concerns evident in the more developed version presented by Robert Cox, who introduced a loosely Gramscian conception of international power relations. His bowdlerized Marxism was heavily centred on the concepts of 'production' and 'social forces', with 'states' and 'world orders' seen as dependent on the 'historic blocs' or configurations of social forces which underpinned them.[41] Gramsci's own work, as we saw in chapter 2, had been concerned with the relationships of consent and coercion, culture and politics, in the nation-state. New Gramscian global theory has centred, from the start, on political economy, and relations of direct coercion, or violence, have tended to be downplayed.[42]

Cox replaced 'complex interdependence' by the 'internationalization of production'.[43] Where Keohane and Nye had seen regimes and international organization, Cox talked of 'the internationalizing of the state'. The potential of this concept was hardly developed, however. This was partly because Cox devoted most emphasis to the *domestic* blocs underlying what he called 'neoliberal' (Western) and 'developmental' (Third World) nation-states. It was also, however, because the concept was internally weak, being defined as 'the global process whereby *national* policies and practices have been adjusted to the exigencies of the world economy of international production'. The problem was not only, therefore, that Cox saw 'internationalization' in purely economic terms. It was also that he saw it primarily as a process whereby national policies were adjusted to the exigencies of international capitalism. Capitalism existed at the inter-

---

[40] Cerny (1990: 225).   [41] Cox (1987).

[42] As Germain and Kenny (1998) argue, Cox and his followers failed to base their work on a close reading of Gramsci, whom they claimed as an inspiration.

[43] Cox (1987: 253–65).

national and global levels, but the state remained national in form: it was internationalized in economic content, but not in political form. Cox recognized the European Economic Community as a major instance of internationalization, but this too was defined in purely economic terms.

While Cox adapted Marxist economics and Gramscian political sociology, he too set a trend, for Marxist-influenced international theorists, in failing to refer to Marx's own writing on the state – with its conception of this institution as comprising 'bodies of armed men'. The military-political side of the state was not even granted the residual role that it had played in the account of Keohane and Nye (who were still debating with realism). In Cox, who seemingly takes this settling of accounts for granted, the state was subsumed entirely in socio-economic dynamics, and world politics defined as the formation of blocs based on social interests. In his shadowy references to military activities and expenditure, military power became a mere function of political economy. Cox's 'Gramscian' account left the state where it had been in Keohane and Nye: as a still-national entity operating in conditions of economic interdependence, now redefined as those of the world market economy and capitalist hegemony. Although the idea of the 'internationalized' state had been introduced, no real attention was given to the structural changes in state power itself.

The significance of state 'internationalization' is more clearly indicated in Stephen Gill's writing on 'trilateralism' that takes its cue from the same Gramscian source. Gill's work is more sophisticated than Cox's, particularly in the way it utilizes Gramscian concepts. Gill's work advances Cox's argument by defining an 'American-centred transnational hegemony' and exploring the trilateral relations between Japanese, European and American power. Gill considers the military dimensions of power more explicitly than does Cox, but still from the point of view of political economy.[44] Finally, he contributes a sociological dimension with his study of the Trilateral Commission as part of an emerging 'international establishment'.[45]

The Marxist basis of the argument is more clearly indicated – but still fails to include the theory of the state, the author preferring to start from world systems theory and Gramsci.[46] Still missing, indeed,

---

[44] Gill (1990: 78–85).   [45] Gill (1990: 201).
[46] Gill (1990: 33–56).

is any explicit reconsideration of the nature of states and state forms in this process of internationalization, and any overall evaluation of the role of military power in the state. This nuanced offshoot of Marxism adds, therefore, a 'sociologism' to the 'economism' of previous post-realist international theory.[47] The sociologistic pattern is also pronounced in Kees van der Pijl's pioneering account of the making of a transatlantic ruling class.[48] He has continued to elaborate this perspective in a series of works, recently focussing on the 'international cadre class', up to the present day.[49] Although van der Pijl presents Western rulers as an increasingly coherent group of power-holders, in an account spanning a century of war as well as economic changes, he has little to say directly about inter- or transnational state organization.

The strongest statement of sociologism is Robinson's. For him, 'Polyarchy, or . . . "low-intensity democracy," is a structural feature of the new world order: it is a global political system corresponding to a global economy under the hegemony of a transnational elite which is the agent of transnational capital.'[50] There is

> a transnational hegemonic configuration . . . conceptualized on the basis of the transcendence of the competitive nation-state framework, yet not on the transcendence of capitalism as a world system. This emergent configuration may be conceived in social (class), institutional and spatial terms. The social composition of the configuration is of class fractions drawn from the different countries and regions of the three clusters and increasingly fused into a transnational elite . . . . The institutional embodiment of this configuration is the TNCs driving the global economy and society, taken together with emergent supranational institutions . . . . A transnational managerial class at the apex of the global class structure provides leadership and direction to such a new 'historical bloc.'[51]

---

[47] Lest the reader be confused, let me explain that by 'sociologism' I mean a one-sidedly 'social' account, emphasizing social forces such as classes at the expense of, for example, state organization. A broader 'sociology' that combines these and other elements is advocated here.

[48] Van der Pijl (1984).   [49] Van der Pijl (1998).

[50] Robinson (1996: 14).

[51] Robinson (1996: 370–1). Robinson takes his sociologism to the extent of criticizing Gill for 'confusing "US" hegemony with the hegemony of a transnational class configuration, on the basis of his realist retention of the notion that, even in the age of global society, analysis in international relations is still centered around nation-states and their roles' (370). This seems to me a misreading of Gill's position.

What is notable here is that the hegemonic formation of globality is identified primarily with the transcendence of the nation-state system by *capital*, rather than through new forms of state. The 'institutional' forms of the new hegemony are once more identified primarily with transnational corporations, only secondarily with 'supranational institutions'. Robinson explicitly considers the question of state internationalization, but sees it as 'lagging behind the globalization of production'. He argues that 'first, predictions or discussion of a world state should be seen in the long historical context; and second, the emergence *at some point in the future* of a world state could come about through a lengthy, tension-ridden, and exceedingly complex process of the internationalization of the state'.[52]

In Marxian and Gramscian international political economy, therefore, the globalization of power is primarily the development of global economic and social forces. The relations and forms of the internationalization or globalization of the state, and especially the role of military power within this, remain highly elusive. Robinson's formulations simultaneously reproduce Cox's restricted concept of state 'internationalization' as the adaptation of the nation-state to globalized production, and at the same time, point tentatively to a more expanded concept. Yet there is no sense here of the *real* historical sequence, in which the profound internationalization of the Western state, rooted in the outcomes of world war, was a structural *precondition* for all the 'globalization' of recent decades.

Craig Murphy is the one writer from this school who has looked in detail at some of the forms of international state organization. He argues that the nineteenth-century 'Public International Unions', the League of Nations system and the post-war United Nations system are not just three successive generations of world organizations. 'We need', he argues, 'to link their history to that of industry by saying that each new generation begins when an agency regulating a revolutionary new communication technology appears.'[53] He argues that the driver for the development of international governmental

---

[52] Robinson (1996: 371–2), emphasis added. Thus 'Weber's definition of the state as that institution which holds a monopoly on the legitimate use of force within a given territory loses its logic under globalization, since global economic and social forces may exercise veto power or superimpose their power over any "direct" exercise of state power in Weber's sense . . .' (370) Note that the overriding forces are seen as economic and social, not military or political.

[53] Murphy (1994: 7).

organizations (IGOs) has been the extension of markets, by facilitating transportation and communication, protecting intellectual property and reducing legal and economic barriers to trade.

Murphy points out that,

> The actual turn-of-the-century trading area that was partly regulated by the Public International Unions extended the continental marker to the overseas dependencies of the European empires. In contrast, the actual trading area partly governed by the IGOs after the Second World War remained smaller than the world linked by radio and the airplane. It covered the Organization for Economic Cooperation and Development (OECD), the club of wealthy market countries linking western Europe, Canada, the USA, Japan, Australia and New Zealand, and all their economic dependencies in Africa, Asia, the Caribbean, and the Pacific, but excluded China and the Soviet Union. Within these geographic limits appeared successive world orders, concrete historical political and economic systems, the 'turn-of-the-century Interimperial Order' and the postwar 'Free World' Order.[54]

What is striking about this account is that it implies that 'world' international organizations are in fact dependent on tighter forms of worldwide state organization, namely the European empires and the Cold War Western bloc. But Murphy does not investigate *these* forms of internationalized state, or the relationship between their political-military functions and the development of Western-dominated world economic orders. And so his analysis stops just at the point where it could really become interesting.

The pervasive socio-economism of the political economy tradition, from the earliest theorists of 'interdependence' to the latest proponents of 'hegemony' in a Gramscian sense, has also affected a wider raft of critical international theory, especially through the debate about 'governance'. 'Global governance' is perceived to develop from the contradiction between the national form of state power and the increasingly global economy and society. In the absence of a world government, such a world order can only be governed, it is believed, through a complex system of governance involving international organizations and civil society institutions as well as nation-states.

Thus James Rosenau and Ernst-Otto Czempiel invite us to consider 'governance without government' within the contemporary world order.[55] For Richard Falk, we are now entering a 'post-statist world

---

[54] Murphy (1994: 8).   [55] Rosenau and Czempiel (1991).

order'.[56] Falk utilizes the concept of 'governance' in a critical mode, contrasting his projected 'humane', democratic, civil-society based governance with the 'inhumane' global governance of the market, corporate power and imperialism. Thus non-statist governance is a normative position as well as an emergent political reality: 'Not necessarily government but governance seems an ingredient of the envisioned promised land. The quest is for the gentlest forms of authority, forms that do not intrude on freedoms, do not create a huge gap between citizens and institutions established for their benefit and yet facilitate security, resource use, and environmental quality.'[57]

Global governance approaches lean heavily on the concept of 'global civil society', strongly rooted in the Gramscian tradition. Civil society is seen as a source of principled, democratic input into an otherwise state- or corporate-based institutional array. The problems of converting the concept of civil society, developed by Gramsci like most other thinkers in a national context, to the global level, are however considerable in practice.[58] As Gramsci saw, civil society exists in the context of the state. Indeed historically, civil society has constituted the 'nation' in the nation-state. As Germain and Kenny point out, international Gramscianism is inconsistent with Gramsci's own project, in failing to identify the state corresponding to global civil society.[59]

Critical international theory of global phenomena thus raises formidable problems. Some globalism is still adjectival, in the sense indicated above. Accounts of transnationalism hardly amount to theories of globality. Moreover these problems are not exclusive to any one intellectual school: radical liberals and neo-Gramscians follow transnational theorists in underemphasizing state transformations and failing to advance a serious theory of the state. Thus the alternative theories of international relations have tended to shift the ground, rather than to confront realism on its own terrain of the state.

The significance of this absence is confirmed by the way in which the literature on global politics focusses on governance at the expense of the state. The revival of the ancient term, governance, is a curiosity of contemporary political discourse. Up to a point, it reflects a valid new understanding: society is now comprehensively governed, by a much wider range of agencies than the coercive, legislative,

---

[56] Falk (1997: 125).   [57] Falk (1995: 151–2).
[58] For a critique, see Shaw (1996), Part II.   [59] Germain and Kenny (1998).

administrative and judicial arms of the state. Governance in this sense has a meaning close to the multi-centred surveillance that Giddens sees as a characteristic of modern society.[60] But the highlighting of broad-based governance is dangerous, if it serves to obscure the state core of contemporary globality.

Transformations of internationality

The most fundamental problem with the governance approach is, therefore, that it does not offer a sharp enough conception of politics, and especially of the hardest forms of political authority, of state power and its military dimension. It is simply not true that we have moved into a post-statist world order, or that multi-centred governance has replaced or is likely to replace the state. The failure of global theory has been, above all, a failure to understand the continuing and changing roles of state power in global change. Truly, it has been a case of *Hamlet* without the Prince. But although the simple remedy to this is to 'bring the state back in'[61] to the discussion of global change, the question is not so straightforward. This project too easily collapses into the global-sceptic attack on 'myth-making' and the substitution of internationalization for globalization.[62]

Of course, it is difficult to conceive of any state globalization that does not depend on internationalization. World government could never be unmediated by local forms, and although in principle these could be world-regional or local rather than national, in practice it is inevitable that any global state forms will have a strongly international as well as transnational character. Not surprisingly, therefore, in international relations, the literature analyses various forms of 'internationalization' of politics, but only hesitatingly reaches towards 'globalization'. Following the literature discussed above, economistic definitions are widespread,[63] but there are a number of ways in which theorists have proposed to analyse specifically state forms of internationalization.

The most basic concept, introduced by Keohane and Nye, is that of 'regimes'. The concept still assumes the prevalence of national state units, and identifies internationalization in their cooperation in spe-

---

[60] Giddens (1985).
[61] As 'the state' was earlier returned to sociology (Evans et al. 1985).
[62] Weiss (1998), Hirst and Thompson (1996).
[63] See for example, Keohane and Milner (1993: 4).

cific issue-areas. It is framed by the problematic that Hurrell describes as 'how is co-operation feasible between states claiming sovereignty but competing for power and influence in a situation of anarchy?'[64] As he points out, regime theorists have seen both law and power as sources of regimes, especially hegemonic power, which of course returns the analysis to the balance of power between the units. Thus regime theory has downplayed ideas of community and justice: 'the role of power and coercion in the implementation of rules remains fundamental'.[65] However, as Meyer, Rittberger and Zürn point out, regime theory explains 'the possibility, conditions, and consequences of international governance beyond anarchy and short of supranational government in a given issue area'.[66] While all recognize that the need for political regulation 'beyond the nation state' has increased dramatically, the premise of regime theory is that the 'modern' response to an extended range of societal interactions, namely the formation of statehood, does not seem viable on the international level.

'Contemporary International Relations scholars agree upon little else', claim these regime theorists, 'but the nonfeasibility of a world state.'[67] However, even they have to admit that 'The image of competitive international politics produced by anarchy among sovereign states is most strongly challenged by the observation of instances of hierarchically ordered supranational policy-making (including implementation).'[68] Certainly, to view cooperative internationality simply under the aspect of serial relations between discrete state entities may reproduce the prevailing political and legal understanding. But it ignores the *comprehensively structured* nature of international 'regimes' as a whole, which brings into question the assumption that these juridical state entities are in fact the appropriate units of 'state' analysis.

One step on from regime theory is the idea of 'security community'. According to John Ruggie, 'NATO has never been merely a traditional alliance; its indivisible and generalized security commitments owe as much to the idea of collective security as to the conventional alliance form . . . over time the transatlantic region has evolved into a "security community"'.[69] For Barry Buzan there is a spectrum, at the

---

[64] Hurrell (1993: 50).   [65] Hurrell (1993: 55).
[66] Meyer et al. (1993: 392–3).   [67] Meyer et al. (1993: 394, 396).
[68] Meyer et al. (1993: 402).   [69] Ruggie (1998: 201).

extremes of which he sees chaos and security. 'Security regimes' are one step up from 'regional conflict formations'; a 'security community' is a further step away from chaos, in which disputes among members are resolved to such an extent that none fears, or prepares for, war. Beyond the security community lies 'regional integration', 'which cods anarchy and therefore moves the regional security issue from the national and international, to the domestic realm'.[70]

The problem with this categorization, however, is that while recognizing change, it does so only in the old clothing of domestic (national) and international. Certainly, Buzan is correct in so far as, if we can define 'state' at all, there must be must be a point at which integration of separate states leads to a new state form, so that external relations between states are transformed into the internal relations of new state power. However, in identifying existing trends within the West principally with the form of 'security community', he leaves us with the view of these as 'external' relations, and underestimates the extent to which the distinction between 'inside' and 'outside' the state has already been brought into question.[71] Behind the idea of the West as a security community lies, however, confusion over the ideas of community and state. The question 'when is a state not a state?' requires a more comprehensive answer (I try to provide this in chapter 6).

Beyond this idea lies the concept of 'multilateralism'. According to Ruggie, 'What distinguishes the multilateral form from other forms is that it coordinates behavior among three or more states on the basis of generalized principles of conduct.' However, he claims that, 'for analytic purposes it is important not to confuse the very meaning of multilateralism with any one particular institutional expression of it, be it an international order, regime or organization. Each can be, but need not be, multilateral in form.'[72] However, just as with (what Ruggie sees as) the more specific concepts of regime and security community, the idea of multilateralism retains the idea of the autonomous national state at its core.

---

[70] Buzan (1991: 219).

[71] See Walker (1993). Although the 'inside-outside' question has been confused in international and political thought, by its identification with the nation-state, it cannot be entirely dismissed. In so far as we can define states as structures, albeit not simply national, the question of inclusion within/exclusion from them remains real for all too many people.

[72] Ruggie (1998: 12).

Indeed for Ruggie, multilateralism is an extension of 'American nationalism'. This, he claims, is 'a civic nationalism, embodying a set of inclusive core values: intrinsic individual as opposed to group rights, equality of opportunity: for all, anti-statism, the rule of law and a revolutionary legacy which holds that human betterment can be achieved by means of deliberate human actions – especially when they are pursued in accordance with these foundational values'.[73] There is a close 'relationship between inter-ethnic accommodation at home and multilateral organizing principles abroad'.[74] Of course, the idea of multilateralism has also been adapted in a more radical direction, for example by Cox.[75]

Close to these perspectives analytically, but more distinctive conceptually, is Alexander Wendt's recent discussion of structural change in international politics. In contrast to his more conservative formulations quoted above, he proposes that there is 'an internationalization of political authority', even 'international state formation'.[76] However, it is a process that has not gone very far 'and even if it continues we are only in its early stages'. It is 'issue-specific (though it may "spill over" into new issue areas), mostly regional in nature (so there are potentially many international states), and a matter of degree. Moreover, there are strong arguments for thinking it will not continue, since it creates fundamental tensions between the national and transnational functions of state actors.'[77]

This tentative trend, however, has two broad theoretical implications. It points 'toward a gradual, but structural transformation of the Westphalian states system from anarchy to authority', and towards '"disarticulated" sovereignty in which different state functions are performed at different levels of aggregation, and/or a "neo-Medievalism" in which political authority is shared by both state and nonstate actors'. Either way, Wendt argues,

> the result is neither anarchy nor hierarchy but the emergence of a new form of state and thus states system which breaks down the spatial coincidence between state-as-actor and state-as-structure. As such the erosion of individual state sovereignty does not imply the erosion of the state. Sovereignty is not an intrinsic feature of state

---

[73] Ruggie (1998: 218).   [74] Ruggie (1998: 219).

[75] Robert Cox (1997) argues for 'a broad view of multilateralism' in which both states and other actors will constitute the 'multilateralism of the future', shaped by and shaping structural change in world economy and politics.

[76] Wendt (1997).   [77] Wendt (1997: 57).

agency but one social identity a state may have. By transferring it to a collective, states may actually strengthen their capacity to solve problems. Internationalization is a way of reorganizing and redeploying state power – not a withering away of the state.[78]

Wendt's formulation here poses the radical possibility that the state system is being fundamentally transformed, albeit that the changes are in their earliest phases.[79] However, there are two fundamental problems with his formulations. First, although the general direction is identified, he does not provide any concrete examination of the processes of historical change. The dynamics, exactly how far they have progressed, what might push them further, what might hold them back, are missing. Second, this is a discussion of change in the state-system de-anchored from the general debates on social change in the present period. Post-Westphalianism is a form of 'post-' analysis, but its links to the larger context of 'post-' thinking are loose, and its connections to global theory are neglected.

Seeking the global Prince

This chapter has suggested that global theory has tended towards economism, sociologism and loose conceptions of 'governance' rather than the state, while theories of change in interstate relations have failed, for the most part, to illuminate their relations to globality. At the end of the twentieth century, there were increasing signs, however, of interest in the political aspects of global change. This has involved redefining internationalization in global terms, as in the claim of Held and his colleagues that 'international regimes mark out the growing institutionalization of global politics' and 'constitute forms of global governance, distinct from traditional notions of government conceived in terms of the specific sites of sovereignty'.[80]

For Held and colleagues, however, global politics was little more than a composite of these trends. 'All these developments', they argued, 'illuminate a shift away from a purely state-centric politics to a new more complex form of multilateral global governance. There are multiple, overlapping political processes at work at the present historical conjuncture.'[81] Thus although Held and his colleagues put

---

[78] Wendt (1997: 61).
[79] Thus Wendt (1997) appears considerably less conservative than Wendt (1999).
[80] Held et al. (1999: 51).   [81] Held et al. (1999: 85).

politics at the heart of globalization, they saw global politics in terms of newly 'multilayered governance' and a 'diffusion of political authority'.[82] Indeed, they emphasized 'the contemporary world order as a complex, contested, interconnected order' and acknowledged 'the "messy appearances" which define global politics at the turn of the new millennium'.[83] From here it was not so far to Ian Clark's argument that the globalization of world politics has been matched throughout the twentieth century by a corresponding 'fragmentation'.[84] Or even to Susan Strange's case: 'we have now, not a system of global governance by any stretch of the imagination, but rather a ramshackle assembly of conflicting sources of authority'.[85]

It is far from my intention to deny the 'complex', 'messy', 'fragmented' and even 'ramshackle' appearances of the world relations of political power that the twentieth century has bequeathed to the twenty-first. Any worldwide political system, coordinating authoritative relations over billions of people living in highly varied social conditions, was bound to be complex. The development of global politics from the historic relations of separated centres of power, through turbulent processes of revolution, counterrevolution and war, was bound to be messy and uneven – we might add, dangerous. No one can deny that emergent globality is deeply contradictory, and possesses all these characteristics in abundance.

This does not mean, however, that we can identify no (relatively) cohesive political forces at work. We saw above that many consider that we live in a 'post-statist' world, in the sense that governance now extends beyond the separated state entities of the national-international era. Likewise, we saw that the 'nonfeasibility of a world state' has been considered axiomatic in international relations. All these arguments demonstrate, however, is the simplicity of their underlying assumption, that a state is an uncomplicated centre of state power, a singular sovereign. Once we recognize the inadequacy of this assumption, we see the emptiness of the claims that are made: both statements are more truisms than truths. If we are looking for the uncomplicated singular world state, if we see only the diffusion of authority in a complex web of jurisdictions, we will miss the more complex global concentrations of state power that have actually come into existence.

---

[82] Held et al. (1999: 62).   [83] Held et al. (1999: 85), citing Mann (1993: 4).
[84] Clark (1997).   [85] Strange (1996: 199).

The title of this chapter suggests that social scientists have written the 'Prince' out of the drama of global change. Such a figure is not to be found, of course, in Shakespeare's sense, or even in Machiavelli's. As Gramsci long ago recognized, the 'modern Prince' is a collective actor. His own answer was that the new Prince was the collective organic intellectual of the proletariat, organized in the revolutionary Communist party, which would develop the 'philosophy of praxis' and guide the historic bloc of the working class towards power.[86] Of course, Gramsci's Prince did not develop as he advocated; communist parties hardly lived up to his model of new political leadership. Nevertheless, the question is an interesting one. What kinds of state and political agency were appropriate in his times? What kinds of state and political agency are appropriate in the global transition? Who or what can be the 'global Prince'?

As Gramsci's discussion suggests, we should treat these questions broadly. Political agency in modern conditions is collective and institutional. Two possible candidates will be examined here. On the one hand, there is the internationalized state that has been glimpsed, but never fully examined, in the intimations of globality that we have considered in this chapter. On the other, there are the very different kinds of revolutionary actor in the transformation of global times, whose agency has been partially recognized in the discussion of civil society and social movements. Of course, no one kind of agent can bear the weight which Gramsci tried to place on revolutionary parties. Transformative global agency is not the exclusive property of state institutions, but neither is it that of civil society, social movements or any other singular kind of agent. The failure of Gramsci's model should lead us to look carefully at the relationships of different types of political actor, in the making of the global world.

The remainder of this book addresses these questions in a number of different ways. First, I develop a historical account of the ways in which twentieth-century historical change have led to the global revolution, asking in what it has consisted, who has made it, what have been the decisive events, and how we should understand transformations of the state and political agency within it. Second, I examine the politics of global change in the revolutionary period of our own times – the beginning of the twenty-first century – and the nature of the global state that is coming into existence. Third, I discuss

[86] Gramsci in Hoare and Smith (1971).

the future course of the global revolution, the unsolved problems and major sticking points, and try to identify the agents of historic advance. My answer to the question of the global Prince will not be as simple as Gramsci's concept of its modern forerunner. But if the solutions are more complex, political agency is still central.

Part II
History and agency

4 Internationalized bloc-states and democratic revolution

In this part of the book I lay out, over two chapters, a schematic historical account of the global revolution. I offer a kind of theoretical history – or historical social theory. I am aware that this undertaking is likely to fall between the stools of theory and history, insufficiently abstract for the former, insufficiently grounded for the latter. I argued in chapter 2 that current theoretical difficulties cannot be resolved at the metatheoretical level. Nor, however, can they be resolved solely at the level of what Mann has called the 'empirical theory' of historical sociology.[1] The large-scale historical narrative has been discredited in recent times, not least because of the failures of Marxism. However, we should not throw out the baby with the bathwater. Conscious of the dangers of determinism and teleology, aware that any such narrative must also be provisional, we still need to get a grip on a historical overview. Otherwise our theoretical assumptions will tend towards 'grand theory' and our empirical study towards 'empiricism', each of them, as Mills pointed out, equally ahistorical.[2]

Here I develop the critique of national and international thought which I presented in chapter 2, as a means to define the principal contours of historical change in the modern era. I relate this account to the issues raised by the critique of recent global thought in the last chapter. We can only understand global change through a theoretically informed historical account, and history cannot be written with a blank slate. To develop an account of the global revolution involves revising how we understand the earlier historical changes of modern times.

In the account which follows, I place state relations at the centre of

---

[1] Mann (1988).   [2] Mills (1959).

modern history. I outline the development of globality from the contradictions of national-international world order. I examine globality as a structure defined by state relations and firmly embedded in economy and society. I suggest the changing relations between the putatively distinct spheres of economy, society and polity in the course of the twentieth century, and discuss their roles in the emergence of a global world. Globality has been widely understood as involving particular kinds of neo-liberal relations in which the economy is abstracted from political control. In this account, I argue that this approach involves a fundamental misunderstanding of the historical processes: state relations remain central.

In the end I do not accept Ian Clark's warning, in one of the few attempts to historicize globalization in the frame of world politics, against seeing the twentieth century as 'a century in two halves'. His 'wider perspective of globalization as a continuing, if periodically accelerating, aspect of the twentieth century as a whole', which has 'become more powerful in the second half of the century', is inadequate. I propose, rather, a variant of the view that he criticizes: 'that [globality] is a new departure: there may have been integration and extension of international relationships before, but [globality] is qualitatively distinct from them'.[3] However, he is right to advise against 'reinforc[ing] the rigidity' of the divided century image. If global changes are rooted in the earlier historic transition of the mid-twentieth century, we need also to see the continuities (in both transitions) with early twentieth-century, nineteenth-century and indeed earlier developments.

Contradictions of the high national-international era

To understand why the national-international order of the twentieth century is giving way to a global order in the twenty-first, we need first to reach back into its nineteenth-century evolution. The nineteenth has often been demarcated by the end of one set of pan-European wars, in 1815, and the beginning of another, in 1914. Michael Mann has however defined it as a 'long' century, beginning with the industrial revolution around 1760, but still ending in 1914.[4] Whether demarcated by war or not, that century has been understood

---

[3] Clark (1997: 19).   [4] Mann (1993).

principally as a period of 'peaceful' economic and change, often contrasted with the 'century of total war' which succeeded it.[5] Certainly, during the hundred years to 1914 there were no Europe-wide or 'world' wars. But wars, albeit more limited than these, were commonplace. The catastrophes of the twentieth century were thoroughly prepared in nineteenth-century developments. The national-international order was consolidated. The economic and political infrastructure for total war was created, and partially demonstrated. Modern mass militarism developed at the core of society: not only in the technological 'industrialization' of warfare, but in the creation of conscript mass armies and other means of modern state mobilization, including the socio-cultural forms of mass society which were to serve total war.

Industrial capitalism developed in Europe within a competitive system of states inherited from the early, pre-industrial stage of modernity.[6] Major states were empires, and in the European expansion they had spread their competing jurisdictions over far-flung areas of the world. Powerful early maritime states such as Spain and Portugal were imperial before they were national in a modern sense; the major continental empires, Austria-Hungary and Russia, were clearly multinational. Although national consciousness developed in the early modern era – for example in Holland and England – the prototype of modern nationalism only emerged in the French revolution.

The modern Europe of nation-states was therefore a nineteenth-century, even a late nineteenth-century, phenomenon. It was consolidated only after the revolutions of 1848 and German and Italian unification in the 1870s, and fully realized through the twentieth century – in the revolutionary waves of 1917–19, 1944–5 and even 1989–91. Although we are accustomed to thinking of these modern revolutions in terms of democracy and socialism, it is important to emphasize the extent to which they have been national movements.

The European state-system therefore attained its fully national-international form, which we take for granted in current debates, only

---

[5] Marwick (1968).

[6] Mann (1984) argues that for this reason we cannot accept the idea that industrialism and/or capitalism qualitatively altered the warlike potential of society, either in a pacific or a militaristic direction, except (and it is a huge exception) in the intensity and scale of conflict.

a little over a century ago.[7] Moreover, the heyday of the nation-state (roughly 1870–1945) was also that of the modern European empire. Even smaller western European states, such as the Netherlands, Belgium and Denmark, were colonial powers. The classic national-international system was a world order of rival empires, an 'Inter-imperial Order' as Murphy calls it.[8] The dominant form of the state was not, therefore, simply a nation-state, but *the nation-state-empire within an interimperial state-system.*

The meaning of this developing Eurocentric world for later global developments is contradictory. On the one hand, nationality-inter-nationality became increasingly the ordering principle of a worldwide system of political authority and social relations. In spatial reach, it touched most areas of the world. But on the other, within the interimperial system, there was also a plurality of national-imperial world orders. Each European nation-state-empire was a world order in its own right – especially in the cases of the largest empires, the British and French, impressively large, diverse, genuinely worldwide orders. Within each imperial order, not only was trade regulated very differently from interimperial trade, but a single dominant language, culture and of course authority structure prevailed.

The national-international, interimperial system constituted there-fore an important dual advance towards contemporary globality, but it was very definitely a *pre-global* order. Certainly, the very development of a recognizable worldwide society, through the dominance of European 'civilization', involved steps towards the recognition of human commonality and universality. The pre-1914 world was liberal as well as national and imperial. European science and high culture crossed national boundaries, as indeed they had done since the origins of the modern era (and long before that). International trade and investment developed apace, so much so that the period has been seen as a heyday of internationalization barely surpassed even in the contemporary global world.[9] As Clark points out, 'To many economic historians, it was the nineteenth century that realized the achievement of an integrated global economy', leading to 'the binding of the whole

---

[7] In this context it is quite curious that international relations conventionally traces the modern international system to the Treaty of Westphalia in 1648. While Westphalia helped to codify the *forms* of state sovereignty, the national-international *content* of the state-system is really a more recent development.
[8] Murphy (1994: 8).   [9] Hirst and Thompson (1996).

world into something very close to an economic unit'.[10] International organization grew apace, as agreements between states provided a worldwide infrastructure for communication and trade.[11]

However, this worldwide society was manifest in *discrete* imperial systems, thoroughly divided by borders of violence. In this interimperial world, stronger, increasingly autonomous national state institutions were becoming deeply embedded in economy and society. Industrialization, the development of transport and communications, and emerging mass media expanded states' capacity to mobilize the infrastructural power of societies. The external war-making capacity of the nation-state grew in proportion to its surveillance capacity in society. The growth of states' power was also the expansion of their capacity for violence against each other. At the same time, each empire was fractured by more or less common racist distinctions between Europeans and non-Europeans. In this context, full human commonality remained a utopian value of liberal and socialist thought. It was upheld by international idealists, against dominant nationalist and imperialist modes of thought.

The realities of the national-international world order therefore belied the nineteenth century's pacific image. This was an era in which warfare was becoming more entrenched in state relations: not only in geopolitical rivalries, but in the way in which state institutions organized economy and society. Military sectors became protected from market vagaries by ongoing state contracts: what would later be called the 'military-industrial complex', the centre of the modern war economy, was born.[12] Militarism grew as a social force, as mass armies trained the entire adult male populations of European states, at any one time mobilizing a substantial proportion as conscripts and the remainder as reservists. Militarism grew, too, as a cultural force, a source of many of the traditions which were 'invented' in the imperial world.[13]

Dialectics of total war

With hindsight, the outcome of the high national-international, interimperial world order was an extended period in the early and mid-

---

[10] Clark (1997: 143).   [11] Murphy (1994).
[12] MacNeill (1982), Pearton (1982).
[13] MacKenzie (1984), Hobsbawm and Ranger (1983).

twentieth century in which total war became a model not only of state power but of economic and social organization. The industrial society of the nineteenth century was giving way to the total war society of the twentieth. However, this centrality of war to twentieth-century society has been explored more by historians than it has been theorized by social scientists.[14] Indeed there is a disturbing irony in the fact that while even popular media recognize the passing era as the 'century of total war', the great modern expansion of social theory has largely neutralized warfare (as we saw in chapter 2).

Because economic, social and political theorists have seen war as an abnormal disturbance of the regular patterns of society, they have failed to grasp the extent to which twentieth-century society was taken over by the dynamics of war. They have taken too literally the 'post-war' rubric which they have liberally applied to the whole half-century after 1945, and indeed still apply even today. By adopting post-war terminology they acknowledge the decisiveness of the 1945 turning-point, but they conspicuously fail to *theorize* the the transition from total war to post-war. Indeed, hiding behind the comfortable veneer of the post-war, they assume *de facto* the achievement of the demilitarized industrialism which Comte anticipated over a century before 1945.

But this is to obliterate the meaning of the militarized state relations of the twentieth century and all their outcomes in society. Capitalist industrialism did not develop simply through its socio-economic contradictions, as nineteenth-century theorists such as Marx believed it would. The theorists of the nation-state have explained how its resources were channelled through the national-international system of war.[15] But in confining themselves to the *role* of war in this system, they too have failed to explain how the *dynamics* of war itself have played a central role in modern society. In failing to incorporate Clausewitz into their theoretical canon, they also failed to acknowledge the processes of warfare as constitutive of modern society. Even theorists of war have failed to recognize the extent to which war in the twentieth century went far beyond Clausewitzian terms – particularly in its industrial technology, social mobilization and genocidal murderousness.[16]

---

[14] For example Marwick (1974, 1989).   [15] For example Giddens (1985).

[16] Thus the idea that modern war is Clausewitzian – in the sense that it has been an extension of state policy – represents a limited understanding. This has implications for the arguments of van Crefeld (1991) and Kaldor (1997) that contemporary warfare is moving beyond 'Clausewitzian war'.

If we are to grasp the sense in which contemporary society is 'post-war', we must also understand the sense in which early and mid-twentieth-century society was a *war society*. Within the national-international world order, states were driven to mobilize bordered economies and societies as resources for war. The protected military-industrial sectors of the late nineteenth century became models for all-embracing national war economies in the twentieth. They were also models for their 'peacetime' equivalents, the 'command economies' of totalitarian regimes and the 'military-industrial complexes' of the Cold War.

Within the national-international world order, states thus assumed an enormous new significance in society. In the nineteenth century, Marx had argued that the separation of politics and economics was characteristic of modern, bourgeois society. He aimed to show that this separation was an artifice: specific historical relations of production between capital and labour underlay the abstracted commodity forms of the market, and the struggle arising from these relations had revolutionary political consequences. This critique was overtaken, however, in the twentieth century, by the universal statization of economic relations, not just in 'wartime' but in 'interwar' periods. Economic relations became directly political, because states increasingly controlled economies in their own interests. In war economies and totalitarian command economies, this control was completely manifest; but it was also very significant in the Keynesian warfare-welfare states of the democratic West.

Statism was not merely an economic phenomenon: it pervaded social, cultural and political relations. Social groups, cultural traditions and artistic forms, as well as political traditions, all became dependent on and entwined with the nation-state. National definitions were reinforced at the expense of the universal and international. Internationalist traditions, such as those of the socialist movement at the turn of the twentieth century, were swamped by the nationalism which total-war mobilization engendered.

What is striking is that warfare became the principal goal and purpose not just of states but of national industrial societies. States became strategic organizers of national economies. The idea of strategic economic planning – which has now mutated into the idea of state-guided economic competitiveness within a global market economy – originated in strategic planning for war. Culture became saturated, too, with ideologies of national military rivalry.

During the era of total war, warfare not only reinforced the national segmentation of society, but even defined different social forms – capitalist and socialist. Sociology treated the Soviet Union as a distinct variant of industrial society and most critical Marxist theories defined it as some kind of post-capitalist social formation. Although it originated in revolution, its subsequent development and expansion into central Europe were largely conditioned by its military rivalry with Western nation-states. In the totalitarian state with its command economy, virtually all social relations became state relations. The state was not simply one set of institutions within society: state institutions defined the nature of society in a comprehensive way, as well as the difference between this form and capitalist societies. The Soviet Union and Soviet bloc-state were therefore extreme cases of the way in which the national-international order came, through warfare, to define the character of society.

In previous work, I unravelled some of the dialectics of total-war society.[17] The nineteenth-century expansion of industrial capitalist society provided the infrastructure – economic, social, cultural and political – for modern nation-states' war machines. The industrialization of weaponry, transport and communications had already transformed war beyond the Clausewitzian model, at the time of the American Civil War (1860–5). In the twentieth century, the transformation was taken much further, so that in the First World War (1914–18), an altogether vaster mobilization of society was achieved. National economy and society became integral components of the supply side of total war. The constraints on war which Clausewitz had termed 'friction' were now represented largely by bottlenecks within the war economy and conflicts in the society within which it existed.

In the First World War, many social trends of the previous century came to fruition. A new 'mode of warfare' (to use the term developed by Kaldor[18]) had developed, which became known as total war. This mode of warfare increasingly *enveloped* the social formations of national-international capitalism, so that social contradictions became increasingly contradictions of the mode of warfare. Social and political revolution did not emerge from class conflict engendered in the cycle of capitalist production, as Marx believed. Instead, revolution devel-

---

[17] Shaw (1988).   [18] Kaldor (1982).

oped from the pressures which total war stoked up in capitalist economies and societies.[19]

Revolution and counterrevolution in the total-war era accentuated the national-international form of world order. Russia, the weakest of the war machines, saw the most comprehensive breakdown of existing state forms, and the only sustained revolutionary success. But the internationalist Bolshevik revolution deepened the conflict between Russia and neighbouring national-imperial states. Out of national isolation and civil war came the nationalized counterrevolution within the revolution itself – Stalin's totalitarian dictatorship, 'socialism in one country' and industrial development for a new war against Germany.

In Germany itself, as in Italy, the dialectics of military defeat also produced revolution, but this was defeated at an earlier stage by counterrevolutions which took high nationalist and militarist forms. The link between the absolute violence of total war and the new Fascist totalitarianism was striking. Fascism and Nazism drew extensively from the militarism of total war – mythologies of national humiliation, idealizations of military comradeship, glorifications of totalized violence and militaristic notions of command all entered into these militarized, mass counterrevolutionary movements of the inter-world war period.

The development of the total-war system, with its militarization of revolution and counterrevolution, contributed to worldwide crisis. The sense of general crisis was strong in the 1930s: for Marxists, it was a crisis of the capitalist system; for others, a crisis of international power relations.[20] It was both of these and more. Centrally, it was a crisis of the national-international world order and the total-war system which it had engendered. The interwar crisis was one of state relations in general: the very structure and forms of state and interstate power, and their embedding in economy and society.

New late modern, incipiently global state relations have issued from this crisis of the national-international order. The Second World War appears, with the hindsight of the beginning of the twenty-first century, as the most fundamental turning-point so far in the transition from a national-international to a global world. The fundamental

---

[19] Thus the major waves of revolution (1917–19, 1944–5) coincided with the concluding phases of wars rather than with economic crises such as that of 1929–31.
[20] Carr (1939).

character of the transition is implictly acknowledged in virtually all late modern social thought, with its ubiquitous references to the contemporary world as 'post-war'. But the depth of the post-Second World War transition has not been recognized, mainly because new state relations were consolidated only through the military rivalry of the Cold War. Moreover, this new order *preserved* the older national-international forms even through fundamental change, and inhibited the development of conscious globality for a generation. This was, in retrospect, the moment of 'pre-global' revolution.

1945 and the national-democratic revolution

In our time, to see the end of the Second World War as a revolutionary moment of any kind, let alone a pre-global revolution, is not easy. The big economic and social changes of mid-century – the Keynesian revolution, the welfare state – are believed to have been undermined by globalization. The principal military result of 1945 was the Cold War, which we now believe we have overcome. In many ways, the world at the beginning of the twenty-first century seems to be finally settling accounts with the world of 1945. Above all, the manifest 'revolutionary' developments of that period were tied to the inter-national Communist movement, which has been so fundamentally defeated and discredited in recent decades.

The Chinese was the paradigmatic revolution of the period. Mao Zedong's revolutionary army, first created in rural isolation in the early 1930s, fought the Japanese from 1937 to 1945, before finally ousting the Kuomintang from China's cities in 1949. In Vietnam in this period, Ho Chi Minh's Communists won power in the North; a further thirty years' war against France and the United States was needed to unify the country under their rule. In Korea, Communists won the North, but the country's division was frozen after the first big hot war of the Cold War era, in 1950–3.[21]

In Yugoslavia as in China, Josip Broz Tito's partisans defeated both Germans and rival Serbian and Croatian nationalists to forge a federal Communist state. In Albania, too, Communists seized power. Else-where in Europe, Communist resistance movements were defeated (Greece) or restrained by Stalin into seeking parliamentary power, from which they were ejected with the onset of the Cold War (Italy,

[21] Cumings (1981, 1990).

France). Communism spread to east-central Europe in the late 1940s, including the eastern zone of Germany, through the consolidation of Soviet power in the region occupied by the Red Army in 1945.

In the Russian revolution of 1917 both the democratic and internationalist impulses had been real – if shortlived. The new Communist revolutions of the 1940s had little room for either. Whether imposed by guerrilla forces or conventional armies, these were militarized revolutions, led by totalitarian parties. Successful revolutions ushered in states modelled on, if not actually 'satellites' of, Soviet Russia. The continuing impulse for change within the elites of these states was, if anything, nationalist. In the last years of Stalin (who died in 1953) and their immediate aftermath, leaders with autonomous national projects were purged. However, Tito's national rebellion against Stalin set a precedent for subsequent fragmentation in 'international' Communism, most notably Mao's split from Khrushchev in 1957.

The most telling feature of these manifest revolutionary developments of the 1940s, seen from fifty years further on, is that the regimes they created appear as obstacles to the global-democratic revolution of our times. In Asia at the end of the twentieth century, the Chinese and Vietnamese Communist states survive, after earlier imposing terrible privations on their populations, only through participation in global markets and accommodation with Western capitalism. Their regimes appear ideologically bankrupt, with weak legitimacy, and hostile to new democratic movements among the people. Cambodian Communism spawned the monstrous Khmer Rouge and the terrible genocide of the 1970s. The North Korean regime remains a similarly hideous caricature of totalitarianism, leading its people into mass starvation in the 1990s. At the beginning of the century, even Fidel Castro's Cuba – the one Communist regime after the 1940s to result from a revolution – appears stagnant and undemocratic, hardly the inspiration for the Western left which it became in the 1960s.[22]

Everywhere in Europe, the Communist regimes created in the 1940s have collapsed. The Soviet satellite states in east-central Europe proved chronically unstable, as a series of major revolts (discussed more fully below) showed. Despite modest rises in living standards,

---

[22] The Nicaraguan revolution of 1979, the other successful revolutionary movement in the Western hemisphere, never produced a Communist regime, and the Sandinista government has given way electorally to a more right-wing government.

in the end only Soviet arms sustained Communist power. The withdrawal of this underpinning led to the relatively swift and peaceful overthrow of Communism in 1989, followed in turn by the collapse of the Soviet Union itself. In Yugoslavia, the regime's national legitimacy was undermined by the national claims of elites in the federation's republics and provinces, leading to disintegration and war in the 1990s. In Albania too, the Communist regime collapsed.

With hindsight, therefore, the manifest revolutionary developments of the 1940s were historic dead-ends. They often removed corrupt, feudal and reactionary local elites, created unified central states (especially significant in China), and achieved significant economic development and social welfare advances. But they hardly created a lasting model: within a decade of the late 1940s, international Communism crumbled and the regimes – exposed as brutal and totalitarian – faced new democratic, national revolutionary challenges from below.

The more durable 1940s revolution must therefore be sought elsewhere. The second main strand of historic transformation, which overlapped with the Communist revolutionary model, was that of national independence. Where China and Vietnam gained national autonomy through revolutionary armed struggle, the emerging national elites of the British Indian empire gained independence through largely peaceful political organization, resistance and negotiation with the imperial power. (Ominously, of course, they were immediately embroiled in inter-communal war that set a pattern for the next fifty years.) In Indonesia, too, a national elite managed to seize power after the Second World War, preventing the restoration of the Dutch colonial empire.

The results of these movements were, in some cases at least, parliamentary-democratic nation-states with far greater legitimacy and staying power than the revolutionary Communist regimes. India and Ceylon (later Sri Lanka) remained democracies throughout the following half-century, despite oligarchic and authoritarian tendencies in their politics; even in Pakistan (and later Bangladesh), parliamentary episodes alternated with dictatorial rule. In Indonesia, however, the outcome was prolonged authoritarian government. Indian independence was the crucial precedent, moreover, for the dissolution of European empires in the late 1950s and early 1960s: in much of British and French Africa and the British West Indies, as well as in other colonial territories, more or less peaceful handovers to local elites occurred and versions of national-democratic institutions were established.

European imperial states varied in the enlightenment of their accommodation to independence, both in general and in the cases of particular territories, and the anti-imperialist forces they faced varied greatly in their politics and strategies. Thus in the British empire, there was serious armed struggle in Malaya, Kenya and Cyprus in the 1950s. In two major centres of the French empire, Vietnam and Algeria, long, bitter wars of independence defined this historic transition. Like the Dutch in the East Indies, the Belgians in the Congo were unprepared for independence, and there was a collapse into war. One of the oldest and smallest of empires, the Portuguese, was the last to disappear, only after armed struggles in Angola and Mozambique precipitated the fall of the authoritarian regime in Portugal itself.

While the independence of colonial territories was the most obvious face of the national movement of the 1940s and afterwards, similar trends could be observed in states such as Iran, Egypt, Iraq and others in the Arab world, which had previously existed in various conditions of subordination to European powers. After 1945, many of these states became more genuinely autonomous and nationalist movements came to power – often through military *coups d'état* – in the 1950s. In the Middle East, much of the nationalist radicalization was centred, ironically, on reaction to the Palestinian Jewish movement's own declaration of Israeli independence in 1948.

This second wave of post-Second World War revolution, like the Communist first wave, was very mixed in its character and results. It spread the system of autonomous nation-states across the globe, and in many cases introduced the idea of democratic government. But it hardly established either a stable order of nations or stable democracies on a wide scale. In many new states, national identity was problematic, parties representing national and tribal minorities opposed dominant elites, and corruption and authoritarianism were entrenched in state institutions. The growth of urban areas was not matched by economic development capable of assuring widespread prosperity. The conditions for social conflict and even war, rather than for democratic transformation, were widely created.

The third wave of post-Second World War transformation – although one which appeared as the opposite of 'revolutionary' change in the predominant Communist mode – was democratic reform in the advanced West itself. As a result of the war, the major

Western democratic states were victorious, and imposed more or less demilitarized forms of parliamentary democracy on defeated Japan and the western zones of Germany. Throughout most of western Europe, some form of parliamentary democracy was restored following the defeat of the Nazi German empire – in contrast to east-central Europe where it was quickly usurped by Communist regimes.

In subsequent decades parliamentary democracies became entrenched in western Europe.[23] The extent and depth of democratic reform in Europe can easily be underestimated since, half a century on, we take much of it for granted. Before 1939, only in north-western Europe was parliamentary democracy well established, and even there universal suffrage was still qualified. In many states, not just Germany and Italy, formal democratic institutions had proved precarious. The western European settlement after 1945 embedded democracy in many states where it had been weak and threatened. Even then, democracy was not universal in the western part of the continent: in southern Europe, authoritarian regimes persisted in Spain, Portugal and (intermittently) Greece until a new wave of democratic revolution overthrew them in the 1970s.

Before 1945, moreover, Western states were democratic only in the limited sense of combining political freedoms and parliamentary institutions. Only in Scandinavia had social democracy advanced strongly at the national rather than the municipal level. Through the Second World War, social democracy became hegemonic in British politics, as wartime participation led to a 'Keynesian welfare state consensus'.[24] In continental western Europe, previously dominant right-wing elites were often compromised by collaboration. Even after the early post-resistance dominance of Communist and social democratic parties was displaced, the new Christian democratic right-wing institutionalized similar Keynesian, welfare-oriented politics. Only in the USA, where the New Deal of the 1930s receded, was this kind of change not consolidated.

We need to assess the overall, combined significance of these three historic transformations after 1945. This can only be seen when we place them in the context of change in the national-international world order as a whole. On the one hand, it is clear that all three waves of change made the *national form* of the state more universal

---

[23] See Therborn (1977).
[24] See Addison (1975) and discussion in Shaw (1987).

and more legitimate. European world empires disappeared between the 1940s and the 1970s, to be replaced by around a hundred new 'nation-states'. Parliamentary democracy, where it was institutionalized in North America, western Europe, the Indian sub-continent and parts of Africa and Latin America, was invariably rooted in national forms. Revolution, even when Communist, was inevitably nationalist.

On the other hand, all three waves involved specific *new forms of internationalization*. The Communist revolutions sprang from a formally internationalist political doctrine which promised new forms of international cooperation. Paradoxically, however, their real internationalism was by far the weakest. The Communist bloc was dominated by the Soviet elite and failed to achieve meaningful integration; those national elites which could escape its grip did so. By the late 1970s, the USSR and China engaged in armed border skirmishes, and their Vietnamese and Cambodian clients were fighting wars.

The post-colonial, national-democratic revolution spawned a new internationalism of the developing world. The Third World, so called to distinguish it from the First and Second worlds of the Western and Soviet blocs, was often a residual category. But it also manifested itself in a form of politics, contesting the remnants of colonialism, Western economic power and Cold War political-military dominance. Although significant in the politics of the United Nations General Assembly, the Third World states formed a disparate movement of democratic, national-Communist and authoritarian regimes, many of which were tied in varying degrees to the major Cold War blocs.

The strongest new internationalism was, in reality, that of the West itself. At the core of the post-war order was the victorious wartime Western alliance of the United States, Britain and France. Democracy was partly a spontaneous demand of people and parties in countries formerly occupied by the Axis powers. But it was also an order imposed by the victors, in Germany and Japan to pre-empt a resurgence of military aggression, elsewhere in Europe to tie nations into the Western bloc, and reinforced by the Marshall Plan. The goal was to co-opt German and Japanese power by demonstrating to local elites that their national aspirations could be met within a US-led orbit. At the heart of the new phase of national-international world order was a form of Western unity in which interstate alliance was linked to democratic political forms.

In order to take further the analysis of the internationalism of the post-1945 era, we need to examine the three transformations which I have identified in the context of the world system. This involves examining their impact on state relations: at the ways in which these changes were entwined with the organization of state power in general, and changes in the structure and relations of particular 'states'. We need to evaluate the Cold War as a particular stage in the crisis of the national-international world, and the transition to a global world.

A post-national, pre-global world

Worldwide changes after 1945 cannot be understood simply within the three kinds of national-democratic transformation that I have described. These processes were all rooted in, and had an impact on, major shifts in state relations which originated in the Second World War. In the organization, fighting and conclusion of the war, changes took place which have had fundamental impacts on the entire post-war organization of the world economy, society and politics.

These changes were of three main kinds. First, the war brought about massive realignments of power between the principal nation-states, which led in turn to qualitative changes in the character of the centres of state power. Second, the war brought about the creation of legitimate, international world state institutions. Third, the intensive, total and extensive, worldwide character of the war meant that it was experienced not only in national terms, but as a common calamity – and victory – for the people of the world. This brought about an unprecedented sense of common worldwide humanity.

Let us take first the changes in the structure of worldwide state power. In the world war, two of the major nation-state-empires, Germany and Japan, were not just defeated. The Western alliance militarily occupied western Germany, and the USA occupied Japan. Just as much of the physical structure of their economies had been razed to the ground, the existing political structures of Nazism and the Japanese empire were largely dismantled. State entities were reconstructed – albeit using some of the old apparatuses and personnel – in forms which expressed their fundamental dependence on the victors. Moreover, the relationship between the principal Western victor-states, the United States and the United Kingdom, went beyond simple alliance. Britain became structurally dependent, militarily and financially, upon the USA. Similarly, other western European states, above all France and Italy, were restored as independent, democratic states mainly through American and British military action, despite the efforts of national resistance movements. These states too were in relations of dependence, due to this fact.

The secondary victor, the Soviet Union, was in *de facto* control of much of eastern Europe, including eastern Germany, which it had liberated from Nazism. The Soviet state was able to engage in far-reaching reconstruction of state, economy and society across the eastern part of Europe – although the new forms did not prove stable over the longer term. Only in relatively weak or backward areas, such as China and Yugoslavia, could independent local forces claim a major share of victory.

The results of the war laid the foundations, therefore, for an unprecedented integration of many hitherto autonomous major centres of state power in the world, under US leadership. The war-time situation had encouraged ambitious ideas for an American-led bloc: as Van der Pijl points out, 'The "Atlantic" predicate of Roosevelt's global design, first articulated in the 1941 Atlantic Charter, foresaw the incorporation of both the British Empire and the Soviet Union in an overarching Pax Americana.'[25] The wartime alliance did not develop into a single internally pacified core of world power, due to mutual rivalries and suspicions between the dominant American and subordinate Soviet and other elites, deepened by differences in their social and political systems and ideologies. According to Van der Pijl, 'It was not until the Chinese Revolution that a more realistic awareness of the limits of American power led to a revision of this strategy. In effect, the Grand Area once again became the dominant concept, with the Atlantic region, in particular, becoming the essential axis . . .'[26]

For Van der Pijl, this was the axis 'along which the internationalization of US capital, the generalization of its most advanced mode of accumulation, and the restructuration of class relations it presumed, took shape'.[27] We do not have to accept his assumption that wartime state strategies were essentially 'class strategies' on the part of the bourgeoisie, determined by the relation to the working class in the labour process and functional positions in the process of circulation of capital.[28] It is important to understand political and

[25] Van der Pijl (1984: 27).   [26] Van der Pijl (1984: 27–8).
[27] Van der Pijl (1984: 28).   [28] Van der Pijl (1984: 31).

military state integration in their own rights; the ascription of class meaning to state actions is intrinsically problematic.

But Van der Pijl is correct to note the way in which the most ambitious designs for world state integration were curbed, by essentially political processes. These were, to a significant extent, about what Kaldor calls 'the imperial nature of the Soviet Union' with its 'totalizing and militaristic characteristics' (stressed by dissident critics in eastern Europe), leading to the 'determination of the Soviet regime to hold on to the territory acquired during World War II'. Moreover, the whole Soviet system was 'built on the notion of threats both internal and external', so that 'mobilization for war was the only way of mobilizing the economy'. In turn, as she argues, 'The West needed a Soviet threat to legitimize the construction of the Western bloc. The Soviet system did represent an undesirable alternative, even though few people at that time viewed it as a territorial threat.'[29]

Instead of a single dominant bloc, therefore, two antagonistic blocs formed, Western and Soviet, through the military dependence (forced, in the case of the Soviet bloc) of the secondary member-states on the respective leading states or 'superpowers'. Within each bloc, the core states had similar political systems and ideologies. As the conflict of the blocs grew, formal military alliances (notably the North Atlantic Treaty Organization and the Warsaw Pact) and other common institutions were developed.

This meant that from the mid-1940s, state power in the northern industrial world was increasingly configured in a radically different way from the whole of the previous historical period. Before 1939 there had been a large number of more or less autonomous nation-states, of which the major states constituted rival world-empires, and between which competition could ultimately lead to a range of possible wars. Now there were two competing state-blocs, whose rivalry dominated world politics, together with a larger number of essentially secondary and minor centres of state power outside these blocs. A world dominated by two blocs, major Western and minor Soviet, was very different indeed from the previous national-international world based on rival European empires.

This was a historic change of the first order. Nevertheless the significance of this change in world order was largely hidden, for two principal reasons – one to do with the content of the relations of state

---

[29] Kaldor (1998: 201).

power, the other to do with their form. On the one hand, at the centre of the world order there was still military rivalry between states. 'Deterrence', Kaldor argues,

> . . . became a way of imagining war, of playing out a pretend war day after day, using real soldiers, weapons, military planners and the like. The point of this imaginary war was to keep alive the idea of interstate conflict so as to legitimize the blocs, to apply nation-state assumptions to the new situation. Yet precisely because the blocs were based on support for ideas about how to organize political and social systems, rather than on territory, neither territorial expansion nor wars of conquest were relevant to bloc expansion. Moreover, the two sets of ideologies were not so much competitive as complementary, each requiring the other for explanation. The elision of systemic and territorial expansion actually served as part of the legitimizing discourse of the imaginary war.[30]

On the other hand, at the centre of bloc rivalries was the conflict of the two 'superpowers', whose 'national' interests dominated bloc strategies. Soviet leaders automatically elided the Soviet Union's interests with those of the wider bloc. American leaders (and thinkers) continued to elaborate an explicitly national ideology, more or less in disregard of the bloc character of the state organizations over which they increasingly presided. Moreover, all states still presented in a national form, and blocs were international alliances, so that even subordinate elites had interests in perpetuating national-international thinking. As Kaldor argues, 'the bloc-system can be said to have prefigured new methods of political organization which arose because of the limitations of the nation-state. The Cold War was a way of reconciling the attachment to the nation-state with the need for larger forms of political organization.'[31]

For these reasons, the continuities in world order appeared to be more fundamental than the changes, and had (and continue to have) an exaggerated significance in the literature of international relations. For, however real these continuities were, they masked a basic change, the most important single change in world politics in recent centuries. The dominant nation-state-empires of the nineteenth and early twentieth centuries were overthrown. With them went the core of the interstate system – which lay in interimperial relations rather than in Westphalian ideas of sovereignty – and the classic meaning of the nation-state. Instead, in the order of blocs, ideologically differentiated

---

[30] Kaldor (1998: 201–2).   [31] Kaldor (1998: 194).

by their different social and political systems, the form of the nation-state was radically internationalized – albeit in contrasting ways.

A major paradox of the late twentieth century was that people often observed a 'decline of the nation-state', and attributed this to global liberalization of markets in the century's final decades. In reality, the major changes in the nature and roles of nation-states took place half a century earlier. The competition between nation-states in world war itself led to the abolition of the classic (imperial) nation-state, and instituted the bloc order, in which the 'nation-state' lived on in neutered form, in most cases a shadow of its former existence.

The principal manifest changes of the period that began in the 1940s – the Communist revolutions, the end of European empires and the proliferation of (often weak and insubstantial) nation-states, the con-solidation of democracy in the Western core – can all be seen as part of this larger transformation in world order. The expansion of Commun-ism in Europe was, overwhelmingly, the consolidation of the Soviet bloc. In Asia, it was part of the wave of national independence and liberation from European empires, the other side of the suppression of nation-state-empires at the heart of the state-system. Democratization within the West responded to the new demands of Western working-class movements, but it also increased the political homogeneity and coherence of the new Western bloc.

Global institutions and consciousness

The pre-global significance of the mid-1940s revolutions can be seen above all in the creation of the United Nations (UN) system of world institutions. These were inclusive interstate institutions which repre-sented the international system as a whole. The founders of the UN acknowledged the limitations of the previous international frame-work, the League of Nations, and intended a far more powerful set of institutions. The UN was an international system of states, and it privileged the victors of the world war (the Western triumvirate of the USA, Britain and France; the Soviet Union; and China, represented initially by the Nationalists) as permanent, veto-carrying members of its Security Council.

However, these new international institutions had a worldwide significance: they represented a common authority framework for the entire world. And although the world of 1945 was a world of nation-states, the roles of individuals and peoples were recognized in setting

up the system. While the UN Charter enshrined the We̶
principles of state sovereignty and non-interference in the int̶
affairs of states, the Universal Declaration of Human Rights pro̶
claimed the place of individuals in the UN-sanctioned world order,
and the Genocide Convention defined the violation of the collective
rights of human groups by states as the most dangerous modern
breach of international law.

ᶜᶜThe setting up of the UN represented more, therefore, than a new
interstate or international framework. It acknowledged common
world interests in human rights and the prevention of mass slaughter.
In this sense, new legitimate world institutions responded to common
experiences of the people of the world in the Second World War. It is
sometimes suggested that nations remain the only possible foundations for political community because they alone are repositories of
common experiences and memories. This is clearly untrue in general,
because all human collectivities are constituted partly by such realities. It is also particularly untrue in relation to the biggest, most
defining historical experiences of modern times, the world wars.ᶜᶜ

The world wars have been experienced, it is true, very much in
national forms. After all, the competitors in these total wars were
nation-states and alliances of nation-states, mobilizing entire nations,
so there have been major national experiences – occupation and
humiliation, struggle and victory – which have had huge effects on
social relations of all kinds. Nevertheless, wars have also been
experienced and remembered through other communities – of race
and ethnicity, sex and class – across as well as within national
boundaries. And world wars – obviously, one might have thought,
because we know them by that name – have also been experienced as
common world events. The Second World War, much more than the
first, was a genuinely worldwide conflict, and huge international and
transnational communities of struggle were formed.

Of course, when wars are experienced as national events, the
experience of individuals and groups within nations varies vastly, and
their interpretation of national significance varies too. Even more, it is
true that the experience of 'world' war varied hugely across the
world. Even among the states involved – and we have to remember
that even in a world war many states, particularly in Latin America,
were not combatants – wartime experience ranged from the physical
extermination meted out to the Jews and other groups, on the one
hand, to the boomtime of American civilians, worried not for them-

...lier husbands and sons across the world, on the

...on experience made from such diversity? Clark
... the First World War) claims that 'Participation in
...ely globalizing experience . . . It is hard to imagine a
...expression of globalization in the lives of ordinary
...ough worldwide communications, people gained some
a. ...the situations of others, and came to see them not simply
as ene... but (to varying extents) as common participants in and
victims of a titanic world struggle. The worst experiences, such as the
destruction of the Jewish people, became emblematic of a worldwide
struggle of good and evil. Although these experiences were those of
particular communities, and even of nations (thus the Holocaust
became part of the founding doctrine of the Israeli state), they were
also world experiences, part of the common memories of worldwide
humankind.

Even the destruction inflicted by the victors, such as the area-
bombing of German cities and above all the atomic bombing of
Hiroshima and Nagasaki, became common experiences and symbols
of human victimization. However, they have been misappropriated by
states – or denied by extreme nationalists – these common experiences
are a prime foundation of contemporary global consciousness. It is
extremely significant that more than half a century after 1945, the role
of the Holocaust and of many other traumatic episodes of the Second
World War is actually growing in both culture and politics. The lessons
of these experiences, as well as of new traumas which compound these
lessons, are fuelling new developments of global law and morality.

The development of the United Nations system responded, initially,
to these human, social outcomes of the world war as well as to the
radically altered interstate relations which resulted. Of course, as the
Cold War bloc-system was consolidated, worldwide community
seemed increasingly a pious aspiration. As a result of Cold War
divisions, the UN settled into an ineffectuality reminiscent of the
League, from which it has only partially escaped. Used briefly – in
consequence of Soviet absentionism – by the Western side in the
Korean war, the UN was subsequently able to act mainly where East
and West could agree.

And yet for both sides, the experiences of the world war were

[32] Clark (1997: 66).

essential to ideology and myth: the common framework continued even in division. For the West, the Cold War was a continuation of the wartime struggle for democracy against totalitarianism. For the Soviet bloc, it was a worldwide struggle against imperialism, continued from the Great Patriotic War. The wartime community of struggle was twisted in ideology, but it was too strong a reference point to deny outright. Furthermore, the very process of conflict in the Cold War created – paradoxically – conditions of cooperation in the world order. The original Cold War of the late 1940s and early 1950s, peaking in the Korean War, was one of largely unmanaged rivalry. It was associated with the most brutal totalitarian phase in the Soviet bloc and with authoritarian anti-Communism in the Western democracies (most notoriously, McCarthyism). It was a dangerous and unstable period, in which the shape of the post-war world was still being forged.

As the Cold War became increasingly understood as an ongoing system of conflict, the superpower leaderships recognized the need to manage their mutual relationships more consciously. With the Soviet achievement of a credible strategic nuclear force in the later 1950s, and the normalization of bureaucratic authoritarianism under Khrushchev and Brezhnev, the conditions for understanding between bloc leaders improved. Even crises, whether internal to the blocs like those of 1956, or between them as over missiles in Cuba in 1961, served – however dangerous they were at the time – to define the limits of the system.

The Cold War thus became a process of power positioning and mutual surveillance by the two blocs. Since crises within the blocs were seen as belonging to the respective superpowers, the two main forms of conflict were direct (over the means of military competition, the arms race) and indirect (over influence in the world outside the blocs, the Third World). Both forms of conflict were increasingly managed from the mid-1950s onwards, through limited measures of arms control on the one hand and manipulation of clients on the other.

Despite these processes of management, of course, the Cold War system remained unstable: crises were caused both by the super- powers' innovations in weaponry and by changing balances of power in Third World regions, and relations were influenced by conflict within the blocs. Throughout the period, the risks – the possible consequences of instability – remained colossal.[33] Although mutual

---

[33] Thus nuclear war became the paradigmatic case of what Giddens (1990) calls 'high- consequence, low-probability' risk.

monitoring became more sophisticated, more integral to the system and even more cooperative, it did not eliminate risk. Indeed, surveillance could magnify the perception of threat as well as providing a way of controlling it.

However, an important element of latent cooperation was built into the manifest Cold War system. This helps to explain why the so-called Second Cold War of the early 1980s could lead, as rapidly as it did, to the winding down of the entire system in the second half of the decade. Through extensive mutual knowledge, closer relationships between the two superpower elites, the development of regular contacts and the 'hotline', as well as common membership of the United Nations system and developing experience of crisis management, war was averted. In the 'Helsinki process', universalist norms of human rights became part of the ongoing relationship between the two blocs. All these developments help to explain why unprecedented cooperation could develop between the West and Gorbachev's Soviet Union in the late 1980s, and remained strong in the relations of the West with the successor states of the Soviet bloc – many of which were led by ex-Communist elites.

Cold War and the integrated bloc-state

The Cold War was therefore a system of war and politics which contained, usurped and distorted the potential for a common, world-wide world order (based on the authority of legitimate international institutions), which had emerged in the first phase of global revolution in 1945. At the same time, however, within this system, the potential continued to develop. We need therefore to understand how, just as the contradictions of the system of nation-state-empires destroyed that system and led to its replacement by the bloc-system, so contradictions within the Cold War system led in turn to its downfall and the global revolution of our times.

The Cold War has been understood in different ways, and it is only now that it is over that we can begin to gain some historical perspective on it. Its manifest centre was an ideologically presented conflict of nuclear-armed state-blocs, which threatened mutual destruction of states and peoples – indeed of planetary life. What it was really 'about', and what its consequences were, are less agreed. For some, it was a great-power conflict of national interests, in new guise. For others, it was a conflict of social and political systems and ideas.

For others still, although it may have begun in such conflicts, it came to be 'about itself' – about the unstable balance of weaponry which came to dominate our civilization, emphasizing its 'exterminist' potential.[34] It was an 'imaginary war' in which total war maintained its hold on state institutions and culture even as much of social and economic development strained ahead.[35]

The Cold War was both more than a traditional conflict of states and less than a conflict of social and political systems. As a new system of military rivalry between state-blocs, it was based on new state relations and forms, and although these differed radically between the two blocs, they were both parts of the same system. The Cold War was in one sense a continuation of the total-war society which had come into existence in the early part of the century. However, it both accentuated some and diminished other characteristics of this set of state relations, and to different degrees in the two blocs. The Cold War continued the total-destruction side of total war, to the point that it threatened instant, total annihilation. In the Cold War, however, the total-mobilization side of total war was weakened, although more so in the Western than in the Soviet bloc.[36]

The Cold War originated in great-power political rivalry, in the aspirations for control and mutual suspicions of American and Soviet elites at the end of the Second World War. It did not originate in a simple conflict of social or political systems. In principle post-revolutionary Soviet Communism could have coexisted with Western capitalism, as indeed was partially envisaged by both sides in 1944–5, during *détente* in the 1970s, and again in the thaw of the mid-1980s. However, the liberal world political-economic order promoted by the United States and its allies at the end of the Second World War potentially threatened total Soviet control over economy and society within its territory.

Effectively the world was divided into 'a sphere in which free trade and currency exchange would increase under the stabilizing *pax Americana*, on the one hand, and an expanded autarchic alliance, the "Communist bloc", on the other'. As Cerny suggests, 'The Cold War was thus rooted in economic policy as much as, and perhaps more than, in political philosophy. "Openness" means just what it says – that the necessity or desirability is accepted of the penetration of the

---

[34] Thompson (1982).
[35] Kaldor (1990, 1998).   [36] See Shaw (1988, 1991).

home society by external pressures.'[37] Thus 'the Cold War brought with it the division of the world economy into the "open" capitalist sector and the "closed" Communist bloc: political and economic structures within each bloc were more tightly interwoven than ever before'.[38]

Moreover, the Western bloc achieved huge economic growth through its open economic system, which was primarily a system of open relations across its own (from the bloc standpoint, internal) borders. As Clark points out, expanded world trade was large within the Western triad of North America, Europe and Japan, so that even Dicken, who accepts the main elements of the globalization thesis, 'readily concedes that the statistics reveal an overwhelming concentration "within the advanced industrial states as the source and destination of foreign direct investment; indeed, some three-quarters of the total"'.[39] Despite impressive growth in the Soviet bloc during the early part of the Cold War period, it was always the minor system, dependent on (and later increasingly integrated with) the West's dominant system.

Differences of political, economic and ideological system fuelled, therefore, the power rivalries that led to conflict, and once begun it was easily understood and presented in these terms. Once begun, too, the Cold War assisted the process of bloc formation and consolidation, the conflict providing a means of disciplining – albeit by different means in the two blocs – both subordinate states and society. In these senses, we can see the Cold War as a dynamic system of state relations, in which both state and society were produced and reproduced in bloc terms. We can also see it as producing distinctive state forms, as both new forms of nation-state and international organization, within and across blocs, were developed. These relations and forms were in some senses common to, but in many ways quite divergent in, the two blocs.

In both blocs, the superpower nation-state functioned as the centre of military power for the bloc as a whole, and to this extent the Cold War was correctly seen as a US-Soviet conflict. Major military decisions within NATO followed from the development of American policy, seen by American leaders as a matter of 'national' interest even as it determined the policy of NATO as a whole. NATO had a

---

[37] Cerny (1990: 214).   [38] Cerny (1990: 216).
[39] Clark (1997: 143), citing Dicken (1998).

collective decision-making structure, but it was hardly here that bloc policy was principally formulated. To the extent that other states were able to influence NATO policy, it was largely through the bilateral relations of major centres (Britain, France, West Germany) with the USA. In the Warsaw Pact, the formally collective nature of the organization made little difference to the simple domination of the Soviet state.

The centralization of military power meant that the bloc-state had a common disciplinary function for national elites and society in general throughout each bloc. The need for bloc unity against the common enemy permeated the politics and culture of West as well as East. However, the discipline of the Soviet bloc was primarily and often simply imposed, overwhelmingly and directly coercive. That of the West was much more voluntary and legitimate. Anti-Communism was indeed a coercive doctrine, orchestrated by state and media, but it had a genuine resonance in Western societies. This was especially true in Europe where invasion (or the threat of it) by totalitarian states was a recent memory and examples of totalitarian dictatorship in neighbouring Communist states were real.

The political relations of subordinate states and peoples in the Western bloc with its American centre were more genuinely two-way than the organization of military power implied. Nation-states lost most of their military autonomy – even Britain and France were effectively constrained in their independent use of force, especially after the 1956 Suez fiasco. However, national centres retained considerable autonomy in their internal economic, social and political relations. Indeed, while shorn of their empires and their classic independent military functions, nation-states were in other senses *more* powerful institutions, and more embedded in national society. Common national experiences of war, the expansion of state socio-economic functions due to war and the consolidation of democracy all meant that the state apparatuses and their leaders were stronger at the national level.

Thus within the West, the nation-state form was actually strengthened *within* and through the bloc-state. Despite overwhelming American military dominance and the lack of real international, let alone democratic control of military policy, national politics within the other states largely supported the bloc during the Cold War. Pro-Western conservative, Christian-, liberal- and social-democratic parties easily prevailed not only over Communist but also over anti-Cold War, neutralist parties. In some phases and places, of course, anti-Cold War social movements did gain significant public support, but this was rarely translated into substantial leverage within political systems.[40]

These relations explain the paradox of Western state forms during the Cold War. Although the outcome of the Second World War had abolished the system of nation-state-empires and subordinated nation-states within larger state-blocs, the Cold War West was constituted as a genuinely international bloc. Despite and even because of the loss of classic national-imperial forms, national institutions, increasingly democratized, were strengthened. Despite fundamental military integration and centralization, the Western state-bloc was both formally and in political substance an alliance of nation-states. The content of national power had been substantially diminished, but the national form of the state was actually reinforced. The cooperative international form, moreover, was given a fundamental new importance in the bloc-state. National state entities were penetrated by the international organizations of the Western state and adapted accordingly, finding new roles in pressing redefined, chiefly economic, national interests within their frameworks.[41]

We can analyse the development, therefore, of *a new form of state: the national and international bloc-state*. The Western state was a largely successful example of this form, rooted in the social relations which produced national economic, welfare and democratic legitimacy as well as international, collective security. The Soviet bloc-state was a much less credible, and ultimately unsuccessful, example of this form. The Soviet state had partial legitimacy within the borders of the USSR, and chiefly in Russia itself – above all as the destroyer of Nazism – even if it was also the outcome of Stalin's genocides against both classes and nationalities. Although this legitimacy was extended in some of the countries liberated by the Red Army in 1945, the Soviet bloc was from the beginning an imposed order. The states of eastern and central Europe, including eastern Germany, had Soviet-type regimes forced upon them through the Yalta agreements, Soviet occupation and political manipulation, with modest or minimal popular support.

---

[40] Thus in the early 1980s, the success of the Dutch peace movement in delaying deployment of cruise missiles was the exception which proved the rule among the five states in which deployment was scheduled. This was due not only to more extensive mobilization but to stronger political influence in governing as well as opposition parties.

[41] See e.g. Cerny (1990).

Soviet-type regimes were styled 'people's democracies' but the people were 'represented' through the party-state rather than anything recognizable as genuine democracy. In the early years, the Soviet Union ruthlessly imposed its priorities on social, economic and political life in the satellite states. Post-war reparations saw factories looted wholesale from Germany and Hungary. Everywhere, forced industrialization was tied to Soviet reconstruction, combined with disastrous policies of forcible collectivization, causing great hardship. National party elites, as well as society, were brutally purged to ensure absolute acquiescence. In these conditions, Warsaw Pact membership was in no sense a choice of nations or governments.

Soviet bloc discipline, like the internal discipline of the Soviet state, was eventually modified. After Stalin's death in 1953 and Khrushchev's 1956 denunciation of his abuses, it became more authoritarian and repressive than totalitarian in the classic sense. This was largely due to the revolts of the mid-1950s, which emphasized the instability of rule based on wholesale repression. After this, national party elites gained some autonomy from the Kremlin in internal economic, social and political matters, if not in military bloc issues. In this sense the Soviet bloc-state appeared as a pale reflection of the Western model, and the autonomy of national apparatuses, although much more limited, gained real significance.

However, the Soviet bloc never gained the cohesion of a successful bloc-state. State relations of all kinds were overwhelmingly coercive, with legitimacy which was at best limited and often minimal. The bloc, as it was consolidated in the 1940s, was effectively an extension of the Russian empire that the Bolsheviks had inherited from Tsarism, and which Stalin had re-entrenched before and during the Second World War. The westward expansion of the Soviet system, to countries of which some at least were more industrially advanced and much more closely linked to western Europe than Russia, created new tensions. 'For an inefficient and uncompetitive system like the Soviet Union, expansion was an extraordinary burden', Cox points out, 'and one likely to grow as the economy began to slow down.' The Soviet Union would eventually do 'as other declining powers have been impelled to do in history: that is, retreat from an empire it could neither afford to support nor hope to control over the longer term'.[42]

The bloc had superficially similar national and cooperative inter-

---

[42] M. Cox (1998b: 162).

national forms to those of the West, but these forms were not solidly embedded in the social relations of state power. The states of the Soviet bloc were not nation-states in the Western sense, with extensive economic, social and political autonomy rooted in a level of satisfaction of social needs and affirmed through national democratic institutions. There was some real progress in welfare provision and consumption from the late 1950s onwards. But Soviet-bloc-states appeared relatively more inefficient than Western nation-states and still had weak national and democratic legitimacy. The extension of national autonomy mainly served to accelerate the trends towards its break-up.

The internationalism of the Soviet bloc, rooted in inadequately national states, remained to the end an imposed form. The Warsaw Pact was never much more than an instrument of Soviet policy. Even if eastern European elites' and peoples' fears of revived German militarism gave some meaning to the Pact's armaments, especially in the early decades after 1945, their real function was much more to do with the internal discipline of the bloc. In practice the Pact was mobilized only to suppress successive national revolts. Not surprisingly, those Communist regimes that came to power independently of Moscow resisted integration into the bloc, and saw it as a threat to their national integrity.

The success of the Western bloc-state and the failure of its Soviet rival were reflected in their contrasting experiences in the development of bloc integration and international institutions. As Clark points out, 'If globalization emerged from the successful creation of an expanding Western system, then a necessary part of its explanation must lie in the failure of the Soviet Union to provide an effective challenge to that political and economic framework: the fate of globalization was contingent upon, not only the fact of the cold war, but also its actual course.'[43]

Ironically, given the significance of international cooperation and planning in Communist ideology, there was little real international planning within the Soviet bloc. The quasi-imperial character of intra-bloc relations, especially in the early years, meant that national elites sought to escape from bloc-level decision-making. The bloc economic institution, Comecon, lost rather than gained significance over time. As east-central European national economies grew more sophisticated,

[43] Clark (1997: 141).

more of their trade was with the West, and world market prices were used ever more as a measure of exchange even within the Soviet bloc.

Indeed as Friedman argues, the Soviet bloc disintegrated, in the end, partly through its relationships to the Western-dominated world economy. There was a deep connection between Western monetary crises and the unravelling of the Soviet bloc (and hence the entire bloc-system). 'Existing socialism', she suggests,

> foundered when the tension between national and bloc organization shifted because of irreversible ties to Western money, energy, and food markets. The Communist Party of the Soviet Union compromised the unity of the bloc in favor of its national interest in hard-currency earnings. The Communist Party of each of the eastern European countries struck out on its own in Western capital markets. The bloc could not hold, and neither could the economies and ruling parties within it.[44]

The collapse of the Warsaw Pact system was thus the culmination of a decade of economic realignments that helped undermine the political institutions of the Soviet bloc. However, it was much more than that, even if few recognized the depth of its problems. As Michael Cox argues, 'the real cause of the failure to anticipate the end of the Cold War lay in a collective failure to recognize the USSR for what it was: a weak and flawed system in terminal decline'.[45]

The economic disintegration of the Soviet bloc, and the growing integration of its more advanced member-states with Western-dominated world markets, contrasted with real economic integration in the West. While the Soviet bloc institutions remained limited, the West generated a more and more sophisticated raft of international institutions which effectively regulated the world economy. As Friedman puts it, 'The economic integration of the capitalist bloc was considerably greater than that of the socialist bloc; . . . whereas Stalinist autarky never succumbed to attempts at bloc-wide planning . . . integration of North American and European economies proceeded very far through sectoral reorganization by private transnational corporations.'[46]

She might have added that it proceeded too through the distinctive international state organizations of the West. The world financial institutions set up at Bretton Woods in 1945, the World Bank and

---

[44] Friedman (1998: 228).
[45] M. Cox (1998b: 166).   [46] Friedman (1998: 228).

International Monetary Fund, became effectively Western-bloc institutions with a world-regulatory role. Through the General Agreement on Tariffs and Trade (later the World Trade Organization), the West regulated its own intra-bloc trade and indirectly at least most of the remainder of world trade. Through the Organization for Economic Cooperation and Development it consolidated a broad Western core, which included neutral as well as militarily allied developed market economies. Later, the Group of Seven major states became a Western and effectively a world leadership forum which linked North America, western Europe and Japan.

Within the Western bloc, therefore, military integration became increasingly a framework for economic integration. Nowhere was this clearer than in the historically fragmented western European core of the state-system. Here limited cooperative institutions such as the European Iron and Steel Community led to the European Economic Community, European Community (EC) and eventually the contemporary European Union (EU). European integration should not be opposed to Atlantic (and hence trilateral) integration: Atlantic unity, as Lundestad notes, *'was* the essential framework into which European integration was to be fitted, and was indeed fitted'.[47]

In these developments, above all, it became clear that the West was far more than the alliance of independent nation-states. It had become an increasingly integrated state-bloc, with a wide range of sophisticated international as well as national institutions which to a large extent regulated the world economy as a whole – Third World and Soviet bloc as well as West. The institutions of both Europe and the wider West were all international in form. They presupposed and to some extent reinforced national forms. But at the same time the integration that they furthered weakened national boundaries and relativized national differences. In this way, the internationalization of the West transformed as well as renewed national-international forms. Friedman notes that 'Rivalries in the Atlantic bloc have so far been contained by deep economic integration, but as Kaldor says, the political disintegration of eastern Europe cautions against complacency.'[48] While this is in principle correct, it is clear that there were structural differences between Western- and Soviet-bloc integration.

Within the internationalized West, democracy was substantially strengthened in several different ways. First, parliamentary democ-

---

[47] Lundestad (1998: 147).   [48] Friedman (1998: 228).

racy was increasingly recognized as a key criterion of membership of the West. In its first three decades NATO always included states such as Turkey and Portugal which had clearly authoritarian regimes. However, neutral, non-NATO democratic states were recognized as part of the West. From the 1970s especially there was a clear trend towards democratization of authoritarian Western bloc-states, encouraged by bloc centres and institutions, notably in the incorporation of Spain into NATO and Spain, Portugal and Greece into the EU. Second, towards the end of the Cold War period, a functioning parliamentary democracy increasingly became a key criterion of admission to Western institutions, particularly the emergent EU, the most thoroughly integrated of them all. Third, some Western-bloc institutions, including NATO, had international parliamentary bodies: eventually, the EC developed the first internationally elected transnational body, the European Parliament. Although the latter's powers were restricted, the idea of transnational democracy which it represented was a radical departure.

The development of the Western bloc-state during the Cold War thus created three of the main conditions for contemporary global state development: economic institutions with increasingly worldwide scope and legitimacy; comprehensive integration of, as well as alliance between, nation-states; and democracy as a normal condition of entry to the dominant world bloc. As Clark puts it, 'the cold war's ultimate effect has been one of integration, not world disintegration, and although it created deep fissures between East and West, this served the purpose of integration within the West, stimulated an attempted incorporation of the Third World into the First, and may potentially contribute to a single global system in the cold war's aftermath'.[49] But while Cold War Western military integration was the starting-point and condition for these developments, they also reflected social struggles against the Cold War and the dominant Western bloc. So long as the Cold War continued, moreover, the global democratic revolution could never realize its full potential.

Democratic revolution, Cold War and war

The relation of democratic change to the Cold War order was always double-edged. On the one hand, democracy was the political system

---

[49] Clark (1997: 123).

of the dominant Western bloc and the ideology of United Nations institutions. On the other hand, the Cold War system as such functioned to contain democracy in all three sections of the world. Within the West, democracy was increasingly institutionalized, but democratic reform remained a movement from below. The democratic revolution continued, therefore, in opposition to the Cold War system and its institutions, in all three sectors of the world order.

Democracy was most clearly a revolutionary movement within the Soviet bloc and other Communist states. As we have already seen, the revolutionary significance of the Communist seizures of power after 1945 was fundamentally flawed by the anti-democratic character of the regimes which were created. Within a few years of their creation, the 'people's democracies' were shaken by profound movements of democratic revolt. Only months after Stalin's death in 1953, workers in East Germany rose up; three years later, in 1956, a fully-fledged revolutionary uprising briefly overthrew the Stalinist regime in Hungary, and a major revolt took place in Poland. The international significance of the Hungarian revolution was clear: it was a direct challenge to the Soviet bloc-state. The revolutionary government under the reform Communist, Imre Nagy, took the decisive step of declaring Hungary's withdrawal from the Warsaw Pact as well as opening up democratic change. Despite and indeed because of this, the Western bloc was unable to intervene – it was held back moreover by its own, simultaneous Suez crisis. Since Western intervention could have led to a world war which the West would not risk, the Cold War system underwrote the Soviet bloc's capacity to suppress democratic revolt.[50]

This lesson was depressingly confirmed in all subsequent movements against the Soviet bloc order, whatever form they took. In Czechoslovakia in 1968, a reformist group led by Alexander Dubček won control of the national party and state – this time without breaking with the Warsaw Pact. But as the government allowed society democratic self-expression, this came to seem too great a threat to bloc order, and the USSR organized the military suppression of the reform movement. In Poland in 1980–1, workers and intellectuals established the independent trade union movement, Solidarity – making no direct challenge, however, to either the Warsaw Pact or the legitimacy of the Communist regime.[51] Although the movement

[50] Lomax (1976).   [51] See Touraine (1983).

lasted much longer than previous revolts, in the end the Polish military themselves quashed it – their leader, General Jaruzelski, later justifying this as the lesser evil compared with direct Soviet military intervention.

In 1956, 1968 and 1981, the West expressed sympathy but was unable to intervene to support the democratic movement. It became clear that the Cold War system itself was a barrier to democratic revolution in the East. So long as the Soviet bloc was locked into conflict with the West, it would be able to sustain the capacity to repress democratic movements, and the West would be unable or unwilling to support them.

In the Western bloc itself, although parliamentary democracy was the dominant political form, the Cold War system also functioned to contain democracy.[52] Especially in the early Cold War period, the USA and the other Western states tended to see movements to extend democracy as manifestations of Communism. Thus they long supported anti-democratic governments in some NATO countries, in order to defeat Communism internally and contain it internationally. They often opposed anti-colonial movements, seeing these as Communist-inspired. Even within core Western states, democratic reform was tarred with the Communist brush.

Democracy was confined, moreover, almost entirely to national institutions. The bloc institutions were the elements of Western state power that were least democratic. Not only NATO but even the bloc economic institutions were subject to minimal democratic control. Other nation-states did not dispute American hegemony over Cold War policy, and within the USA, as Mills argued, the 'highest level' of power was also the one over which democratic institutions and publics had least purchase.[53] Cold War policy was seen, as Mann points out, as an area of 'geopolitical privacy' of elites.[54]

Thus the extension of democracy within the West was a product not simply or mainly of state elites, but of struggles by oppressed groups and social movements. From the mid-1950s to the mid-1980s extensive social movements in Western states themselves maintained the

---

[52] It is noteworthy that Francis Fukuyama, while admitting that 'formal democracy alone does not always guarantee equal participation and rights' and that 'Democratic procedures can be manipulated by elites', nevertheless appears to defend the separation of liberalism and democracy: 'It is possible for a country to be liberal without being particularly democratic, as was eighteenth-century Britain' (1992: 44).

[53] Mills (1956, 1958).   [54] Mann (1987).

impetus for democratic reform. Many of these were directed against the Cold War system itself and its military manifestations – notably the nuclear disarmament movements of the late 1950s and early 1960s, and again of the early 1980s, and the anti-Vietnam War movements of the late 1960s and early 1970s. In Europe, anti-nuclear weapons campaigns also attacked American control over Western bloc policy.

Others challenged, however, many undemocratic features of Western states and societies: the civil rights movement against American racism in the early 1960s, the student movements of the late 1960s (destabilizing, notably, the authoritarian Gaullist regime in France), the women's movements from the early 1970s onwards, and the 'green' movements against unaccountable corporate power from the late 1970s. Throughout this period, the 'public sphere' in Western states was expanded by the action of what were seen as 'new' international social movements, based on minorities or issues rather than classes, and organizing transnationally across boundaries.

These social movements radically extended the scope of democratic demands. Democracy was seen not as a purely political process, or even as a means of state intervention to extend democratic rights in economy and society (the social democratic extension). It was also seen as applying in social relations within the workplace (although this was an old idea of pre-statist socialist traditions), in the family and sexual relations (an idea developed by earlier feminists which now became much more part of the democratic mainstream) and in the control of the environment. Social movements also extended, therefore, the content of the democratic idea, so that democracy was understood as participatory, broadly and deeply embedded in society, rather than purely representative and located in state institutions.

The conflict between the Cold War system and democratic change was even more obvious on the margins of the Western bloc than at its core. During the early Cold War period, as we have seen, authoritarian regimes remained in southern Europe. In the 1970s, the democratic movements which fanned out after 1968 swept away the remaining dictatorships, leading their transformation into liberal democracies. In the Portuguese case, this upheaval also stimulated the break-up of the last European colonial empire. In the post-colonial, so-called Third World the opposition between the Cold War system and democratic change was fundamental. Throughout the non-Western world, Western governments and especially the USA continued until the

1980s to support corrupt, authoritarian, military and anti-democratic regimes as bulwarks against Communism. The Soviet bloc, equally, supported undemocratic nationalist and Communist regimes which aligned with it against the West. Third World independence movements from the 1950s to the 1970s often took the form of armed struggle against Western-backed colonialism, and developed authoritarian regimes partly in consequence. Many 'democratic' governments in newly independent states also gave way quickly to Cold War-sponsored authoritarian, military and oligarchic rule.

The democratic revolution continued in the non-Western world, but without decisive support from the West – even where Western governments paid lip-service to change. The National Party regime in South Africa, for example, which came to power as the Cold War began, survived until its very end, giving way to democratic reform only in the early 1990s. Throughout this period, Western governments, while eschewing the principles of the apartheid regime, nevertheless sustained it in power and refused more than token support to its opponents, who therefore looked for Soviet-bloc support. Within democratic opposition movements in many colonial and Third World states, indeed, there were tensions between demands for genuine extensions of democracy and the compromises which the blocs (and their respective Communist and anti-Communist politics) more or less forced on movements in return for the blocs' support.

Towards globalism

Throughout the Cold War period democratic movements linked across the three sectors of the world order – the two blocs and the Third World. The West was the pivot of these linkages. Although Western states often had an interest in maintaining undemocratic regimes in the Third World, just as they were constrained by military dangers from offering more than token support to Soviet-bloc democrats, Western civil society was sometimes able to give effective support. Here a developed, relatively well-resourced civil society and relatively open media were able to exert pressure on a state order based on democracy – not only for further reforms in its own institutions, but also for support for democratic change elsewhere.

However, it was difficult for democratic movements in the three sectors to form a common, worldwide movement during the Cold War. This was primarily because of structural constraints, but also because of ideological inhibitions – many internalized the bloc ideologies. From 1956 onwards, however, when the coincidence of Hungary and Suez highlighted the common militarism and repression of the two blocs, movements across the world increasingly saw common interests in opposing the bloc order and the Cold War system itself. At the level of states, the Third World movement was limited by the repressive character of many of the member-states and their ambiguous relationships to the blocs. But the idea of a 'third camp' of democratic – including independent socialist – opposition was influential.

From the 1960s, moreover, new social movements arose with worldwide goals and impact. The student movement of the late 1960s, for example, originating in American and pan-Western opposition to the Vietnam War, grew into a worldwide democratic movement. The May 1968 uprising in France was followed by democratic student movements in eastern European states – notably in Poland and Yugoslavia as well as Czechoslovakia – and in many Third World countries as well as across the Western world. As Harman points out,

> 1968 was the product of contradictions which had developed in the years that came before and which continued to explode in the decade afterwards. The French May was followed by the Italian hot autumn of 1969 . . . The student riots in Warsaw in March 1968 were followed by the much more serious challenge to Stalinism of the Prague Spring and by the even greater challenge of *Solidarnosc* . . . The Polytechnic of Athens rose up in November 1973, numbering the days of the Greek dictatorship. The chimes of freedom were still ringing in Lisbon, Portugal, in April 1974 and in Vitoria, Spain, in March 1976.[55]

However, if most of the new social movements had internationalist or even global goals, they were not able to pursue them with anything like comparable effect in each sector. The difficulties of the 1980s peace movement, which consciously fought against the division of Europe, are indicative. While hundreds of thousands of people might

---

[55] Harman (1988: 7). It is also notable that Fukuyama is completely out of sympathy with the spirit of 1968: 'Those students who temporarily took over Paris and brought down General de Gaulle had no "rational" reason to revolt, for they were for the most part pampered offspring of one of the freest and most prosperous societies on earth. But it was precisely the absence of struggle and sacrifice in their middle-class lives that led them to take to the streets and confront the police. The substance of their protest, however, was a matter of indifference; what they rejected was life in a society in which ideals had somehow become impossible' (1992: 330).

demonstrate in any one of western Europe's capitals, it was difficult to get even hundreds together anywhere in eastern Europe. The movements might then be more effectively dismissed by states – labelled as tools of the other side in the Cold War, when in fact they generally opposed both blocs.

Nevertheless, we can say that a globalist potential was burgeoning, especially in the 1960s, 1970s and 1980s, and pushing against the limits of the Cold War system and world order. This potential had many strands. There were movements such as the campaigns for nuclear disarmament which sought to break down the division of Europe and the world into blocs. There were democratic movements everywhere which supported or sympathized with each other's aims. There were movements concerned with global economic and social inequality, between North and South, and which advocated a 'one world' approach. There were new environmental movements which promoted a view of a common world environment. And finally, there were universalist movements such as those of women's liberation, which transcended borders.

Globalism took a variety of forms – from relatively spontaneous social movements to the coordination of elements in established civil society institutions such as churches, parties and trade unions. The principal globalist campaigns of today were founded during this period – for example, Amnesty International in the early 1960s, Greenpeace in the 1970s. While their influence was much more limited than it has become since the end of the Cold War, they already pointed the way. Their influence was not limited to the West, or even to the more democratic states of the Third World, but was also felt inside both Communist and pro-Western authoritarian regimes. In the later stages of the Cold War, it became easier for democratic voices to be heard in eastern Europe, albeit still with great difficulty.

The real 'revolution in the revolution'

Throughout the Cold War period, moreover, the worldwide democratic revolution faced formidable opposition. The bloc-states, especially the superpowers, devoted part of their enormous military forces, as well as a battery of intelligence services, propaganda arms and cultural agencies, to containing change.[56] Democratic movements

---

[56] Stonor Saunders (1999).

were crushed militarily not only in the Soviet bloc but in pro-Western authoritarian states. Both sides in the Cold War supported and condoned large-scale repression, even to the point of genocide – for example in Indonesia in 1965, when over half a million people were killed.[57]

The democratic revolution came up against the limitations of conventional models of revolution and the inherently anti-democratic bias of the use of armed force. Not only within the Soviet bloc, but in the independent Communist states established in the revolutions of the 1940s and after, revolutionary regimes were from the start repressive and anti-democratic. The democratic revolution of the Cold War period was directed against these so-called 'revolutionary' forms, and met drastic repression from the Communist regimes. This was not only in eastern Europe: in China, too, the revolution quickly showed its brutally repressive character.

People in Western democratic movements often had difficulty in understanding the character of Communist revolutions. Just as in the 1930s, 1940s and 1950s Western socialists and democrats had often idealized Stalin's Russia, in the 1960s and 1970s many developed romantic illusions about China, Cuba, Yugoslavia – even Albania. During the Vietnam War, support for national liberation and opposition to American bombing often led Westerners to neglect the anti-democratic character of Vietnamese Communism. An even more blatant case was the so-called Chinese 'Cultural Revolution' of late 1960s, in which educated urban groups were ruthlessly victimized; many of their counterparts in the West ignorantly idealized this as an 'anti-bureaucratic' movement.[58] Where people were aware of the realities, these were often dismissed as secondary blemishes, or excused by the different economic or cultural contexts of Third World societies.

In retrospect, it is clear that military force and war were becoming more than ever a counterrevolutionary force during the Cold War period. Military force became the prime involvement of superpower and bloc rivalry, threatening mass extermination on a historically unprecedented scale. For the declining imperial states (especially France, Britain and Portugal) it remained a way of trying to stem national independence. Within many new nation-states, it became a means of repressing national minorities and democratic dissent, as

---

[57] Palmier (1973).   [58] Thurston (1988), White (1993).

well as of pressing new rivalries with other states. Many new states in Africa and Asia, like corrupt pro-Western regimes in Latin America, became military dictatorships. Among warring states, war generally led to the restriction or suppression of democracy.

The model of revolution-as-war, symbolized by Mao Zedong and Ho Chi Minh, continued to inspire many suppressed groups in independent Third World states, as it had done liberation movements in the old colonial empires. In historical retrospect, however, guerrilla war appears very much as a variant of total war. It belonged to the period of the world wars and had few major successes after the 1940s. The Vietnamese Communists finally succeeded in 1975 in unifying the country under their rule, but it was unlikely that any similar movement would be able to repeat their success. The Cuban revolution was attractive to radical Western youth, but the killing of its icon, Che Guevara, in Bolivia underlined its limited potential for repetition. It hardly seemed the 'revolution in the revolution' which the French enthusiast Regis Debray naïvely proclaimed.[59] The legacies of the Vietnamese and Cuban revolutions were stagnant, repressive, bureaucratic regimes – now targets for new democratic movements in the global era.

The other faces of revolutionary war were even darker. In recent decades they have been epitomized by the Khmer Rouge regime under Pol Pot in Cambodia, and the last surviving old-style Stalinist totalitarianism in North Korea. Formed in conditions of the Indo-China war, the Khmer Rouge seized power after the American bombing of the country – the last new Communist regime of modern times. They initiated the purest genocide of the Cold War era (one which, since it was directed primarily against large sections of the Cambodian population, negated the national, ethnic and religious confines of the international legal definition of genocide). Like Mao in the Cultural Revolution, Pol Pot targeted the urban, educated population who formed the most plausible social supports for democracy.[60]

This mutation of revolutionary violence into genocide was a dreadful conclusion to the Communist project, and in no way a local aberration. In the global era, post-Communist regimes such as Slobodan Milosevic's in Serbia have shown a continuing capacity for genocidal practice. The Cambodian case was particularly emblematic of the Cold War, too. After the Soviet-backed Vietnamese government

---

[59] Debray (1967).   [60] Evans and Rowley (1990).

overthrew Pol Pot's regime in 1979, not only did China – which invaded Vietnam in turn – support its continued rebellion but the USA and Britain tacitly backed it, supporting its retention of Cambodia's UN seat and covertly training its forces. It would be hard to find a more convincing symbol of the corruption of the Cold War system.

The deepening anti-democratic meaning of war was also indicated by other experiences of struggle. One of the most significant was that of Palestine, where the Israeli state was created by warfare in 1948, driving many of the Arab population from their homes and villages, and perpetuated through successive waves of war against both the Palestinian people and Arab states. Although the Israelis succeeded in creating and maintaining their state, they did not achieve security and seriously compromised Israel's democratic credentials. Their Palestinian opponents, on the other hand, succeeded through violent counter-attacks mainly in bringing superior Israeli might down on their people. By the end of the Cold War era, the Palestine Liberation Organization was forced to agree a precarious peace on poor terms.

A more positive confirmation of the same lesson was provided in South Africa. Here the African National Congress (ANC), outlawed by the apartheid state in the early 1960s, resorted to 'armed struggle' from exile, leading to authoritarian practices in the movement and weakening its position in South Africa and the West. However, successive waves of resistance among young people inside the country, from the 1976 Soweto uprising onwards, produced a reorientation in its thinking. By the end of the Cold War the leaders of the regime sought an accommodation with the ANC in a process of democratic reform, through which the ANC abandoned armed struggle and achieved power electorally. In these later stages, war was initiated by elements of the old regime and the ANC's Inkatha opponents, who wished to prevent peaceful democratic reform.

A worldwide democratic revolution had therefore emerged during the Cold War era, leading to three general conclusions. First, democratic change challenged Communist models of revolution, and especially the association of revolution with organized violence. Indeed organized violence, including war of all kinds, had become associated with anti-democratic forces and even genocide. Second, democratic movements were in conflict with the dominant forms of Cold War bloc-states: they were directed at the overthrow of not only Communist but also pro-Western authoritarian regimes, as well as radical reform even inside the Western democracies. They often faced opposition from Western states, although they gained much strength from the democratic relations and forms of the state in the West, in particular from the space and resources open to civil society. Third, although democratic movements existed worldwide and took increasingly international and pre-global forms, they could not become fully global movements within the fractured world order of blocs. Linkages between movements in different sectors were constrained by the deep structural divisions that the Cold War system produced. The problem of democratic change was not merely one of national or local, or even bloc-level power, although all of these were important. It was also about the overthrow of the Cold War world order itself. The pre-global democratic revolution was leading to global change.

5   Global revolution, counterrevolution and genocidal war

It is widely recognized at the beginning of the twenty-first century that world politics are undergoing fundamental change. However, neither in the analytical nor in the historical accounts of 'post-Cold War' transformation has a successful synthesis been achieved between structural change and the role of agency conceived as purposeful social action. As we saw in chapter 3, attention has focussed either on transformed socio-economic relations, or on relations between national state and other entities conceived within the loose categories of 'regime', 'community' and 'governance'.

In the expanded discussions of civil society and social movements, their contributions to the transformation of state relations have hardly been considered. Correspondingly, the connections between structural change and revolutionary social movements in the historical upheaval remain largely unexplored. Even prominent analysts of earlier radical waves have explicitly denied the revolutionary character of our own times. Thus for Eric Hobsbawm, 'the world at the end of the Short Twentieth Century is in a state of social breakdown rather than revolutionary crisis . . .'[1] For Fred Halliday, there is a 'permanence of unrest', but the agenda of change that the classic revolutions inaugurated may now be achieved through reform: the revolutions of 1989 (and, for that matter, 1956 and 1968) don't really count.[2] For these analysts, schooled in earlier Marxist traditions, this is not a change in the character of revolution, but a transformation of revolution into something else.

The role of an increasingly global democratic revolution in the

---

[1] Hobsbawm (1994: 459). This assertion is quoted with approval by R. Cox (1999: 3).
[2] Halliday (1999: 334–5).

144

messy, uneven transformation of the bloc-state system of the Cold War era into an incipient global state-system, has thus been little explored. In this chapter I examine how the crisis of the bloc-state system and the transformation of the democratic revolution have combined to produce a new set of historic conditions. In contrast to those accounts of globality which plot the extending worldwide web of economic and cultural linkages, I focus on the traumatic political upheavals at the centre of global political transformations.

The final crisis of the bloc-system

Although the structure of Cold War state relations constrained the democratic revolution, the Cold War was also a highly dynamic system. The original period of high Cold War tension gave way in the mid-1950s to the beginnings of cooperative management of bloc rivalry. By the mid-1960s, after the Cuban missile crisis, some limited arms control was in place. In the late 1960s and early 1970s, the danger of linkage between the Vietnam War and the overarching Cold War rivalries was contained. Paradoxically the 1970s, the final decade of war in south-east Asia, became the era of *détente* between the superpowers.

However, the results of war were profoundly significant for the Cold War system. The USA's first ever major military defeat, at the hands of a small, poor nation and amidst great social unrest, deeply affected the American state, the crisis of which was magnified by the disintegration of the Nixon presidency. At the same time the entire Western world, which had suffered unprecedented economic and social unrest since the late 1960s, was convulsed by the first serious economic recessions of the post-war period. As the oil-producing states garnered unprecedented economic and political leverage, there was a deepening sense of instability in the economy, society and politics of the West, and above all of the United States.

In these circumstances, both inter- and intra-bloc politics underwent great upheavals. Modest strategic advances by the Soviet Union came to be seen in some American quarters as fundamental threats. The USSR was moving towards something like nuclear parity with the USA – albeit at the cost of a crippling burden on its much more backward economy. It also achieved a modest expansion of inter-national political leverage, in countries such as Angola, Mozambique, Ethiopia and Afghanistan. The idea that the Soviet bloc had seized a

145

'window of opportunity' due to American weakness, and that this needed to be redressed by strong new American leadership, became a cornerstone of the 'new right' in American and later British politics. At the same time, the expanding European and Japanese economies gave new confidence to non-American Western elites, leading to extravagant predictions of a new contest of 'Europe versus America' or 'the disintegrating West'.[3]

A new phase of intense inter-bloc conflict, the 'Second Cold War', was the product of these contradictions.[4] The December 1979 Soviet invasion of Afghanistan, in support of its client regime,[5] coincided almost exactly with a NATO decision to introduce new 'intermediate-range' nuclear missiles into western Europe, including Pershing II missiles which could be delivered from Germany to Moscow in ten minutes. The new right-wing US president, Ronald Reagan, supported by his British counterpart, Margaret Thatcher, launched a rapid drive to raise military spending, introducing new weapons and strategic defence systems that would restore clear Western superiority. The threatened Soviet leadership responded in kind, so far as it could afford, and the nuclear arms race accelerated. Within the blocs, discipline was reasserted: the Solidarity movement was crushed in Poland, and nuclear disarmament movements were defeated politically by concerted right-wing leadership in western Europe.

From this heightening of Cold War tension to the recognizable end of the Cold War order was a matter of a few years. Just as the contradictions of the interimperial order led to the war of 1939–45 which ended that order, so the contradictions of the Cold War gave rise to the rather different crisis of 1989–91 and the subsequent transition. These were not, however, the contradictions of the Cold War simply as an interstate system, but those of Cold War *state relations* as a whole. Caspar Weinberger, Reagan's cold-warrior Secretary of State, was not wrong to suggest that their escalation of the arms race helped to crack the economic foundations of the Soviet regime. But this was only a part of the story. The democratic revolution also played a key role in the crisis of the 1980s. The decade began with hundreds of thousands on the streets of west European capitals; it ended with similar numbers on the streets across eastern

---

[3] Mandel (1974), Kaldor (1979).   [4] Halliday (1982).

[5] The invasion was a sign of Soviet weakness, not strength, but it concretized the spectre of the new Soviet threat.

Europe. The fall of the Berlin Wall, on 9 November 1989, was a supreme moment of people power, a great symbolic linking of Germans and Europeans that ended Cold War division.

This was much more than a piece of street theatre accompanying inevitable structural change. To understand this revolutionary upheaval we need to chart, briefly, the transformations of state relations through the Cold War decades. I have noted how the extreme bloc discipline of the early Cold War gave way through the 1950s and 1960s to more moderate forms. In the Soviet bloc, there were 'normalized' bureaucratic politics, greater national autonomy, modest market reforms, improved living standards, and some expansion of cultural and intellectual (but not political) freedom. The infrastructure of statism, militarization and the command economy remained largely intact, however, from the high Stalinist era of total war.

In the West, on the other hand, from the 1950s onwards there were more radical changes from the period of total war. While wartime statism was extended into general economic management and social welfare reform, direct controls over the economy increasingly gave way to more liberalized markets. Eventually state ownership, expanded in the immediate post-war years, began to be 'rolled back'. The mass armies of the early Cold War period gave way to smaller, more professional armed forces, and conscription was abandoned by the states of the Western bloc 'offshore' from continental Europe.[6] There was a great expansion of consumption, mass culture and new lifestyles, liberated from the statism of the total-war period.

While Western economies and society were more dynamic and Western institutions more able to accommodate change, social change generated new forms of protest and oppositional politics. Conflict in pre-Second World War Western societies was based largely on classes, and especially working-class movements, and most opposition to dominant elites had been led by social democratic and Communist parties. In the post-war West, two major structural changes led to new political outcomes. First, the main working-class movements were increasingly embedded in the Cold War international divide and developed opposed bloc allegiances. While social democracy became Atlanticist, tied into the Western bloc, Communist parties were linked to the West's Soviet opponents. Second, economic changes led to a great expansion of professional and white-collar occupations, seen by

[6] Shaw (1991: 83–93, 174–7).

many as the growth of a 'new middle class'. In these conditions, a new 'middle-class radicalism' erupted, largely focussed around 'international' contradictions of the Cold War bloc order.[7] This new radicalism first manifested itself in the anti-nuclear weapons movements of the 1950s and early 1960s, but then spread to movements against the Vietnam War and to the associated student movements of the later 1960s and early 1970s. Later in the 1970s, movements against nuclear power developed, from which grew widely focussed environmental movements. From the late 1960s onwards, too, the new radicalism generated very broadly based women's movements, and other movements concerned with sexual politics.

Oppositional politics developed very unevenly, of course, between the two blocs. Western (especially European) new lefts overlapped with mainstream liberal and social democratic parties, and connected with successive mass movements. Soviet-bloc oppositionists were confined to small groups, without the possibility of party or movement bases except in rare moments of uprising. Where Western critics were mainly anti-Cold War in general, seeing their own state-bloc as representative of the Cold War order, Eastern critics, conscious of their more immediate oppression, tended to be more anti-Soviet than anti-Cold War. Because of these radical differences in situation, relations between the two groups were often difficult. Soviet-bloc oppositionists tended to appeal to Western democracy as a whole, and were often suspicious of the Western opposition – not least because it contained within its ranks a pro-Soviet element.

Despite these differences, social movements in both West and East played critical roles in the 1980s dissolution of the Cold War world order. In the Western bloc, a new wave of nuclear disarmament movements was anticipated in the 1970s by campaigns against the so-called 'neutron bomb' – 'theatre' nuclear weapons designed to halt tank advances through radiation without causing large-scale physical destruction. After the dual crisis of late 1979 – the Soviet invasion of Afghanistan and NATO's decision to introduce new intermediate-range missile systems – a rapid growth of mass movements took place across the Western half of the continent during 1980–2. Unlike the more nationally based movements of two decades earlier, the new nuclear disarmament movements were not merely international in outlook, but pan-European and trans-bloc in their aims and

[7] Parkin (1968).

organizing intentions. Significant groups in the new movement saw its aim as being to unite Europeans across the Iron Curtain, to undermine the bloc-system, and to create a nuclear-free Europe 'from Poland to Portugal'. E.P. Thompson argued that combined citizens' movements could take Europe (and hence the world) 'beyond the Cold War'.[8]

In practice, of course, 'peace movements', as they became known, were far more directly influential in western Europe than in the Soviet-bloc countries. Coordinated mass demonstrations created a huge momentum, and churches and opposition parties rejected new missile systems, while opinion polls showed majorities everywhere for these aims (but not for dismantling existing systems or NATO itself, both of which retained strong support). In the Netherlands where the movement was strongest, even members of the ruling coalition opposed new missile systems, and deployment was long delayed. In Germany and Britain, the two most important states in which the largest deployments were planned, strong campaigns by conservative governments led to both winning their 1983 elections, thus defeating the disarmament movements. In the United States, a parallel 'nuclear freeze' movement gained widespread support, but had little effect on the rearmament policy of the first Reagan administration (1980–4). However, although defeated, these movements had demonstrated that large-scale support for disarmament and *rapprochement* existed, especially in western Europe, and it had forced Western governments to devote great political energies to deflecting this.

In the Soviet Union during the 1980s, the depth of the regime's stagnation was manifested in the succession of partly incapable elderly leaders – Brezhnev, Andropov and Chernenko – at more or less yearly intervals. Although the regime responded to new Western missile deployments with new systems of its own, it simultaneously participated in the Helsinki process for political cooperation in Europe, while encouraging the pressure of the Western peace movements on NATO. At the same time as the Soviet government repressed dissidents, including a few independent peace activists – and the Czechoslovak regime suppressed the Charter 77 movement – it tolerated the unprecedented Polish Solidarity movement for well over a year before the Polish military suppressed it.

Much more than in the original Cold War of the 1950s, in the Second Cold War there were therefore complex trans-bloc political

---

[8] Thompson (1981).

Learning Resources
Centre

processes, involving relations between states and social movements. Western peace movements elicited responses both from Western governments, which sought to contain them, and Soviet-bloc regimes, which sought to exploit them internationally, while limiting their influence within eastern European society. They also had some limited success in stimulating independent peace activism in the East, as well as in dialogue with Charter 77, Solidarity and other democratic oppositionists.[9] Although Soviet-bloc independent peace movements were counted in dozens or at best hundreds of participants – rather than the hundreds of thousands of the West – they had an importance beyond their numbers.[10] Like other democratic movements in the bloc, they pointed the way to an alternative future. Unlike some of the other movements, they underlined the inescapable conclusion that that future involved the end not only of the Soviet system, but of the Cold War with which it was intimately bound up.

The importance of these developments became clear in the dynamics that led to the end of the Cold War. These were rooted, above all, in the manifold crisis of the Soviet system – economic stagnation, political decay, cultural atrophy – and the inter-bloc conflict and arms race of the early 1980s comprised only one component of that crisis. The Soviet crisis in the 1980s was at the same time a crisis of state relations within the USSR, a crisis of 'international' structure of the state-bloc, and a crisis of relations between the Soviet and Western blocs. In this sense the crisis can only be explained by understanding the links between all these levels. It cannot be explained by one of them in isolation.

By the 1980s, the Soviet state and bloc were manifest anachronisms. The Soviet state retained the total-war command-economy model of relations between state and society. The Soviet order still had many characteristics of the classic European empires, all other examples of which had fallen apart after the First and Second World Wars. In both its internal and bloc forms it remained quasi-imperial, as close to the old model of empire as to the new model of the contemporary Western state-bloc. The social relations of state power in the bloc were extreme, ossified forms of relations which had long since been transformed in the more dynamic West. The Soviet state blocked any

---

[9] Wylie (1999) argues that in the case of Poland the effect of this dialogue – 'détente from below' – was limited. However, no one would argue that Poland was a strong case of this link.

[10] Tismaneanu (1990), see also Raina (1991).

self-organization by society, and any democratic accountability. In many ways, therefore, the Soviet state and bloc were survivals from the eras of empires and total war, and contained only limited mechanisms for internal renewal. Hence the crisis would inevitably mean a dramatic upheaval; but given the centrality of the Soviet bloc to the whole Cold War system, this upheaval would be a change in world order, not merely a change in one sector.

Revolution and counterrevolution, 1989–91

The global revolution was anticipated by the crisis of the Cold War system in the 1980s. A few thinkers in that crisis anticipated the unravelling of the system in something like the way in which it occurred.[11] However, it is fair to say that virtually no one, in any sector of the world, or in either state elites or oppositional movements, anticipated the process as a whole in all its main respects, least of all in its timing or the apparent completeness of its outcome. However much, in the early 1980s, some people could see beyond the Cold War, few if any had more than a sketchy idea of how it could happen or what it would mean. The actual process of change took virtually everyone by surprise, and its implications have continued to disorient people since.

In particular, very few understood the depth of the crisis in the Soviet bloc-state. 'In effect,' as Cox has pointed out,

> most of us assumed continuity in world politics would continue to involve irreconcilable opposition between well-established social systems. The idea that either of them would actually fail seemed beyond the bounds of possibility, a mere fantasy indulged in by utopians but not to be taken seriously by mature commentators. Yet the USSR did implode, and as a result the Cold War came to an end, suddenly and without much warning. But who anticipated this? Hardly anybody.[12]

[11] Thompson's partial equation of the two blocs, understandable since he wished to assert the political independence of the peace movements from both, nevertheless limited his understanding of the historic consequences of the success of democratic movements in the Soviet bloc. The unwinding of the Cold War did not pose so radical a challenge to the structures of the Western bloc as to those of the Soviet, because both the relations of national entities and the relations of society and state were more consensual in the West. The dissolution of the Soviet bloc did not necessarily entail the parallel disintegration of the West.

[12] M. Cox (1998b: 158).

Further, the relations between revolution and counterrevolution in the changes of 1989–91, or later in the 1990s, are hardly grasped. The relations between elite processes and social movements are generally obscure. The links between upheavals in the Soviet bloc and transformations of world order, including the role of the Western bloc, are confused. Not surprisingly, therefore, the global revolution as a whole, of which the transformation of the Soviet bloc is the key element, has hardly been recognized.

It is important to recall that the upheavals in the Soviet bloc in the late 1980s were anticipated by the democratic revolution throughout the Soviet bloc over the previous three decades. In 1953, 1956, 1968 and 1980–1 there had been great national movements in one or more of the bloc's member-states in central Europe. There were revolts, too, within the Soviet Union – in the Vorkuta slave-labour camp complex in 1956, in Novocherkassk in 1963 – but never on a national scale even within a republic, let alone on a pan-Union scale. Change within the Soviet state had been led from the top, responding mainly to passive dissatisfaction in the population, to anticipations of revolt after the central European examples, to the criticisms of courageous 'dissidents', to external pressures and demands, and to the problems of the ruling elite itself.

The changes of the mid- and late 1980s were initiated, once again, from above. Mikhail Gorbachev, when he became general secretary of the Soviet Communist Party in 1985, clearly understood the crisis of his regime as complex. If he sought economic restructuring (*perestroika*), political openness (*glasnost*) and international *détente* for their own sakes, he also saw their close interlinkage – in particular, he recognized the burden of military competition on the Soviet economy as a crucial impediment to economic reform. Gorbachev came to power, however, at the point when Reagan and his allies had largely accomplished the USA's massive rearmament, restored Western supremacy in the arms race and apparently defeated the peace movements. Within the Soviet bloc, too, opponents such as Solidarity had been put down. In all these senses, pressure for change in the Cold War order was blocked, and Gorbachev's initiatives were crucial.

Nevertheless, this was hardly a pure elite process. Gorbachev was aware that movements such as Solidarity testified to the instability and unsustainability of the quasi-imperial bloc order. He was aware that the peace movements demonstrated deep Western support for *rapprochement*, which he could mobilize with proposals for East–West reform. In developing his disarmament proposals, Gorbachev even picked up Reagan's 'zero option' of no intermediate-range nuclear missiles in Europe – proposed originally as a propaganda bid to undermine the peace movement, at a time when it was assumed that the USSR would not accept it.

In these senses, the impact of democratic, anti-Cold War social movements was evident, however indirectly, in Gorbachev's reforms. But he himself saw them initially as ways of modernizing the Soviet system. Like reformist leaders in eastern Europe before him, he saw openness as a means of mobilizing support against the entrenched dominance of conservatives, as much as an end in itself. Gorbachev's equivocal attitude towards democratic principles was manifest in the limited nature of his reforms of Soviet institutions. His failure to seek electoral support for his own position as Soviet president proved a critical mistake, once Boris Yeltsin used his position as elected president of the Russian Federation to challenge Gorbachev's legitimacy.

Similarly, Gorbachev undoubtedly sought reform of the Soviet bloc and the Cold War world order, rather than their collapse. He encouraged reformers in the East German leadership to seek democratic change, but he hardly envisaged that this would dissolve the Communist state into the Federal Republic. He encouraged reformers across eastern Europe, but hardly expected that this would lead to the repudiation of the Warsaw Pact and the embrace of NATO by eastern European states. Likewise Gorbachev encouraged reformers in the republics to seek new constitutional relationships within the Soviet Union; he hardly anticipated that they would seize power and dissolve the Union altogether.

Gorbachev's importance was that he gave a clear indication to all those who sought change of any kind, that the Soviet state and bloc and the Cold War order could not continue in the old way. His partial reforms opened up the Soviet system to all kinds of forces, from within the party-state bureaucracy, from society across the bloc, and indeed from the Western world. Gorbachev's failure to develop a radical democratic project, and to embed that in the kinds of economic and social reforms that would have given it popular support, was a large part of his downfall. His contribution was decisive, and while it is difficult to imagine that anyone could easily have ridden the processes of change that he unleashed, the limitations of his project were central to his undoing. As Cox suggests, the 'temporary cult of Gorbachev' in Soviet studies (which made 'a number of well-known

Western scholars virtual cheerleaders for perestroika abroad') obscured from view what was actually taking place in the USSR. 'The common wisdom was that Gorbachev was renovating the Soviet Union: in reality,' Cox points out, 'the combination of changes he was implementing accelerated its decline and fragmentation.'[13]

Nevertheless Gorbachev did define – and symbolize – some of the themes of the global-democratic revolution which ended the Cold War. However uncertainly in practice, in theory he embraced democratic change in the fundamentally authoritarian structures of all the Communist regimes. He still identified with the interests of a Soviet state, but his programme for change within that state was accompanied by a wider agenda of change. It included transformed relations within the wider Soviet bloc and across Europe ('our common European home'), and the ending of the arms race and Cold War division of the world. However poorly implemented, and whatever the limitations of his concepts, the linkages of democracy and global change were Gorbachev's themes.

The radical exposition of these themes belonged, however, elsewhere, to those who took Gorbachev's reforms into their own hands. By 1988, the Hungarian Communists had agreed democratic reforms that would lead to their own surrender of power. In 1989, following Gorbachev's visit to East Berlin for (ironically) the fortieth anniversary of the Communist state, mass movements developed on the streets of Leipzig, Berlin and other cities, as well as among refugees trying to reach West Germany via Hungary. By early November, the East German dictator Erich Honecker had been purged by his Politburo and as the new leadership accepted the reality of the refugee flows, the Berlin Wall – the prime symbol of the Cold War division – was breached. It did not 'fall' or 'collapse', however: it was opened through popular protest and, in powerful symbolic action, partially dismantled by people on the streets.

The revolution spread rapidly from Germany to Czechoslovakia and then Romania by the end of 1989. In Czechoslovakia as in East Germany, the regime capitulated and the revolution was again peaceful – the famous 'Velvet Revolution'.[14] Only in Romania, where the national regime of Nicolae Ceaușescu was an extreme relic of Stalinist totalitarianism, did the old order resist. Here the revolution took a

---

[13] M. Cox (1998b: 168–9). See also Walker (1986), Galeotti (1997).
[14] Wheaton and Kavan (1992).

more violent form – the Ceauşescus were summarily shot – but the fighting was short-lived. In Poland and Bulgaria, as in Hungary, the Communist one-party state gave way to democratic elections without uprisings, although in all of these social movements played important parts.

The peaceful – even evolutionary – character of the revolution was more finely balanced than appeared. In both Germany and Czecho-slovakia, elements of the regime prepared the use of force that actually occurred in Romania. That, in the end, this movement was unprece-dentedly peaceful reflected not only the democratic goals of the opposition movements, but the recognition by Communist elites that their time was up. This in turn reflected the movement's origins in Gorbachev's reform process in the USSR, together with the inter-national character of the revolution. While historic revolutions had led to war, civil and international, because they challenged the dominant world powers, this revolution involved an accommodation with the dominant Western bloc. The revolution was partly about the end of Cold War division: about peace, not war.

The leaderships of these revolutions were varied. In East Germany a radical democratic citizens' movement, New Forum, played a leading role; this was emulated by Civic Forum in Czechoslovakia. In Romania – where in contrast to the other countries no independent action at all had been possible in previous years – relatively unrecon-structed but anti-Ceauşescu Communists initially seized control. In Hungary, Poland and Bulgaria, reform processes were initiated by reformist or opportunist elements in the Communist parties, but rapidly slipped from their grasp as other parties and movements emerged.

In no country did the groups who were most closely involved in making the revolution actually run the state in the aftermath. In part this was because there were no revolutionary parties, only loose intellectual groups and coalitions of activists, in the leadership of the revolts and reform movements. The Czechoslovak case provided the closest example: here parties spawned by Civic Forum dominated the first elections, and the best-known dissident, Václav Havel, became first president of the new Czechoslovakia. The more radical activists were marginalized, however, as the more right-wing of the post-Civic Forum parties won power, leading within a few years to the (fortu-nately peaceful) separation of Slovakia from the Czech Republic. In East Germany, radical activists lost out to the established West

German parties and their state was reunited with the Federal Republic. In other countries liberal and conservative parties, based partly on the dissident opposition and partly on the remnants of pre-Communist era parties, succeeded to power. In most cases, the reconstituted Communist parties and their allies were forced initially into opposition, although in Hungary and Poland they resurfaced as social democrats and did not have to wait long to regain at least a share of power. Here the post-Communists adapted relatively quickly to a new liberal, democratic, pro-NATO free-market European order.

In central Europe, therefore, the democratic revolution, which had been prepared in the embryonic civil society which oppositionists had nourished, was relatively smooth and also relatively successful.[15] Although many lost through market reforms, there was no catastrophic impoverishment. Despite rapid disillusionment with aspects of parliamentary democracy, the change as a whole had high legitimacy. In central Europe, moreover, the transition was clearly part of a major international reorientation. In reclaiming independent nationhood, the new democracies were also reintegrating themselves into Europe and the West.

In the Soviet Union itself, the quasi-imperial centre of the bloc-state, the democratic revolution was much more poorly prepared and weakly executed, and it faltered early. Both democratic and pro-Western, European impulses were weaker, except in the Baltic republics. Gorbachev and his fellow reformers in the party elites substituted for the civil society movements that were important in central Europe. Their economic reforms led to widespread misery without real improvements. They failed to follow through on democratic reform. This allowed the process of change to be taken over by those within the ex-party elites who were better able to ride the nationalist element in popular feeling. Gorbachev tried to manage the process of change from within the remnants of the party machine, and lost out to more opportunistic, demagogic, nationalist forces. Yeltsin, with a stronger instinct for the exploitation of democratic forms, outflanked both Gorbachev and the unreconstructed Communists to seize power in Russia. He achieved this, however, at great costs for the democratic revolution in the Soviet area and the direction of worldwide change.

The revolutionary momentum that began with Gorbachev and reached its peak in autumn 1989 in central Europe quickly gave way

[15] See Kavan (1999).

to counterrevolution. Even before the East German and Czechoslovak upheavals, of course, it had received a decisive check to its worldwide momentum in China. Here Gorbachev played a role superficially similar to that which he had played in East Germany. Visiting, he signalled the desirability of change simply by his presence and what he generally represented. But whereas the German Communist state was a dependency of Soviet power, so that Gorbachev's signals had a direct meaning for a regime as well as people engulfed by a sense of impending change, the Chinese Communists had their own power base, and the reform movement was not so strong. The People's Liberation Army gave the democratic movement a lesson in repressive power that the central Europeans mostly escaped.[16]

In the Soviet Union itself the outcome was not such a simple victory of counterrevolution. The successful Yeltsin-led resistance to the anti-Gorbachev *coup* of 1991 was, in one sense, the decisive victory of change, which dealt a deathblow to the old regime. But in the same fateful moment, the form of this triumph accelerated the fragmentation of state power across Soviet territory, and its consolidation in the hands of often corrupt, authoritarian and nationalist elites in the newly independent republics, at the expense of fuller democratic transformation. In Russia itself, Yeltsin's rule took the form of a ruthlessly opportunist, authoritarian and semi-monarchical regime. Yeltsin balanced elements of democratic and market reform (from which his family and entourage enriched themselves) and the strong militarist, nationalist elements of the state machine, especially in the armed forces. Within two years of his victory, Yeltsin's tanks were bombarding the *duma* building, crudely bringing an unruly parliament to heel. Not long afterwards and equally fatefully, Yeltsin indulged his military in their disastrous attempt to crush the independent government of Chechnya, a republic within the Russian Federation. (The Chechen regime was also corrupt and militarized, like many of the post-Soviet elites.)

The Chechen war of 1994–6, renewed in 1999–2000, was the sole conflict in which the Russian state was a principal, direct protagonist. However, it was only one of many wars that resulted from the break-up of the Soviet Union. During the Gorbachev years, the opening up of the state had already produced the first tensions between national elites in the Soviet republics, spreading into society. In 1988, there

---

[16] Cheng (1990), Baum (1991).

were already pogroms of Armenians in Baku, the capital of Azerbaijan. By the early 1990s, the newly autonomous Armenian and Azerbaijani state machines were at war over the Armenian-populated enclave of Nagorno-Karabakh in Azerbaijan. Similar patterns were reproduced across the post-Soviet region. There was a major civil war in Tajikistan. South Ossetian and Abkhazian separatists fought the new Georgian state, within which there was also fighting between supporters and opponents of its authoritarian first president. Russian-speaking separatists fought the Moldovan state. In all these wars – before Chechnya – the armies of Yeltsin's Russia were involved to some degree.

Minorities within republics often had genuine grievances, as of course did minority republics and their (majority) peoples against the Soviet state. However, the rapid, widespread resort to war can be seen as a profoundly counterrevolutionary tendency, opposed to genuine democratic change. Everywhere, militarization was a means by which elites (old ex-Soviet and new nationalist) stifled nascent democratic and pluralist tendencies. In the regions affected, war led to even greater economic problems and social misery than elsewhere in the ex-USSR. While combatants often looked to states and diasporas beyond the former Union for support (Azeris and Tajiks to the Islamic world, Armenians and Georgians to the West), war slowed real integration of affected states and peoples into the world economy and global institutions.

From counterrevolution to genocide

The link between war and counterrevolution was even more apparent, and most clearly exposed its genocidal content, in Yugoslavia. Independent from Moscow, with a more liberal economy and more prosperous than other Balkan Communist states, Yugoslavia had stood between East and West in Europe. It is salutary to recall that in the 1980s it was seen as likely to gain membership of the European Community. However, as Communism fell across Europe, the Yugoslav party, already fractured into competing national elites in the Federation's seven republics, metamorphosed into a variety of post-Communist parties seeking electoral legitimacy through inter-republican confrontation.

In Slovenia, the party managed to develop democratic national forms similar to those of the West. In Serbia and Croatia, however, elites mobilized national support by arousing hostility towards ethnic minorities. In 1988–9 Slobodan Milosevic sought to consolidate his rule in Serbia by campaigning against the majority Albanian population of the autonomous southern province of Kosovo.[17] Milosevic scrapped Kosovan autonomy, dismantling institutions that were legitimate in the eyes of the majority of the local population, and instituted repressive Serbian direct rule. This was a directly counterrevolutionary move, pre-empting democratization that would have led inevitably to an Albanian-majority administration in Kosova. In response, Albanians established parallel unofficial systems of administration, education, etc., creating a prime example of the unstable situation known to earlier Marxist analysts of revolution as 'dual power'.

Simultaneously, the Croatian nationalist regime of Franjo Tudjman sought to create an ethnic Croat state and discriminated against the Serb minority. In 1991, the Slovenian and Croatian governments reacted to Serbia's crude dominance of the Yugoslav Federation by moving towards secession.[18] Milosevic unleashed wars against these states, and another, against Bosnia, followed in 1992. Internally, Milosevic's Serbia was the most extreme example of the way in which nationalism and militarism opposed democracy. The regime used censorship, intimidation and war propaganda to defeat the opposition and ensure that – despite impoverishment and the misery of war – it maintained control in successive elections. In Croatia, Bosnia and Kosova, Milosevic used the Yugoslav National Army together with police, paramilitary gangs and political clients to brutally 'cleanse' non-Serb populations from areas Serbian nationalists aimed to control. The wars in Croatia and Bosnia were campaigns against the populations, as much as against opposed armed forces or states, to seize substantial parts of these republics from non-Serbian populations.

In Bosnia, Muslims were killed, raped and expelled from towns and villages, their mosques razed. Plural urban communities such as Sarajevo and Tuzla, which defied the ethnic ideal, were systematically attacked. In Bosnia, these processes culminated in the massacre at Srebrenica in 1995, in which thousands of Muslim men were executed.

---

[17] According to the majority Albanian population, the area is known as Kosova.

[18] It is widely argued that premature (German-led) recognition of Croatia's independence by the European Community precipitated the Yugoslav wars. In reality the fundamental mistake of Europe and the West was not to recognize earlier the political disintegration of the Yugoslav Federation and seek to regulate it more forcefully.

Later, they were renewed in Kosova, culminating in the war of 1998–9. Similar policies were pursued by the Croatian state, both in Bosnia, in its war with Bosnian forces and the Bosnian Muslim population in 1993–4, and in re-taking the partly Serb-populated 'Krajina' region of Croatia in 1995.

By the early 1990s, therefore, 'new wars'[19] were authoritarian nationalists' principal means of counterrevolutionary opposition to democratic transformation, especially where the latter involved issues of relations between different ethnic communities and secession. In these wars, as in the Nazis' war against the Jews,[20] the expulsion and killing of civilians were not simply brutal accompaniments to orthodox interstate war,[21] but prime modes of violence. In terms of the international convention, according to which genocide is the deliberate destruction of a national, racial, ethnic or religious group 'in whole or in part',[22] these wars were clearly genocidal.[23]

Worldwide scope of revolutionary change

In the final decade of the twentieth century, the most intense and critical phases of the global-democratic revolution and counterrevolution were centred in the formerly Communist regions of Europe and Asia. Because the world bloc order itself was based in the North, especially in Europe, this order could only be overthrown within these regions. The revolutionary events in the ex-Soviet Union and eastern Europe should not be seen, however, as purely or even mainly regional events, let alone a simple wave of national movements. These

---

[19] The term 'new wars' is Kaldor's (1999).

[20] Davidowicz (1985).

[21] However, as the International Criminal Tribunal has recognized in its application of the laws of war, these were indeed 'international' wars, pitting Serbian, Croatian and Bosnian states against each other.

[22] For the full definition see Guttman and Rieff (1999: 142).

[23] Moreover, since our 'genus' or species is humankind, not any one type of social group, the only theoretically defensible definition of genocide is that which concerns the intentional destruction of any human group. In this sense, therefore, the international legal definition cannot be regarded as fully adequate. Most would agree, for example, that there was genocide in Cambodia in the 1970s; but although the Khmer Rouge targeted ethnic minorities, most victims came from other social groups (the urban, the educated) identified as enemies of the new regime. Moreover it is mistaken to take the supposed discrimination of the *génocidaires* as the defining characteristic of genocide; mass slaughter always becomes fundamentally indiscriminate. I expand this argument further in ongoing work.

were global revolutions in a number of senses. First, although the global revolution has been centred on the ex-Soviet bloc, it also had genuinely worldwide scope. Second, they helped to break down the bloc-system, the final form of national-international relations, and helped to create the conditions for globality. Third, these changes were not merely unintended consequences of national or anti-Soviet revolt. Of course the participants in the revolutions did not foresee the way the larger history would develop; but in many ways they intended the global unification which occurred, and willed their absorption into a unified Western-led world order based on democracy.

The worldwide global-democratic revolution has had a sharp but not yet decisive impact on the remaining Communist and left-wing regimes. As we have already noted, it received an early – and still its most serious – setback in China, where the example of Gorbachev's Russia inspired the democratic movement which was crushed in Tiananmen Square in 1989. The regimes in China, Vietnam and Cuba have survived, however, through different sorts of economic and political accommodation with the West. They have allowed chinks for controlled democratic forms – the continued liberal system in Hong Kong after the 1997 handover, greater intellectual and cultural freedom in China's cities, a new tolerance of religion in Havana. However, there is a clear sense that further democratic change is inevitable, even if its timing and mechanisms are far from certain.[24]

Other old-style revolutionary states allied with the Soviet bloc have also faced rapid change. In Afghanistan and Ethiopia, Soviet-backed regimes fell to the *mujaheddin* and to Eritrean and Tigrean nationalist guerrillas, respectively. In Angola and Mozambique, the end of the Cold War meant that the regimes lost Soviet and Cuban backing, but their South African- and US-supported guerrilla opponents also lost much of their support and legitimacy. (The UNITA movement in Angola, however, exploiting mineral wealth, continued as a powerful military force.) In Nicaragua, the Sandinistas, who made the last revolution of the bloc era, gave up power electorally to a centre-right government, while the USA ended its support for *contra* (counter-revolutionary) guerrillas. In Cambodia, the Vietnamese-installed regime of Hun Sen survived a UN peace process through which it had

---

[24] The North Korean state represents a different case: at the end of the twentieth century, still unreformed, economically bankrupt and militarily offensive. It is unclear whether it can survive as a state in the face of an increasingly democratic South, or if it can change without provoking interstate conflict.

to share power with royalists, and saw off the Khmer Rouge, who finally lost their Chinese backing. In most of these states, electoral processes played a part in the changes, although democratic reform could not be said to have advanced far.

The worldwide influence of the global-democratic revolution has not been confined, however, to the former Soviet sphere of influence. On the contrary, US- and Western-backed authoritarian regimes have been toppled on a wide scale. In Latin America, the change pre-dated the end of the Cold War in Europe. The 1980s were the decade of democratic transition, as military regimes almost everywhere handed over power to elected governments. In Argentina, whose military *junta* had invaded the Falkland Islands (Malvinas) in 1982, in Brazil, even in Chile where the brutal Pinochet dictatorship seized power with American support in 1973, elected governments had taken over by the early 1990s. In Mexico, the long-standing one-party state finally opened up to genuine electoral competition. While democratic rights often remained problematic, social inequalities vast and many regimes inclined to authoritarianism, this amounted to a substantial shift.

In Africa, trends have been more mixed, and dramatic changes more clearly synchronized with the Cold War transformations in Europe. The most significant democratization has been that of South Africa, where the Nationalist F.W. de Klerk's attempt to reform apartheid bore some resemblance to Gorbachev's reform programme. Despite centrifugal tendencies and extensive and continuing violence, it was a more successful transition: South Africa remained a unitary state, and parliamentary institutions were democratically transformed. Since the African National Congress had overwhelming majority backing and an exemplary conciliatory leader in Nelson Mandela, legitimacy was high. Serious localized war between Inkatha, backed by counterrevolutionary elements of the old state machine, and the ANC was contained.

Elsewhere in sub-Saharan Africa, democratization has also been a trend, with the transition from military to electoral government in Ghana and the ending of post-independence one-party rule in states such as Zambia, Malawi and Kenya. Many electoral processes remain less than fully open, however, and authoritarian tendencies have often quickly appeared in the new regimes. In Nigeria, the continent's most populous state, a repressive military regime clung to power throughout the 1990s, but reform processes were developing at the end of the decade. Elsewhere, moreover, far from democratization, authoritarian governments held sway or states have fragmented amidst violence. In Sudan, a repressive regime continued to fight a long-running war with southern secessionists, causing extensive misery. In Ethiopia, the new regime renewed the war with Eritrea at the end of the 1990s. In Somalia, a central state has still not been reconstituted after almost a decade of war. In Liberia and Sierra Leone, warlords and gangsters remain powerful, any form of central government precarious.

In Rwanda in 1994, an ethnic-particularist regime met the prospect of reform with the worst recent programme of mass killings anywhere in the world. The genocide has left a deeply traumatized and divided society. In these circumstances, it is hardly surprising that the new Rwandan Patriotic Front (RPF) government, which defeated the *génocidaires*, has not created a mature democracy. As in Uganda, where the murderous Idi Amin dictatorship was overthrown in the 1980s, the existence of a moderately stable regime with an approxima-tion to the rule of law is widely seen as an achievement. The 1996–7 overthrow of the Mobutu regime in Zaire (Congo), instigated by an alliance of the Rwandan and Ugandan governments with internal opposition, appeared to spread this phenomenon. However, the new regime of Laurent Kabila degenerated quickly into corrupt authoritar-ianism, spawning a new civil war, into which other central African states were drawn, and in turn sharpening the tensions between authoritarian and democratic trends within some of these, notably in Zimbabwe.

The removal of manifestly brutal, parasitic dictatorships, and their replacement by regimes which are at least partially responsive to popular needs and human rights, is a limited sign of advance in the global-democratic revolution. But the circumstances of society and the instabilities of states in much of central, western and north-eastern Africa mean that reform is problematic. Democracy can hardly be embedded in societies where even subsistence production is threa-tened by violence. Ruling elites across much of the continent show an alarming tendency to view their interests as served by war, and to construct volatile alliances with state and parastatal movements involved in wars. Half a dozen states were involved in the new Congo war of 1999–2000; an equal number were named by the United Nations in 2000 for breaking sanctions designed to halt UNITA's continuing campaign in Angola.

In much of Asia, the situation in the 1980s and early 1990s appeared to be less favourable to democratic change. Civil society and democratic culture were weak even in Japan, where parliamentary institutions are well embedded. Other parliamentary democracies were virtual one-party states. Authoritarian and semi-authoritarian regimes delivered considerable economic advance. The Asian 'tiger economies' – Hong Kong, Taiwan, South Korea, Singapore, Thailand – were paradigms of this kind of progress, and China itself was increasingly seen as an example. The idea of 'Asian values', in which relatively authoritarian traditions are upheld, was widely promoted in the early 1990s as a counterpoint to Western liberal and democratic ideas. However, parliamentary-democratic institutions have progressed in many Asian countries and elsewhere, and remain embedded, despite many contradictions, in India. Openly authoritarian regimes, such as the military regime in Myanmar (Burma), were under obvious pressure at the beginning of the twenty-first century. Although a military *coup* overthrew the elected government in Pakistan in 1999, the new rulers faced immediate pressure to restore a parliamentary regime.

Moreover, as in Europe democratization was not a purely elite concern. Despite many uncertainties, the democratic revolution was also spreading in Asia. We can trace a pattern of major revolts, from the Philippines in 1986 (the overthrow of the Marcos dictatorship), to the uprising in Korea in 1995 and the student-led movement in Indonesia in 1998 (that overthrew Suharto). In Malaysia, a democracy movement challenged the autocratic parliamentary government of Mahathir. Revolts often lead – as in the former Soviet bloc – to the replacement of open dictatorship by corrupt elite rule within democratic forms. Thus democratic change remains generally very incomplete, but it moved forward dramatically in the 1990s. Bruce Cumings has argued that the Korean movement of 1995 'ultimately went beyond anything in the global transition from authoritarianism that the world has witnessed in the last decade' and that 'the contribution of protest to Korean democracy cannot be overstated'.[25] The extended Indonesian transition has had comparable scope. Student-led movements in the capital and big cities have combined with secessionist movements – not only in East Timor but in Aceh, Ambon and elsewhere – to force fundamental changes. However, movements for change have faced extensive terror and repression from the armed

[25] Cumings (1998: 24–25).

forces and paramilitary groups. At the beginning of the twenty-first century, the situation remained finely balanced between democratic change and violent reaction.

A full decade after the 1989–91 upsurge in Europe, the Middle East remained the world region in which the influence of democratic and globalist forces was most obviously limited. Ironically given the cultural unity of the Arab world, in which many states are products of early twentieth-century colonial mapping and manipulation, 'national' power structures here were more isolated and sharply constraining of any kind of democratic reform compared with any other world region. Powerful states, hugely armed and towering over nascent civil society, have been long buoyed by massive oil revenues which have fuelled arms spending and regional rivalries, which in turn have confined the space for political change.

In the Middle East in the 1980s, there were moreover revolutionary developments of older kinds. The Iranian revolution of 1979 was a mass uprising, the democratic potential of which was quickly destroyed in the creation of a theocratic state. Nationalist movements, from the Palestine Liberation Organization to the Kurdish parties in Turkey, Iraq and Iran, sustained an older model of guerrilla struggle. Islamic states also sponsored guerrilla, or terrorist, movements – especially in Lebanon. In the 1990s, however, there were limited democratic developments, raising the prospect of a wider transformation. Reforms in Iran created genuine electoral processes in which more secular forces have gained ground, even if they are still highly threatened by religious reaction strongly embedded in state and society. The Palestine National Authority, likewise, has been constructed on partially democratic foundations. Israel itself, of course, remains internally democratic, and there has been a sharp conflict between political tendencies which has largely determined the progress of the 'peace process' with neighbouring Arab states and peoples.

In the wider region, many authoritarian regimes appeared increasingly stagnant, and their leaders aged, at the end of the 1990s. Oil no longer supplied unlimited resources to sustain military power. This declining resource base could be a source of tensions – such as those which precipitated Iraq's 1990 invasion of Kuwait and the subsequent wars. But it was also a factor that might constrain elites' military ambitions and lead to accommodations with both regional rivals and world powers. At the end of the twentieth century, the global revolution had hardly progressed very far in the Middle East, but there were reasons to identify a potential.

The echoes of democratic revolution could be found also in the more stable, formally democratic, Western countries. The drastic upheaval of Italy's corrupt Cold War party system was one manifestation; the removal of Thatcher and the triumph of the centre-left across western Europe others. In the West, democratic movements often took more subtle forms, from the diversion of parliamentary fora at European and regional levels, on the one hand, to social movements for the democratization of everyday life, on the other. The depth of the latter trend should not be underestimated: Margaret Thatcher's campaign to restore 'Victorian values' was an ignominious failure, in contrast to her success in promoting the deregulation of markets.

Global-democratic revolution and state formation

The worldwide scope of democratic transformation does not, by itself, render it global. The paradox of (in Robertson's phrase) 'a universalistic entitlement to particularism' has been noted, as a phenomenon of the earlier part of the twentieth century.[26] As Clark points out, the idea of national democracy as a universal political form can be traced back to the establishment of the League of Nations after the First World War. However, the longer-term effect of the League was not to diminish the role of the separate state but, on the contrary, it lay (as Giddens put it) in 'consolidating conceptions of national sovereignty as the "natural" political condition of humankind, via a particular interpretation of the sovereignty-citizenship relation.' In short, it stimulated 'the primacy of the nation-state as the universal political form of the current era'.[27]

It cannot be denied that there was a dramatic shift towards the realization of these norms in the second half of the twentieth century. The number of distinct 'national' state entities dramatically increased, to around 200, and in the final decades of the century far more of them were to some degree democratic. 'In 1975 at least 68 per cent of countries throughout the world were authoritarian', Potter et al. claim, but 'by the end of 1995 only about 26 per cent were authori-

---

[26] Clark (1997: 62), citing Robertson (1990).
[27] Giddens (1985: 259, 258), cited by Clark (1997: 62).

tarian, all the rest having held some sort of competitive elections and adopted at least formal guarantees of political and civil rights.'[28]

The number of states in an in-between condition, with some elements of democracy but not others, had increased. In many, there might be 'low-intensity democracy', 'functioning as a cosmetic cover for continued foreign domination or domestic authoritarianism, generalized corruption or social anarchy'.[29] Nevertheless, by any standards, 'The 1980s and early 1990s saw a dramatic wave of democratization sweep across the developing world, recalling the similar wave following decolonization in the late 1950s and 1960s. It surged over the three continents and affected both developmentally successful and unsuccessful countries across the political spectrum. Though the wave met resistance at times . . . authoritarian regimes toppled in profusion, to be replaced by regimes organized along liberal democratic lines.' According to Luckham and White, 'The wave had already begun to recede by the mid-1990s as entrenched regimes either resisted the trend or merely went through the democratic motions, or as newly democratic regimes succumbed to various forms of authoritarian reversion.'[30]

Nevertheless democratic norms have become commonly established as more serious standards for national political entities. By the end of the twentieth century, virtually all states, even the most authoritarian, paid some sort of lip-service to them. In genuflection to the democratic spirit of the age, authoritarian nationalists often organized elections in the aftermath of genocide. Indeed by expelling – if not killing – other groups, and intimidating and manipulating their own ethnic populations, nationalists created more or less homogeneous and obedient electorates, which legitimated their power. The homage which these most abusive forms of political power often paid to the idea of democracy showed how entrenched it had become – but also how malleable.

The global character of the contemporary democratic revolution is rooted in the extent to which (as we saw in the last chapter) democracy and human rights have become universal values to which individuals and groups can appeal, if need be over and against national state institutions. During the Cold War, when the 'democratic' West tolerated authoritarian state entities in its ranks and

---

[28] Potter et al. (1996: 7).
[29] Luckham and White (1996b).   [30] Luckham and White (1996b).

encouraged anti-Communist repression worldwide, such universal norms were widely limited in practical significance. In the worldwide democratic revolution of our times, however, they have a new role. Oppressed groups widely appeal, not only to the founding documents of universal human rights, but to the international institutions of a Western-led world order as guarantors of those rights.

In this sense the revolutions of 1989, with their explicit aspirations for integration in an internationalized, democratic world, have set the benchmarks for subsequent movements – not just in Europe, but worldwide. Everywhere, the oppressed and those who champion them appeal to common, global democratic values. The more extreme the plight of oppressed groups, the more explicit, in general, the global appeal. In this sense the democratic revolution is now becoming global. People fight for accountability and freedoms at a national level, but they increasingly locate these ends within a global context.

The character of the revolutionary wave has been transformed by the new conditions in which it now operates. This movement always showed the potential to spill over into each and every state, invoking universal principles. Before 1989, however, its actions were framed within the Cold War division of the world. There was no way in which democratic movements within the Soviet bloc could receive large-scale, practical assistance from the West, or in which the United Nations' Universal Declaration of Human Rights could be implemented in the Third World client states of either bloc. At the beginning of the twenty-first century, this was starting to change: democratic movements were not only worldwide in scope and international in their repercussions, but also global in consciousness.

Of course, some reject the idea of common global values because their expressions are mostly Western in origin. However, all world religions contain recognitions of the human commonality on which globality builds. The attempt to assert that there is a 'clash of civilizations',[31] stronger than those things pulling world society together, is not supported by the evidence. Whether in Tehran, first centre of the Islamic revolution, or in Beijing, Jakarta, Kuala Lumpur or Rangoon, where rulers have proclaimed 'Asian values', campaigners work for democracy and human rights according to universalistic, global conceptions. Of course, people interpret common

[31] Huntington (1996).

values in the contexts of specific nationalities and religions, and they often have justified suspicions of Western leaders and world institutions. But none of this negates the strong drive towards commonality in what is now a global-democratic transformation.

The specifically global phase of democratic revolution began in the Soviet bloc, and was part of the process by which the bloc-system was dissolved. The continuing impact of global-democratic upheaval is felt, however, everywhere that state power remains authoritarian, or where democracy has not been clearly consolidated, and has a powerful pull on public consciousness in the West. There are four reasons for insisting on the revolutionary character of contemporary democratic movements. First, they involve challenges to the national structures of authoritarian state power quite as fundamental as those made by classic revolutions. Second, they are rooted in widespread popular agency and deep-rooted aspirations in a similar way to previous historic upheavals. Third, they are connected to fundamental changes not only in national structures but also in international relations, and in the ways these two are connected. And last but not least, the changes that they produce show every sign of durable impact on the forms and character of power. These are not fundamental socio-economic revolutions, but they do represent historic political transformations.

How this global-democratic revolution relates to statehood is also essential, in theory and practice. In the national-international era, revolution was understood as a question of political sociology, relations between states as the subject of international relations. Of course, as we saw in chapter 2, theorists have recognized how the two affect each other: revolutions had repercussions for relations between states, and international relations, especially wars, were part of the conditions for revolution.[32] Today, because of structural changes that are partly products of the new democratic movements, the basic compartmentalization underlying these analyses no longer works. Global-democratic revolution is not just about the form of government within individual states, but about the shape of world order.

Similarly, wars, traditionally thought of as being fought between centres of state power, are now mostly between states and peoples as well. And yet they are not simply 'civil wars', in the old sense of conflicts within a single state. 'New wars' are about the shape of civil

---

[32] See Skocpol (1979), Halliday (1999).

society and the state. They mobilize cross-border alliances of ethnic nationalists, on the one hand, and of civic nationalists with global humanitarians, on the other.[33] In reality, most wars of the twenty-first century (and some are not so new) are wars of the anti-democratic, anti-globalist counterrevolution. War is the tool of authoritarian and semi-authoritarian regimes threatened by democratic movements – and particularly by secessionist demands from oppressed minorities that inevitably accompany democratization. In the hands of this kind of state machine, war is almost invariably genocidal to some degree.

The global-democratic revolution and the wars that surround it are about the future shape of states. Most obviously, they concern the transformation of authoritarian and semi-authoritarian state power. However, they also have critical importance for the development of state power in general, on a world scale. Local episodes of both democratic revolution and genocidal war are transformed, especially through their mediation in Western civil society, into 'global political crises'.[34] They have manifest significance for the development of state institutions at a global level, for example in the development of new forms of 'international intervention' or 'international law'. But they also have a deep significance for the development of the major centres of state power.

Looked at sociologically, what we have here is state formation on a global scale. One of Marx's most interesting ideas was that all previous revolutions had always 'perfected this [state] machine instead of smashing it'.[35] He thought that the proletarian revolution would be the exception, but historical experience has hardly been kind to this idea. The tendency of revolutions to encourage the growth of the state may be a general law. In the next part of this book, I examine its significance for the global-democratic revolution.

---

[33] Kaldor (1999).   [34] Shaw (1996), chapter 1.
[35] Quoted by Miliband (1965: 290).

Part III
State

6   State in globality

The problem of globality for the social sciences is not, as most debates have suggested, just how to understand global change. The defining issue is how to understand society, culture and politics in the global revolution. As Mann noted of an earlier period, 'In major transitions the fundamental interrelations, and very identities, of organizations such as "economies" or "states" become metamorphosed. Even the very definition of "society" may change.'[1] What is at stake is no less than whether and how we should reconstitute the central concepts of social science in global terms.

In the existing literature, the need for such a reconceptualization has hardly been recognized, let alone realized. In no area of social thought, probably, is this problem greater than in the understanding of the state. Despite some limited recognition of the inter-nationalization of the state, the state of the globalization debate remains (as we have seen) overwhelmingly the nation-state. Hence the focus on the ultimately sterile issue of whether state and nation have or have not been 'undermined' by global change. The key issue has barely been part of the discussion: could what these categories refer to itself have changed?

In this chapter, my goal is to explore what state means in the context of global transformation. However, the category of state cannot be understood apart from other social categories. If we are to grasp the contemporary significance of Mann's point, it will help if we begin with some of the most fundamental of the categories of social science. In this section, I discuss how three key concepts of social theory – society, economy and culture – should be re-examined, as a

---

[1] Mann (1993: 9).

basis for my later reconsideration of the concept of state. I take these concepts together not to conflate them or to deny the need for specific consideration of each, but because they pose the same central issues in the global context.

Globality and social categories

Fundamental social concepts such as society, economy and culture all have a double meaning, embodying a fundamental contradiction. On the one hand, they can all be understood in a generic sense as process. Society has the meaning of social relations in general. Economy has the meaning of the social organization of human resources. Culture has the meaning of the symbolic aspect of social relations, or symbolic interaction in general. In the generic sense, society, economy and culture are all intrinsically open-ended, rather than bounded. 'Culture is open', Raymond Williams proclaimed,[2] and this applies to economy and society too. The scope of social relations is constantly expanded through new interaction. Hence society, economy and culture are intrinsically dynamic, involving constant transformation and change, rather than fixed.

On the other hand, we have ideas of *a* society, *an* economy and *a* culture, or societies, economies and cultures. These meanings particularize the generic concepts and introduce the idea of bounded entities of social, economic and cultural interaction. In some versions, these are seen as relatively static, closed systems. A classic case was Talcott Parsons' self-regulating 'social system' with its functionally interdependent sub-systems, criticized on many grounds including the fact that it equated social system with national context.[3]

Conceptual discussion of societies, economies and cultures in this sense has fallen out of favour, reflecting the greater interest in the open-endedness and dynamism of social relations. The interesting questions appear to be about how boundaries are broken down, or at least reinterpreted, in an era of rapid social change and globalization. But if conceptual discussion has faltered, particularist concepts are still widely used. Domesticated sociology and politics routinely assume national societies and employ the comparative method to analyse their differences. Economists still assume that national economies are real units. Anthropologists have not stopped describing and analysing

[2] Williams (1958).   [3] Parsons (1972).

particular cultures. Cultural theorists have even particularized cultures further as sub-cultures. Although this idea also acknowledges the layering of cultures, it additionally presumes we can identify main cultures which include the sub-versions. International relations theorists, newly incorporating the idea that society and culture are important, often fall for traditional particularisms, closest to statist conceptions. Thus when Ole Wæver recently defined 'societal security', he identified society with national, ethnic and religious communities rather than with more open, plural or transnational relations.[4]

We need to adjudicate the status of particularist concepts. Neither society nor economy nor culture has ever been fully defined by boundaries. The implicit openness of all social and cultural relations means that boundaries were always there to be crossed, relative and subject to transformation. Even the most isolated tribal societies were defined by relations with 'other' societies. Although often seen as relations between social wholes, such 'inter-societal' or 'inter-cultural' relations can only be genuinely understood as interactions between people, that were more or less institutionalized by the bounded entities concerned.

In the national-international era of modernity, national societies and cultures have always been highly permeable. There have always been manifold, complex and highly significant relations across national boundaries, even when states have attempted to develop autarkic economies and closed social political and cultural systems. In the heyday of the nation-state system and the early Cold War, when such attempts at closure were at their peak, most such relations came to be seen as international. However, many relations were really transnational rather than international, in the specific sense of being defined by the fact that they existed between national entities.

The more sophisticated forms of social analysis have emphasized the complexity of the levels of social organization. For Mann, for example, 'societies are constituted by multiple, overlapping networks of interaction'.[5] But this approach, while avoiding dogmatic closure, does not deal with the problem of what defines when sets of networks become societies – or economies, or cultures. Clearly we could reject such concepts altogether. We could argue that there are only social and cultural relations and multiple networks of such relations. We could then hold that to conceptualize these as relations within and

[4] Wæver (1993).   [5] Mann (1993: 728).

between particular units is illusory and ideological because it reifies boundaries.

But this goes too far: social life has always been and still is informed by particularistic concepts. Boundaries, while relative, are real. Thus it makes partial sense to talk of, say, British, Kurdish or Zulu society, as well as many other networks and sub-cultures of sub-national and transnational kinds. We need to examine in what sense particularist concepts can be upheld. What is important is that they must always be understood within the generic meanings of society, economy and culture, rather than defined in opposition to them. All differentiations of particular entities and their boundaries are abstractions from the flux and openness of social relations. Societies, economies and cultures are forms through which relations, understood as process and relationship, are fixed and delineated. Such fixtures or delineations are never absolute, but always relative and subject to transformation.

The critical question is: what is it about those networks of relations, which we call societies, economies and cultures, that differentiates them from other networks to which these terms do not apply? This question requires a general answer: it cannot be circumvented by saying that national (or any other kind of) entities are by definition the basic units of social life. The general answer that makes sense of the ways in which such units are commonly recognized is as follows. Societies (or economies, or cultures) are those contexts of relations which are understood as *inclusive* and *constitutive* of social (or economic, or cultural) relations in general in a particular time and place. A society, economy or culture is a context of relations, by which other kinds of social, economic or cultural networks are seen as being defined, or of which they are component parts.

This definition suggests that the understanding of what makes a complex of relations into a society, an economy or a culture is subject to change. (This conclusion is immediately plausible because the concepts of society, economy and culture are themselves modern. If applied to earlier periods, they represent the interpretation of the past in terms formulated within modernity.) What is more, the definition suggests that the degree of inclusiveness or constitutiveness of a particular society, economy or culture is subject to variation and transformation. Not all contemporary national societies, economies or cultures, for example, are inclusive and constitutive to the same degree. Likewise, the same national units are more or less inclusive and constitutive in different historical periods.

Since the boundaries of societies, economies and cultures are relative to society, economy and culture in general, a range of particularistic concepts may coexist and overlap. Thus Mann suggests that sociology's use of its master concept, society, has oscillated between broad civilizational meanings – connected to the Western multi-power-actor civilization, or industrial or capitalist society – and narrower national meanings.[6] Likewise, it may make analytical sense to talk simultaneously of Welsh, British, European *and* Western, or of Kurdish, Iraqi *and* Islamic, or of Zulu *and* South African societies and cultures. In none of these three ranges are the different terms mutually exclusive, although there are clearly tensions between them.

As these examples suggest, moreover, while societies and cultures may largely go together, we cannot assume that their boundaries are equivalent. Moreover if we substitute economy for society or culture in the ranges just listed, we may find them difficult to sustain. The possibility of non-equivalence of the boundaries of, say, economies and cultures is a feature of the generally overlapping, permeable and non-exclusive character of bounded social entities.

Tensions between overlapping concepts of society, economy and culture are therefore normal in modernity. A number of different contexts of social relations have strong claims to constitute each of these in a given time and place, and to include other kinds of relations. None, however, can be said to be, in any absolute or complete sense, either constitutive or inclusive. There are always competing ideas of which context is constitutive. Of course, for any of them to be at all definitive, there has to be some stability in their defining character, over a period of time. In the modern era, national-international ideas of society have complemented and mutually constituted each other as well as forming poles around which competing particular definitions of society, economy and culture have formed. Thus Welsh and British, Kurdish and Iraqi, Zulu and South African are all in different ways competing versions of nationality. European, Western and (in a rather different way) Islamic are versions of the more general, civilizational context of society, which in the modern era has largely been defined as international.

Following this general conceptual unpacking, we can begin to understand the significance of *global* society, economy and culture. Any of these can be said to exist to the extent that global patterns of

[6] Mann (1993: 9).

relations have become inclusive and constitutive of these relations in general. The concepts of global society, economy and culture, as of other such entities, do not represent static systems or end-states. They are abstractions from the flux of relations, they vary over time and they coexist – and are in tension – with other more particularistic concepts. Moreover since a society, economy or culture is an inclusive set of relations, it does not consist merely of relations at its particular level. National entities partially include and constitute not only sub-national relations of many kinds, but also international relations. Likewise, global society and culture partially include and constitute relations at other levels – world-regional, transnational, international, national, local, etc.

It makes most sense to emphasize that global society, economy and culture are emergent realities. They are becoming *more* defining frameworks, while national-international frameworks – although still important – are becoming *less* defining. The global is not only inclusive of contemporary national and international relations in general but also constitutive of them in a way in which they are not of it. Similarly transnational and regional relations are informed by a sense of the world as a common social and cultural context, more than this global sense is informed by the international, regional or transnational.

Global society, economy and culture are actually particularistic concepts in the sense defined above. However, the comparison of them with all previous concepts of this kind emphasizes the distinctiveness and novelty of these forms. Global entities are not bounded in the same way as every other kind, since they can be said to include contemporary society, economy or culture as a whole, in the generic sense of *all* such relations. These are maximum concepts, defined not like national or tribal entities in relation to others of the same kind, but in relation to more particular forms which they include.

Global concepts are in many ways extensions of existing general concepts of society, economy and culture, as Western, capitalist or modern. However, they are more inclusive than any of these. These older concepts always implied possibilities such as non-Western, pre- or post-capitalist, or pre-modern society. Globality, in contrast, does not so easily define an other (except, of course, pre-global). A global society is one in which a general commonality or unification is implied. Clearly these processes are highly problematic, in something like the same way as the earlier extensions of Western power relations to the world scale. They include and reproduce manifold forms of domination, difference and inequality. Global like national entities can be defined as socio-spatial forms of capitalist society; but no more than national society can globality be reduced to the latter.

To define global society, economy and culture as emergent, increasingly constitutive and inclusive frameworks of relations implies, in the light of this discussion, that the relations between global and other potentially defining frameworks are a key issue. In particular, national-international structures are still of great importance. On the one hand, globality is historically counterposed to nationality-internationality and transcends the classical forms of the latter. On the other, it also depends on transformed nationality and internationality. Rather than pursue the implications of this argument abstractly here, I shall return to it in the next chapter in the context of forms of state. It is important to grasp, however, that national forms of society, economy and culture, already increasingly internationalized, are now also becoming globalized; while globality, an unprecedentedly inclusive and complex framework for worldwide relations, depends on transformed national and international forms.

The singularity of state

There is a generic concept of state, just as there is of society and of culture. Social and political theory has been full of debate about 'the state'. However, this literature has nearly always meant the state in the context of a specific society – usually national society or something approximating (however imperfectly) to such a society. The state has most commonly meant a complex of legitimate power to which individuals relate in the context of a nation, or resulting from the clash of social interests within the national context.

For international theory, on the other hand, states have been unitary, competing actors within an international system. The system as a whole has sometimes been seen as constituting the basis for an 'international society' of states, but a 'society without a state'.[7] If there is one thing on which international relations has been agreed, it is on the 'anarchy' of the international order produced by its lack of a central political authority. As we have seen in chapter 3, new global theory has often reproduced this understanding of world anarchy in new forms. This has meant that although global economic, social and

[7] Bull (1977).

cultural relations are increasingly understood, the prevailing under-standing of the state as a nation-state remains largely unchallenged, with little more than the beginnings of recognition of the 'inter-nationalized' state.

For the literatures in both the domesticated social sciences and international relations, the state in general cannot be separated, therefore, from the plurality of nation-states. Statehood, the only way we have of talking of the quality of state, has been understood exclusively through two sets of terms: anarchy, plurality, competition, sovereignty and violence *between* separated centres of power, and authority, monopoly, control and suppression *within* the societies of these separated centres. The question arises: is there any way of specifying statehood other than in these terms? Can we make any useful comparison between our understanding of generic and par-ticular concepts of society, economy and culture, and similar concepts of the state?

State appears on first examination to be significantly different from society, economy or culture. The latter all constitute spheres of social action, and suppose complex relations between individuals, loosely coordinated in a variety of ways, informal as well as formal, inter-personal as well as institutional. All of them are broader-based than a single system of coordinated action: they include such systems and involve the relationships between them. State, on the other hand, involves, seemingly by definition, the formation of unified, formally defined institutional entities. State has meant the consolidation of a *centre* of social power, differentiated from society, economy or culture in general. State involves not a general flux of relations between individuals, but an authoritatively coordinated complex of relations, which acts as a framework for the looser patterns of relations which make up society, economy and culture.

State is not of course a uniquely modern phenomenon. Throughout the millennia of recorded history, state – in the sense of some specialized, authoritative institutional form of the organization of violence – has been a widespread feature of human society. It may not have been universal: small-scale stateless societies are known. In this sense, the category of state is different from that of economy or culture, or society itself – all of which refer to features which are in some sense necessary, without which it is difficult to imagine human social life. While authority and force are general features of social life, their coordination in a distinct centre of power appears to be a phenomenon of more developed and complex societies, not a strict universal. Further, statehood has not always meant the nation-state or a specifically international system. However, if the modern form of the separation of state from society and economy is distinctive, the separation in general is as old as state itself and is part of what state means.

Moreover, the existence of the state as a distinct power centre has been inseparable, historically, from the competition between different centres. Much – although not all – of the distinctiveness of societies, economies and cultures has derived from the characters of the different centres of state power which have attempted to coordinate them. Much history and tradition, especially recorded, written versions, has been centred on and produced within or concerning state institutions. In the history of organized statehood, the competitive relations of different centres – constituting, thereby, interstate systems – have generally characterized state power.

However, some forms of state, notably classical empires, have maintained relatively unitary authority systems over very large areas. Considering the limited means of transport and communication then available, empires often maintained such systems over areas which were relatively much vaster than those of the entire world today. Imperial orders constituted veritable universes for those who lived within them: although society outside the empire was usually known, for those who lived nearer their centres the state could be effectively singular. Of course, imperial orders of this kind, however dominant over large areas and over generations, were always prone to external pressures and internal fissures, both of which reproduced the contest of violence. Giddens argues, moreover, that in pre-modern states, the distinction between 'external' and 'internal' violence was not so clear as it has subsequently become. Only modern nation-states, capable of more intensive surveillance because of the improvement of communications, constitute the 'bordered power containers' which today we think of as the state.[8]

We can say, therefore, that because statehood involves the concentration of social power, it necessarily implies the potential for competition from those excluded from direct participation in any given concentration. This competition can arise from both 'within' and 'outside' the territory that a given centre claims. State, by defini-

[8] Giddens (1985).

tion, implies the possibility of multiple, autonomous centres of power – of states. However far-spread the authority relations that a particular state spins, the possibility of concentrations of power outside its web, or of new centres arising from within, is omnipresent. The near-ubiquity of actualized violence and military power in classical imperial rule suggests that there has been little escape from this condition of state.

However, there remains the theoretical possibility of a singularity of state. It is possible that there could have been, historically, a single centre of state power within a given self-sufficient society for a certain period. Since we know that historically no societies have remained indefinitely isolated and self-sufficient, such a singularity of state would have been superseded eventually, but it is conceivable that it could have existed. No one would disagree that in the modern world, a complex plurality of states has been normal. But social theory has more than once posed the theoretical possibility of the formation of a single state out of many.

In the early twentieth-century Marxist literature, the prospect of 'ultra-imperialism' was raised by Karl Kautsky. If capitalism were to renounce destructive conflicts and anarchic competition for raw materials, regulating trade in a higher phase of 'international mono-polism', then a new phase of capitalism was conceivable beyond the imperialist phase that had culminated in the world war. This would be the phase of 'ultra-imperialism', the danger of which would take a different form, not that of an arms race and threat to world peace. 'If such an era of ultra-imperialism should come to pass', Kautsky wrote, 'then it is possible that at least the trend toward the moral bankruptcy of capitalism could be temporarily mitigated.' If, on the contrary, the imperialist trend prevailed, a 'second world war' would become 'inevitable'.

Kautsky outlined the ultra-imperialist alternative as follows: 'In the event that an accord of nations, disarmament, and lasting peace are achieved, then the worst of the causes which were increasingly leading to the moral bankruptcy of capitalism would recede . . . ultra-imperialism would initially usher in an era of new hopes and expecta-tions within capitalism.'[9] 'We must even consider', he warned his comrades, 'the possibility that the world may see the spectacle,

---

[9] Salvatori (1979: 193).

shameful for us, of the realization of the International of the imperialists before that of the International of the socialist parties.'[10]

Kautsky's ideas, denounced by Lenin[11] (who according to Salvatori considerably distorted them[12]), have an uncanny resonance. Although the ideas of disarmament and lasting peace still have a utopian ring,[13] Kautsky meant them in a distinctive context, namely military competition between imperialist capitalist states, which has indeed been suppressed. His essential error was to foreshorten the historical possibilities which he disclosed: the developments to which he referred would only come about *through* the 'second world war' which he saw as the *alternative* to them; they did not result from the 1914–18 war.

However, the suppression of war between the major Western states after 1945 did eventually usher in what Hobsbawm has called the 'golden age' of post-war peace and prosperity, albeit in the context of the new deadly rivalry of the Western and Soviet blocs.[14] The resolution of this last phase of major military rivalry between great centres of state power has also ushered in a new phase of 'global' prosperity, at least within the advanced West. In these contexts, it would be reasonable to claim that Kautsky's prediction of a new 'moral' credibility for capitalism was borne out.

Although Kautsky gives us considerable insight into the state relations resulting from 'ultra-imperialism', he only explored one side of the state forms which would result from the abolition of war between major imperial centres. In opposition to Lenin and others who saw world war as resulting in the end of democracy in imperialist states, Kautsky foresaw the strengthening of democracy in a pacified international capitalism. Although he talked of the 'international' of the imperialists, he failed, however (and perhaps understandably), to foresee the *internationalized* forms of modern state which have developed in the eras of blocs and globality. Indeed, although Kautsky (like Bukharin[15]) gave distinct weight to military as opposed to economic competition between imperialisms, he antici-

---

[10] Salvatori (1979: 198–9).   [11] Lenin (1964: 192).
[12] Salvatori (1979: 200).
[13] Thus even Salvatori, a careful and sympathetic intellectual biographer, criticizes him for imagining that ultra-imperialism 'would be fully compatible with a utopian degree of international peace, with the restoration of parliamentary democracy and the strengthening of the united energies of the socialist proletariat' (1979: 200).
[14] Hobsbawm (1994).   [15] Bukharin (1972).

pated the trend among later Marxists in failing to make a clear enough distinction between capitalism and the capitalist class, on the one hand, and state development on the other.

It is not only in Marxist theory that we find indications of the internationalized state. Weberian sociology also proposes a hypothesis which can be developed in this direction. Max Weber's idea of the tendency towards 'pacification' of society is developed by Giddens as a normal component of the consolidation of nation-states. In his account, however, internal pacification is the corollary of external warfare: peace within states, maintained by extensive surveillance, is a mutual condition of expanded violence between them.[16] Nevertheless, Giddens also introduces the idea of the system of nation-states becoming 'a reflexively monitored system', in which the centres of power constantly carry out mutual surveillance, on a global scale.[17] Surveillance has not been limited to the internal relations of discrete states; it has also become a normal condition of relations between them.

If surveillance was expanded to the point at which it led to extensive pacification of interstate relations, then effectively the separate centres of power would be combined. If this tendency was carried to its logical conclusion, a single pacified centre of state power could come into existence. The separate centres of state power would have been subsumed for practical purposes into a single state. Albrow proposes that this is actually occurring, that 'in the Global Age the state is decentred, crosses nation-state boundaries, penetrates and is realized in the daily activities of ordinary people'. However, he qualifies this by saying that 'the world state exists at the moment more as potential than as reality'.[18] He also argues that

> the world state does not operate as the nation-state writ large. It originates out of quite different conditions – not from rivalry over territory and the insecurities of ruling classes, but in joint endeavours to control the consequences of technical advance for the environment, in shared interests in human rights and in a common fear of a nuclear catastrophe. It represents a new stage in the idea of the state, taking it beyond that configuration of monopoly of legitimate violence, nationality and territoriality.[19]

As my historical discussion in chapters 4 and 5 suggested, this highly optimistic view is only partially true.

[16] Giddens (1985).
[17] Giddens (1985: 263). See also Rosenberg (1990).
[18] Albrow (1996: 172–3).   [19] Albrow (1996: 173).

Thus from more than one direction, singular statehood, which no one claims has actually existed, is recognized as a theoretically possible *tendency* in specifically modern conditions. There is no claim in this book, either, that it has been achieved in the simple sense. However, the trend towards a *complex unification* of state power is real and of crucial importance to understanding contemporary world politics. This discussion raises the question: under what conditions could separate centres be said to have actually merged to form the super-imperial states of Kautsky's conception, or the larger pacified complexes implied in my extension of Giddens'.

Behind this question are others which are more relevant to the condition of a plurality of states. What is it that demarcates separate 'centres' of state power? What enables us to say that a given complex of power constitutes a distinct 'state' within a plurality? How are states bordered? When, indeeed, is a state a state? Such questions need to be answered before we can settle the character of contemporary statehood.

Defining state in plurality

Contemporary social scientists have given far too little attention to these issues, usually preferring to assume that they know what states are. The normal modern form of state, it is widely agreed, is the nation-state – and we know one when we see it. Where political science and international relations have addressed these questions, they have generally hinged their answers on the concept of sovereignty. A state is a state when it is recognized by its citizens and/or by other states as a sovereign, i.e. supreme, authority within a given territory. A sovereign state is thus a nationally and internationally legitimate institution of power. Sovereignty has been seen by international relations, moreover, as conditioned by the anarchic relations between separate sovereigns. Some such definition has been widely agreed in the national-international era – this partly explains the 'taken-for-grantedness' of statehood. However, it is also accepted by many scholars that it is no longer applicable, at least not in any simple way.

We can identify three main reasons why sovereignty is now seen as more problematic. First, states have increasingly 'pooled' their sovereignty. Through permanent interstate institutions, sovereignty has been internationalized in new forms of its cooperative exercise.

Second, individual states' jurisdictions are increasingly understood extraterritorially as well as territorially. Hence territorially they overlap rather than being mutually exclusive. Individuals, collectivities and institutions based in one state increasingly operate in the territories of other states; their 'home' state continues to claim jurisdiction alongside, and overlapping with, the territorial states within which they act. In some circumstances, moreover, 'national' state institutions act extraterritorially on their own accounts. Third, and possibly most important, juridical sovereignty, constitutionally and legally defined, is often seen to have diverged from the substance of power relations. This is largely because power is recognized as residing in economic rather than formal political relations.

These transformations in the understanding of sovereignty clearly make the identification of distinct states more difficult. While national units are still seen as the sources of sovereignty, partially pooled and overlapping jurisdictions imply the complex internationalization of nation-states. When, we may ask, does such an internationalized nation-state remain a 'distinct' centre of state power, a 'state' in its own right? When does it become primarily a component of a larger entity, however much it retains some distinctiveness? If the answer to these questions simply refers back to the underlying international juridical understanding of state sovereignty, then how far does the internationalization of law have to go before the locus is understood to have shifted – if not to international institutions as such, at least to a mutually constituted complex of national and international state organizations?

The difficulty of finding a clear and settled contemporary juridical answer (to the question of when a state is a state) is emphasized by the growing tendency to treat sovereignty as an economic rather than a juridical condition. Since 1945, the autonomy and sovereignty of states have increasingly been understood to reside in their control over the national economy. Hence states' sovereignties are said to be undermined when globalization appears to weaken their control. The argument that economic power is the real substance of sovereignty has been supported by the apparent hollowness of sovereignty in many Third World states – dependent on Western banks, states and international institutions, or incapable of exercising real authority in their territories.[20] It has been reinforced by the ways in which juridical

---

[20] Thus for Jackson (1990) many African 'states' are 'quasi-states'.

sovereignty has itself become a commodity, as national entities become 'competition states', competing to offer favourable economic conditions to corporations and rich individuals utilizing a variety of 'offshore' statuses.[21]

If, however, real sovereignty lies in economic power, then what remains of states? How does a state differ from a firm? The answer to the question 'when is a state a state?' surely cannot be reduced to 'when it is a corporation'. It is true that twentieth-century states have accumulated economic (and social) functions which their predecessors mostly did not possess,[22] while even some core functions of states have been privatized to corporations. These transformations are certainly very significant in the context of global change. But no more than the changes in the juridical conditions of statehood can political-economic changes, by themselves, tell us what a state is, even in the twenty-first century.

Historical sociology has offered, as we saw in chapter 2, credible accounts of statehood in the national-international era. Marxist theories of the state (curiously neglected in international theory's re-appropriation of Marxism) emphasized organized violence and coercive apparatuses as central to state power. However, their explanations of these aspects of statehood have been curiously skewed towards class-based, 'internalist' explanations. These appear inappropriate considering that interstate rather than class violence has been dominant in modern times. Marxists neglect the obvious fact that it is wars, rather than class struggles, which have forced the major transformations of states in the twentieth century.[23] But despite this major defect, the classical Marxist tradition did take the coercive state seriously.

The broader sociological tradition, eschewing Marxist class reductionism, offers an even more relevant beginning. As we have seen, Weber's definition of the state has provided a benchmark for later debate: 'A compulsory political organization with continuous operations will be called a "state" insofar as its administrative staff successfully upholds the claim to the monopoly of the legitimate use of physical force in the enforcement of its order.'[24] This monopoly, of course, refers to a given geographical space or territory.

---

[21] Cerny (1990), Palan and Abbott (1996), Palan (1998).
[22] See Gough (1984).   [23] Shaw (1984).
[24] Weber (1978: 54–56), cited by Mann (1993: 55).

As we have seen, Giddens followed Weber to define the modern nation-state as a 'bordered power container'.[25] Especially before 1945, but also since, state leaders (and others) often acted as if this definition was true and they did in fact hold a monopoly of legitimate violence within their territories. By the same token, in a world of nation-state-empires, the demarcation of one state from another was the potential for violence between them. The borders of states were not merely administrative divisions but potentially, at least, lines along which large-scale violence might erupt. States were typically autonomous territorial centres of political-military power whose conflicts were capable of developing into violence.

Even in the high national-international era, however, this was too simple a view of statehood. The tight territorial monopoly of the bordered power container was a norm to which few states approximated in any simple way. Within large-scale states such as the British empire there were multiple, overlapping centres of power. Many of these centres had some purchase on force, and they were often imperfectly coordinated within a single authority structure. Borders of violence were ultimately sharpest between rival imperial centres, but lines of violence existed, too, between imperial states and colonized peoples, and sometimes between imperial centres and colonists. These demarcations also had clear territorial characters, and can well be seen in many cases as conflicts with rival state forms, pre- and post-colonial.

Not surprisingly, therefore, Mann proposes, as we saw in chapter 2, a looser version of Weber's definition:

1 The state is a differentiated set of institutions and personnel
2 embodying centrality, in the sense that political relations radiate to and from a centre, to cover a
3 territorially demarcated area over which it exercises
4 some degree of authoritative, binding rule making, backed up by some organized political force.[26]

As Mann points out, this is an institutional rather than a functional definition. Crucially, it abandons the idea of a simple monopoly of legitimate force; there is merely 'some degree of authoritative rule making' and 'some organized political force'. This definition is an advance in that it allows for the imperfections of states' authoritative

---

[25] Giddens (1985).   [26] Mann (1993: 55).

claims and their capacities for enforcing them. 'Like cock-up-foul-up theorists', Mann states, 'I believe that states are messier and less systematic and unitary than each single theory suggests.'[27]

By implication, Mann's definition allows for both competing and overlapping 'states' within a given geographical area. It raises the prospect that, just as there can be multiple layers of society and culture, there can be a layering of state. However, it raises the same problem that we found above: we need criteria for adjudicating the claims of various possible state centres. We need to be able to decide how, in these terms, distinct states are differentiated – which actually make up more or less individual centres of state power.

Not every layer of state power constitutes a distinct state. For example, it would generally be agreed that municipal authorities within centralized nation-states are not states in their own right. Similarly, although interstate international organizations are also a layer of state power, they have generally been seen as derivative of the nation-states which established and comprise them. We may agree with these common perceptions, so far as they go. It may be empirically correct to regard these layers of state institutions – respectively 'below' and 'above' the nation-state – as constituted largely by the latter. However, we should note that there is no reason to regard any particular layer of state power as intrinsically incapable of constituting statehood.

Thus it is generally accepted that in both ancient Greece and early modern Europe, cities were also states, while many would agree that the contemporary European Union has an increasing number of the attributes of a state. These examples illustrate the fact that, while we may use the same names – 'city', 'nation', 'international organization' – to refer continuously to given layers of state power over time, the defining locus shifts. The city-states of the early modern period increasingly gave way to nation-states. The latter are giving way, at least in part, to European and other international state institutions. In each historic transformation of statehood, previously dominant layers remain in existence, to a greater or lesser extent, but their significance for defining the contours of distinct states diminishes. The question which these processes raise is that of why a given layer or form of state is seen as defining in a particular period.

---

[27] Mann (1993: 88).

We need therefore to add a new criterion to Mann's definition: that to be considered a state, a particular power centre must be

5 to a significant degree *inclusive* and *constitutive* of other forms or layers of state power (i.e. of state power in general in a particular time and space).

Thus, in the national-international era, nation-state-empires could generally be said to be inclusive and constitutive of municipal state forms. Nation-state-empires could also be said to be constitutive of interstate international organizations, and inclusive of them to the extent that such institutions remain essentially within their control. (Inclusion is not necessarily territorial, and does not always involve the priority of larger over smaller units.) The point at which, for example, the European Union could be regarded as seriously autonomous is the point at which its constituent nation-states are no longer simply inclusive and constitutive of the Union, but are becoming constituted by and included within it to significant degrees.

So far I have allowed the European Union to stand for the internationalized state, as an example which will be readily understood. There is, however, a fundamental problem with regarding it as a state in its own right. While it increasingly possesses the forms of statehood, the Union crucially lacks a significant element of 'organized political force' belonging to it – rather than to its component nation-states or to the North Atlantic Treaty Organization of which most member-states are also members. There have been, of course, increasing attempts to form the basis of some such force, as for example in the moves towards a common defence and security policy and in the formation of joint German, French and Dutch brigades. As yet these are dwarfed by, on the one hand, the continuing transatlantic Western military-political thrust led by the United States, and on the other, the dominant role of particular national states such as Britain and France, even in 'European' crises such as those in the Balkans.

The case of the European Union presents us, therefore, with a paradox. Juridically and economically, the Union is more tightly and comprehensively developed as a form of state power than, say, either NATO or the United Nations system. Juridically and economically, the Union is clearly constitutive and inclusive of, at the same time as it is constituted by and included in, its nation-state members. And yet from the historically central criterion of organized violence, Europe remains a secondary, derivative form of state. There is clearly a

European layer of state power – in the uncontentious sense in which there is also a municipal layer – but there may not be yet a European state, if we retain and strictly apply the criterion of force.[28]

We could, of course, argue that force is no longer so important, that military organization is no longer determinant of the 'shape of the state', as Hintze put it.[29] The economistic-sociologistic tradition in international thought (which I discussed in chapter 3) suggests that there is no longer a 'hierarchy among issues' in which 'military security . . . consistently dominate[s] the agenda', as Keohane and Nye classically suggested.[30] And yet, as we saw, this tradition largely failed to problematize the meaning of state as nation-state, accepted from realism. It led to the false conclusion that military force now had a 'minor role' in international politics.

It is not so difficult, indeed, to justify the notion of the continuing salience of violence, in the face of the juridical and economistic misunderstandings of statehood which have increasingly prevailed in contemporary international relations. At the root of all the complex forms of authority in the modern state lies the control of violence. The extent of contemporary pacification and surveillance testifies not to the irrelevance of violence, but to the increasing – but necessarily partial – success of states in securing control. The very complexity of the pacified world creates, however, multiple, new, points of potential contestation. New challenges of force and violence remain ever-possible, as phenomena such as wars of state collapse, terrorism and organized violent crime quickly suggest. The authoritative control of violence must be constantly reproduced through repeated reinvention of its forms and means.

In this sense it remains true that at core, state power is about the relations between authority and force – if not in Weber's tight sense of the 'monopoly' of violence, then in Mann's looser sense of 'authoritative, binding rule making' backed by 'organized political force'. It remains true that states are demarcated one from the other by the potential for violence between them. What remains uncertain, however, is how we understand the forms which state and states take in the global transition.

---

[28] Mann has investigated 'the degree of internal coherence and external closure of European social networks' and comes to the conclusion that 'Euro has been strengthening but does not seem yet to be a particularly coherent or closed network of interaction.' (1998: 205).

[29] Gilbert (1975).   [30] Keohane and Nye (1977: 24–5).

Global state: singularity and plurality

Following the two lines of argument above, first about globalizing social categories and second about the nature of state, we can now begin to pose the question of state in globality. Global statehood can be said to be coming into existence, to the extent that global state relations and forms are inclusive and constitutive of state relations and forms in general. However, the global state coexists and is in tension with other more particularistic forms of state. The central paradox of contemporary statehood lies in these changing relations between singularity and plurality. The nature of the coexistence and the tension between these two aspects will be explored in more detail in subsequent chapters. In the remainder of this chapter, I shall try to pose this relation as a general problem of state power in globality.

There are two defining features of contemporary statehood. On the one hand, it is now possible to pose much more concretely (than in previous periods) the possibility of identifying the concept of state in general with a single complex of state relations and forms. *The* state, as it has traditionally been known, has moved from the realm of fiction – since there was previously only a plurality of states – to that of historical possibility. The idea of a unified centre of state power which generates a worldwide web of authoritative relations, backed up by a more or less common, world organization of political force, is now partially – even if, as we shall see, very imperfectly – realized. State power is generalized in ever larger complexes bound together by common relations of authority and the control of force.

On the other hand – simultaneously and relatedly – the plurality of state power is reproduced in new forms. Both the resilience of some national centres and the continuous emergence of new centres of would-be authoritative force constantly reproduce the contest of violence. In this sense, the plurality of states remains the general form which state takes in contemporary society. In this sense, too, global state relations remain truly anarchic.[31]

State in globality is constituted, therefore, by the relations and

[31] In this sense, therefore, Clark (1997) is correct to rewrite the history of contemporary world politics in terms of the dialectic of 'globalization' and 'fragmentation'. Where he is mistaken is, first, in underestimating the decisive changes linked to the end of the Second World War and to that of the Cold War, and second, in not clarifying the more fundamental question of what constitutes the 'globalization' of state power, which is discussed here.

forms which produce both a new generalization and a new particular-ization of state. There is thus a dual globalization of statehood. First, there is the development of a *single dominant centre* of state power, which is far larger than its central nation-state entity and projects its power on a world scale. In this sense, there is the emergence of a global state, the structure of which will be discussed in more detail in the next chapter. Second, there is the complex implication of *all* centres of state power in global state relations and forms. Thus even those nation-states which remain manifestly 'outside' the dominant state centre are involved in the generalization of statehood which emanates from this centre.

The roles of secondary centres of state power are therefore contra-dictory. Some traditional nation-states are sufficiently inter-nationalized within the dominant global state as to no longer constitute distinct states in any meaningful sense. At the other extreme, state-like institutions, including some which are not widely recognized as states, become effectively new centres of state power – new states – through conflict with the global state. They back their claims to legitimacy with the mobilization of force, and despite coming into conflict with the global state, they often gain recognition in the process.

Global state relations thus involve *a double realignment of centres of state power within society on a world scale*. On the one hand, there are new relationships between centres of state power, in which there is both a concentration and a fragmentation of statehood. On the other hand, there are new relationships of state and society. The emergence of the global state corresponds (as both cause and effect) to the globalization of society, economy and culture. The fracturing of statehood, on the other hand, corresponds to new zones of extreme dislocation of social relations, in which society is impoverished, threatened, even destroyed.

Global state forms articulate these contradictory transformations of state relations. The dominant trend is the complex globalization of authority. This involves the extension of globally legitimate inter-national institutions. It also involves the transformation of national forms of state – including concepts of sovereignty. Linked to both of these is the globalization of democratic norms and values and a normalization of democratic political forms. However, at the same time there is a dissolution of legitimate national authority which produces atavistic, exclusive, ethnic-nationalist caricatures of state power. These apparently opposing tendencies meet in two places. Within the global state, elites subordinate the development of legitimate institutions and norms to their own power interests. Within nation-states on the fringes of and beyond the global state, authoritarian elites attempt to maintain power by subverting globally legitimate democratic forms.

The global structure of state power involves, therefore, new relations and forms of both authority and violence. It extends and deepens a particular but problematic form of order; but it also reproduces war between the global state and other states. Despite the manifold gains for global democracy, there is a real and troublesome anarchy in the contemporary world. This anarchy needs to be understood in terms profoundly different from the dominant understandings of anarchy in international relations. This is not the traditional, competitive rivalry of 'sovereign' states in the 'international system'. Neither is it the benign 'post-statist' community of communities looked for by global civil society theory.

The new global anarchy corresponds, therefore, not only to continuing mobilization of violence by state centres outside the global state, but also to continuing lawlessness and war-proneness even at the heart of the global state. The global state system is one in which the global-democratic revolution is profoundly incomplete. The institutions and elites of the global state respond to the movements for global-democratic change. But they also balance these against their interests in maintaining elements of the old relations and forms, and compromise even with the most virulent forms of counterrevolution. These contradictions of global state development are explored further in the next two chapters.

7   Relations and forms of global state power

Throughout this book, I have proposed that we understand state in terms of the twin concepts of state relations (or the social relations of state power) and state forms (the formal institutional expressions of these relations). Both of these concepts are broad in character. To the extent that states have become ever more powerful in society, more and more social relations have had, directly or indirectly, the character of state relations. Society in general has been increasingly incorporated into the mode of reproduction of state power. This was most evident in the era of classic total war, in the ways in which war and war preparation included more and more areas of social relations. There was an extensive statization of social relations, which was reflected in the comprehensive restructuring of state forms. States as institutions became formally concerned with ever larger areas of social life: with economic management and social welfare as well as war and law.

In principle we can see states as 'janus-faced', looking both 'inwards' to society and 'outwards' to interstate relations,[1] or concerned with both surveillance and warfare.[2] This understanding of the state, common to most historical sociology, is an advance on the concepts of domesticated political science and sociology, on the one hand, and international relations, on the other, which simply reproduce the separation of the two sides of the state without grasping the relations between them. However, this separation has become, especially in the twentieth century, much more one of form than of content. It becomes increasingly difficult to separate the social relations of external and internal state power from each other, as well as from other kinds of social relations.

[1] Skocpol (1979).   [2] Giddens (1985).

195

Thus the idea of society as pacified and interstate relations as warlike, which is given its fullest expression by Giddens, is far too simple even for the high national-international era, and even more so for the period of global transition. Mann has emphasized the implication of civil society in the violence of colonization – wars against indigenous peoples were fought by settlers as well as empires.[3] There are echoes of this even today in the violent expropriation of land by 'internal' settlers in the Brazilian Amazon and elsewhere. Even at the heart of imperial nation-states, moreover, violent contestation of central state power never disappeared, even (or especially) in their heyday. As historical sociologists have emphasized, an 'international-national-international' loop of war and revolution was quite normal.[4] Although in principle we can distinguish war from revolution, the revolutionary character of war and the militarization of revolution make this distinction far from certain in practice.

In modern revolution, moreover, the distinction between class-based movements which aimed to reconstruct the existing territorially constructed state, and national movements which aimed to deconstruct its territorial basis, was also problematic in practice. Since major states were generally empires, class contestation in the imperial core and national contestation in the periphery were often complementary. Social revolutionaries were forced to recognize this in practice, hence Lenin's embrace of 'national self-determination' – initially a strategic development of class politics. In the hands of many Stalinized Communist parties this became the basis for both the nationalization of revolution and the transformation of social revolution into revolutionary guerrilla war.

The partial truth in the idea of pacified society and warlike states was that in the heyday of the nation-state-empire, the violence of interstate war dwarfed the violence of revolution and even of revolutionary war. But intensified surveillance never implied complete pacification. Nor was surveillance ever only one way, as insurgents developed their own means of monitoring as well as tapping into those of central states. Moreover, in highly surveyed (and thus partially pacified) societies, mass media amplified the effects of even small or isolated acts of violence, giving their practitioners political significance out of proportion to their numbers. While it has been difficult for insurgents to win against highly surveyed, especially

---

[3] Mann (1996). [4] Halliday (1999), Hobson (1998).

democratic states, it has also been difficult for states to stamp out violence. (Hence the contemporary tendency towards negotiated settlements of insurgency.)

Centres of power, borders of violence

Borders of violence in the modern world have never coincided at all fully, therefore, with the formal boundaries of states. In the high national-international period, at least it was true that the latter were the most important lines of violence, compared with which violent divisions of society 'within' states appeared secondary. Imperial nation-states approximated, even if they were not at all completely, 'bordered power containers'. After 1945, however, most major nation-states gradually shed the character of formal empires. In the emerging world of blocs, the major borders of violence were simplified to the lines between 'East' and 'West' which were named for their decisive characters – the 'Iron Curtain' in Europe followed by the 'Bamboo Curtain' in Asia.

There were of course other lines of violence between states, mainly between the blocs and secondary centres of state power, but also between the latter and within blocs. Most violent conflicts were, however, 'within' juridically defined states: as any list of the wars of the Cold War era will confirm, major interstate wars such as those in Korea, Vietnam or the Middle East (all of which had important 'internal' aspects) were few in number compared with intrastate conflicts.[5] The dominant borders were the bloc divisions: although Cold War rivalry did not fully determine the secondary conflicts, the latter were often assimilated to bloc rivalry.

Within the Cold War blocs, 'nation-states' were therefore no longer 'bordered power containers'. National state entities (especially subordinate states) opened their borders to each other's armed forces (particularly those of superpowers). Even within the looser and more mutually constituted Western bloc, only Britain and France retained both the military capacities and political scope for large-scale military power-projection independently of the USA. Even in these two cases the opportunities were mainly of a 'post-imperial' kind, increasingly constrained in practice (notably after the failure of the 1956 Suez

[5] Shaw (1991: 59).

intervention, of which Washington disapproved); the independence of their nuclear forces was more apparent than real. If any kind of unit resembled a bordered power container, it was increasingly the blocs themselves. National state entities within the blocs were increasingly interpenetrated.

Despite the reality that many key lines of violence were between blocs or 'within' national entities, the formal construction of blocs on a national-international basis meant that the importance of national forms of state was actually reinforced. The nation-state form was also strengthened from another direction. The break-up of European empires led to the establishment of a large number of 'independent' nation-states. Both bloc ideologies, American liberal and Soviet Communist, legitimated national autonomy as a universal value. However, state-blocs widely oppressed or subverted the real autonomy of their constituent or client national centres. And while national independence was clearly of great significance in cases such as India and China, it was understood on all sides that in the cases of smaller countries, statehood might imply the trappings rather than the full realization of 'sovereignty'. A model for clientelistic independence already existed in Latin America, and was theorized in the 1960s in the widely applied idea of 'dependency'.

Within the evolving juridical and normative world order, restructured around the United Nations, blocs were organized and understood as comprising overlapping layers of 'international' organization. There were three principal layers: bloc bodies such as NATO (and within it the European Economic Community) and the Warsaw Pact; international bodies such as the Bretton Woods institutions which in theory were world organizations but in practice were dominated by the major Western bloc; and those bodies which more genuinely included other states, such as the UN itself, but within which the voices of the blocs were still dominant.

In the inter-bloc order, all of these international organizations were understood to derive their legitimacy from national state entities. However, the United Nations Charter, the Universal Declaration of Human Rights, the Genocide Convention and other aspects of the evolving framework of international law had created a 'universal' legitimation framework, a foundation for 'global' order, based on individual human beings as well as states. Although established by states, this framework always had the potential to go beyond them: a tension between historic nation-statist and emergent globalist definitions was built into international state forms themselves. Before 1989, however, this tension was largely contained by the bloc-system.

The idea of a divergence between real and formal statehood has therefore been widely understood in the past half century. Following ideas of imperialism and dependency, it has been grasped, however, more as a disparity between economic and juridical statehood, than as a manifestation of transformed relations of violence. Only in relatively recent times have the latter come to be seen as the main problem, for example in the examination of 'quasi-states'. Jackson has argued that 'The juridical cart is now before the empirical horse', because 'Ramshackle states today . . . are not allowed to disappear juridically – even if to all intents and purposes they have already fallen or been pulled down in fact. They cannot be deprived of sovereignty as a result of war, conquest, partition or colonialism such as frequently happened in the past.'[6]

And yet states that face organized challenges to the monopoly of legitimate violence within their territory are only one case of how contemporary 'nation-states' fail to correspond to the classic idea of the nation-state. States which face no such organized challenges, but which have overwhelmingly pooled their armed and authoritative resources within a larger bloc, are no less cases of this contemporary gap. In order to grasp contemporary statehood in its complexity, we need first to conceptualize the major categories of bordered centres of state power within which the authoritative control of violence is coordinated. These are, therefore, the three main types of state in the contemporary world (although there are also other kinds of 'state' entities which do not constitute distinct centres). In the following sections I shall discuss how these three kinds of state relate to the global layer of state power.

The global-Western state-conglomerate

Of the first main type of state, there is only one example. The globalized Western state-conglomerate, or global-Western state for short, is an integrated authoritative organization of violence which includes a large number of both juridically defined states and international interstate organizations. This centre of state power is an outgrowth from the bloc-state of the Cold War, but in many respects

[6] Jackson (1990: 23–4).

its evolving twenty-first-century form is *sui generis*. Many core features of this Western state originated in its earlier 'bloc' form, but it is being substantially developed in the processes of global transformation. This organization of violence should be considered as a new type of state – rather than as an alliance or a complex set of alliances of states – for a number of reasons.

First and most critically, the Western state functions as a single centre of military state power in relation to other centres. It has functioned in this way over a considerable period of time and in relation to different adversaries. The core nation-states of the bloc (USA, UK, France) fought an integrated campaign in the Second World War. The bloc itself matured during the Cold War against the Soviet bloc. Since 1989 it has operated against a wide range of other state centres, most notably against Iraq in 1991 and Serbia in 1999.

Second, the integration of what are conventionally considered distinct 'states' into the Western state is now multiply determined by a complex, overlapping set of relations and institutions. The relations of the formally distinct centres of state power are mediated by highly developed and still extending linkages of economic and cultural as well as military-political kinds. The institutions involved also include dense, fast-evolving webs of bilateral as well as multilateral relations.

Third, the Western state's authoritative deployment of violence is now structurally reinforced by its increasing, if problematic integration with the legitimate international and world authority-structure of the United Nations. Not only is Western state power exercised worldwide, but it has a general (if strongly contested) global legitimacy.

The global-Western state, as a centre of power, includes the juridical 'states' of North America, Western Europe, Japan and Australasia. Although this centre's most defining institutional networks are military alliances which bind together most of the entities, the Western state clearly includes not only states which are formal military allies, but 'neutral' states bound to the larger West in other ways. This inclusion is recognized in the membership of some 'neutrals' in the European Union and the latter's edging towards military roles within the larger West. While the defining relationships of the Western state as a whole are its military relations with other centres, inclusion within the conglomerate cannot be reduced to any one institutional form, even membership of NATO and other military alliances centred on the United States.

The criteria of inclusion can be defined, rather, as that, first, entities of the Western state depend on it as a centre of violence *and* second, that their potential to act as organizing centres of legitimate violence in their own rights is clearly subordinated to this dependence. Thus most member-states of NATO maintain some secondary 'national' military capabilities, but alliance roles are the major context in which their military roles are determined. Clearly non-NATO entities in western Europe, including 'neutrals' like Ireland, Finland and even non-NATO, non-EU Switzerland, can be regarded as components of the Western state, because *de facto* they are militarily dependent as well as comprehensively integrated at other levels. A NATO member-state such as Turkey, on the other hand, can only be regarded as very imperfectly integrated, not only because of its lesser degree of incorporation into secondary institutional networks (e.g. excluded from the EU), but because it retains substantial military capability which could override its participation in the Western state.

In this sense too, many smaller 'states' outside the West as generally understood, especially in central and eastern Europe, Latin America, east Asia and Africa, may be seen as so closely dependent on and increasingly integrated with the Western state as not to constitute autonomous centres of state power. Most of these are much more loosely integrated, however, than those which I have defined as inside the Western state. From the point of view of understanding this state in general, however, the issue of precisely which conventional 'state' units should be seen as included is less important than how it operates. Although this state has borders which demarcate its potential for war with other states, it operates militarily, politically and juridically beyond its territorial base. This is a defining characteristic of its global role, and means that the borders of the state also shift according to the extent of incorporation of given territories and their local state apparatuses.

Thus the Western state has a territorial base (indicated above), which is defined – albeit complexly and with varying degrees of integration – by the areas controlled by its component state units. But the state both tends to expand its territorial base (for example by the expansion of NATO, the EU, etc.) and operates extraterritorially on a large scale. It can be seen as a conglomerate of state power in a way which is loosely analogous with corporate conglomerates. Corporations may take over other corporations, to produce larger and larger, more or less integrated units of commercial power, which penetrate more and more markets. Thus the Western state both incorporates, in complex ways, more and more local state machines, and penetrates territories which remain outside its full scope. The term 'bloc', used in the Cold War context, is increasingly inadequate as a way of defining the Western state. This is both because it has developed comprehensive economic, legal, social and cultural forms of integration, beyond its Cold War base, and because its world role has been significantly enhanced and modified in a 'global' context, as I discuss further below.

As we saw in chapter 3, global integration has also been indicated in the concepts of interdependence, internationalization of states within the capitalist world economy, global governance, regimes, security communities and hegemony. However, all these ways of understanding power have equated the state with the sovereign nation-state, and have failed therefore to identify the consolidation of Western state power in a larger conglomerate. All have therefore defined power relations as looser than they really are. They have focussed on the complex relations of national and international organizations within the Western conglomerate, rather than on the relations of the Western centre with other centres of state power. They have therefore missed the striking difference between nation-states within the West and outside it.

Within the Western state, national entities no longer function as classic nation-states did, as more or less autonomous quasi-monopolists of violence, power containers divided by borders of violence. Instead, nation-states are all – albeit in considerably different ways – radically internationalized by their incorporation in the larger bloc of state power. They remain accountable to democratic political institutions which are still largely national in form (although internationalized politics is growing rapidly, especially in Europe). But their core state functions are now essentially organized through institutions of the expanded bloc-state, while even nationality is redefined in terms of the 'cosmopolitan nation'.[7] In this sense too, many smaller 'states' outside the West proper, especially in central and eastern Europe, Latin America, east Asia and Africa, may be seen as so closely dependent on and increasingly integrated with the Western state as not to constitute autonomous centres of state power. The partial integration of such units with the Western state is only one

---

[7] Giddens (1998: 144–6).

instance, however, of the generally variable role of national entities which I consider further below.

As the integrated character of Western state power has been belatedly recognized, Marxist and other critics have predictably seen in it a new form of imperialism.[8] Undoubtedly, there are huge disparities of resources between the integrated Western state and even the largest non-Western centres. Figure 1, using military expenditures as a measure of state power, demonstrates the extent of Western dominance, reinforced by the substantial power of the West's regional allies. In one sense, this map understates the general economic and social differentials between West and non-West, as major non-Western states generally spend higher proportions of their gross national products on military purposes than does the West, as Figure 2 indicates. (Offsetting this, lesser costs in non-Western states, e.g. lower soldiers' wages, may mean that dollar estimates of military spending understate military capability.) Clearly, such large inequalities of power both reflect and reproduce the dominance of the Western state in the world system. The question, however, is whether 'imperialism' is a useful category for analysing this dominance.

Clearly contemporary Western power can be traced back to the historic European empires, as well as more directly to the Cold War Western bloc, often seen as 'neo-imperial' in relation to the Third World. However, if this is any kind of 'imperialism' it is considerably removed from the specific set of features associated with imperialism in classic Marxist writings: incorporation of pre-capitalist regions, export of capital, dominance of bank over industrial capital, aggressive national state capitalism, colonialism, wars of redivision.[9] If it is any kind of imperialism, it is something like Kautsky's 'ultra-imperialism' (discussed in chapter 6), with many of the progressive implications of that concept. Even in terms of Doyle's 'behavioral definition of empire as effective control, whether formal or informal, of a subordinated society by an imperial society', it is clear that 'not every form of international power can be defined as imperialism'.[10]

The global form of Western state power is based on a radical modernization, in which the imperial character of its old nation-states has been transcended. Western state power, as Table 1 shows, exhibits

[8] See for example *New Left Review* (1999).
[9] See Lenin (1973), Luxemburg (1963), Bukharin (1972).
[10] Doyle (1986: 30, 34).

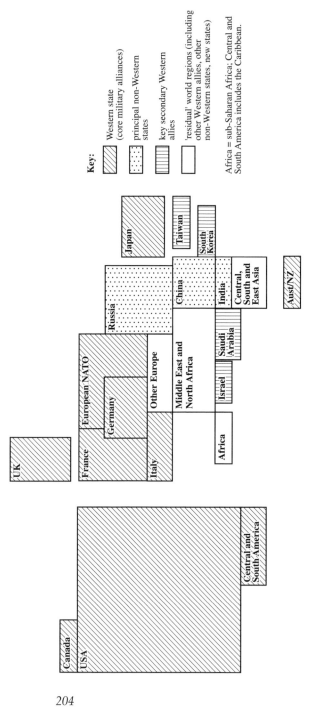

Figure 1 *Worldwide state power at the end of the twentieth century by military expenditure*

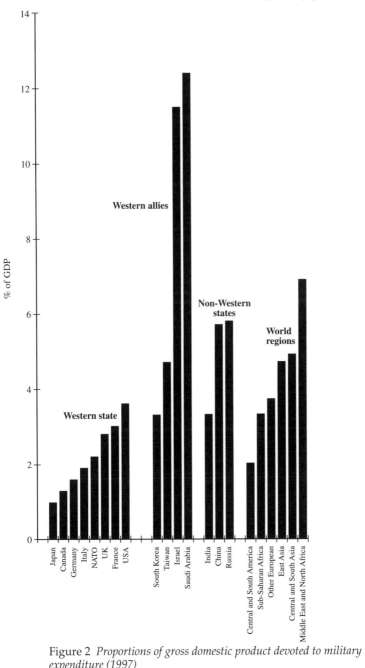

Figure 2 *Proportions of gross domestic product devoted to military expenditure (1997)*

Table 1. *Characteristics of the Western and the major non-Western states*

	Western state	Major non-Western states
Military inter-nationalization	Relatively cohesive and enduring bloc of military power, centred on NATO and other alliances (notably USA–Japan), has survived the end of the Cold War and is held together by the challenges to its common interests in the new world situation; has clearly gone beyond simple alliances of national entities.	Survival, or even development, of the historic national monopoly of violence, and the pursuit of state interests including to the point of inter- and intrastate war.
Economic inter-nationalization	An increasingly complex institutionalized framework of pan-Western political-economic organizations through which the West manages its common interests in the world economy.	Weak integration into Western-led world political-economic organizations.
Inter-nationalization of law	A framework of internationalized law and regulation through which national jurisdictions are harmonized and transnational mobility by corporations and individuals is made possible.	Weak involvement in the internationalization of law and regulation.
Regional inter-nationalization	Highly developed formal internationalization of pivotal European region; formal and substantive democratization increasingly reinforced; significant elements of internationalized citizenship are developing.	Weak, superficial internationalization at best; persistence of major regional rivalries, including in military and even nuclear forms.
Relation to global institutions	Ambivalent (especially USA), but increasingly utilizing UN system to legitimize its worldwide hegemony, and supporting extensions of international law, economic management, political and military intervention.	Ambivalent, but tending to be suspicious of Western-led international innovations; utilizing UN system negatively, to restrain West and inhibit international authority impinging on nation-state prerogatives.

Table 1. (*cont.*)

	Western state	Major non-Western states
Democratization and civil society	Political democracy normalized within West, and increasingly deeply rooted, reinforced by internationalization; relatively strong civil society; democracy and human rights promoted outside West by both civil society and states.	Authoritarian or semi-authoritarian regimes and weak democratization, in which formal electoral democracy (if it exists) is often crudely manipulated by elites; political and social freedoms are weakly recognized and enforced; civil society weak but emerging.
Social inequality and welfare	Despite large socio-economic inequalities, some combination of state and private welfare systems which supports the majority of the population.	Large socio-economic inequalities, with very inadequate or no social welfare systems, and coercion of both urban and rural society.
National and ethnic conflict	Increasingly multi-ethnic societies with relatively sophisticated mechanisms for managing national and ethnic conflicts; so that these are contained without the enormous disruptive potential which they have had in the past and continue to have outside the West.	Multi-national societies in which the relations between states and peripheral, minority and indigenous groups are quasi-imperial – these groups have little protection; national or ethnic conflicts are often violent and these are 'managed' with fairly crude coercion.
Media and propensity to war	Expanded media spheres which sensitize publics to military violence and make the management of conflict problematic for state power.	Only partially open media, in which the abilities of state elites to manage news and opinion and fight wars is greater than in the West, but not unlimited.

economic, regional and legal internationalization; formal and to some extent regional democratization are thoroughly entrenched; it has developed new means of managing national conflicts within its borders; mass mediation of conflict constrains the exercise of military power. Finally, and crucially, the dominance of Western state power is closely linked to the development of the global layer of state, legitimated by the participation of virtually all state entities and of society, which is discussed more fully below.

Quasi-imperial nation-states

If all of this makes it difficult to characterize the Western state as imperial, other states *can* more plausibly be categorized in these terms. Outside the giant Western conglomerate there remain many lesser but still large-scale centres of state power, with significant independent military capacity and scope. As Table 1 suggests, we can contrast the modernization of state power in the West with the relatively unreconstructed character of state power in some major non-Western states. It is clear that despite some democratic reform, authoritarianism is still well entrenched; internationalization and regionalization have only weakly progressed. The quasi-imperial character of many non-Western states is often a source of intense conflicts, which are often 'managed' only with brutal and indiscriminate force. Moreover, for many non-Western states, the developing global layer of state power is deeply problematic, and they are only weakly and partially integrated into it.

The second type of state can be defined, therefore, as the quasi-imperial nation-state, the kind of state centre which most approximates the classic nineteenth- and early twentieth-century model. Numerous major non-Western states, across Asia, Latin America, Africa and the Middle East, provide examples of this type at the beginning of the twenty-first century. Obviously the extent to which such states can be defined as quasi-imperial varies significantly. Nevertheless, not only the largest – Russia, China, India, Pakistan, Indonesia, Brazil, Argentina, Nigeria – but also those which are medium-sized to small in population terms – Serbia, Iran, Iraq, Saudi Arabia, Israel, Vietnam, North and South Korea, Zimbabwe – are very significant military centres. Among these states, a number possess and many have the capacity to obtain nuclear weapons. These are all 'national' centres of importance in the old sense that their rivalries remain capable of producing large-scale, conventional interstate wars. They are also, in many cases, centres whose 'internal' conflicts have the capacities to produce war.

Most contemporary 'national' states are not, indeed, mono-national. A principal reason that we can see them as resembling classical nation-states is that they approximate, to greater or lesser extents, the model of the nation-state *empire*. This is especially true of the largest non-Western states, some of which are the remnants of historic empires. Russia, indeed, once an imperial centre, then centre of a Cold War state-bloc, is now the centre of a residual 'nation-state' with a continuing imperial character. Despite having shed much of the old Russian empire as well as the expanded Soviet bloc in Europe, Russia still retains substantial non-Russian territories within its Federation. China likewise is a historic empire which has been refashioned in the twentieth century as a 'nation-state'. Similarly, India has an imperial history of its own – not only as the British Raj.

Nation-state building, in the post-colonial and Communist states of the Cold War era, has involved many quasi-imperial processes. Core ethnicities, such as the Russians and Han Chinese, dominated. Neo-colonial settlement was common, so that the Russian and Javanese populations of many peripheral areas of the former Soviet Union and Indonesia respectively now match the numbers of local ethnic groups. Centres generally exploited and/or neglected peripheries. The general authoritarianism included systematic and often ruthless discrimination against peripheral, especially indigenous, peoples such as the Naga in India or the tribes of Brazilian Amazonia. Moreover it was not only the largest states which had a quasi-imperial character: so did many of the medium-sized and even smaller centres such as Iraq, in its relationship with Kurds and the Shia Muslims of the south.

We can therefore distinguish three kinds of possible war involving quasi-imperial nation-states, prefigured in major wars of the Cold War era and demonstrated in the wars of the global transition. First, there are wars between major non-Western centres, on the model of the Iran–Iraq War or as threatened by Indo-Pakistani nuclear rivalry. Second, there are wars between non-Western centres and the Western conglomerate, as in the 1991 Gulf conflict with Iraq or the 1999 Kosova war with Serbia. Third, there are wars between state centres and proto-state forces and society 'within' quasi-imperial states, of which there are many examples. In practice, many wars are combinations of these three categories: the Yugoslav wars involved all of them.

The continuing possibility of conventional – or even nuclear – wars involving formal centres of state power gives superficial credibility to the traditional model of an anarchical interstate system. While the danger of war should be taken seriously, it can hardly be understood in terms of such a model, for two main reasons. On the one hand, the weight and character of the Western state conglomerate transform 'interstate' relations beyond the traditional model, even more than the rivalry of state-blocs did during the Cold War, so that local wars become 'global' crises. On the other, we can now see that 'interstate' rivalries, as traditionally understood, almost always involve complex relations with what are conventionally seen as 'intrastate' conflicts. Interstate wars, especially between the Western state and non-Western centres, are as likely to grow out of genocidal 'new wars' of the anti-globalist counterrevolution, as out of simple interstate rivalries.

In the global revolution, general demands for democratic freedoms have intertwined with particularist demands for autonomy from subordinated groups in these states. The dynamic relations of democracy and neo-imperialism are well demonstrated in the case of Yugoslavia, which under Tito was a multinational state with a unique system of checks and balances inhibiting simple ethnic domination. Here, the inevitability that democratic reform would lead to even greater autonomy for other nationalities contributed to the attempt of the Serbian leader, Slobodan Milosevic, to recast the Federation in a more overtly imperial form. This in turn precipitated demands for independence, in which nations were mobilized by state or proto-state elites to form new centres of state power. These conflicts resulted in war both between the newly autonomous 'states' and between the Serbian (rump Yugoslav) state and non-Serbian social groups.

Contemporary nation-states, 'interstate' conflict and war cannot be understood, therefore, without reference to conflicts and wars involving groups which are not formally or legally recognized as 'states' in international law. These conflicts have been seen traditionally as involving 'civil' as opposed to interstate wars. During both the age of empire and the Cold War period they were the most common form of war, outnumbering interstate wars (although the latter involved of course far more combatants and victims). In the global transition, they have been seen by some as involving a 'privatization' of violence, since they seem to involve both a fragmentation of traditional states and the decline of traditional revolutionary challenges to state power. However, as Kaldor points out, the new conflicts are not simply privatized; they still involve forms of politics, if not simply those of conventional states.[11]

---

[11] Kaldor (1999).

New, proto- and quasi-states

Extending this argument, we can identify a third type of state, in addition to the Western state and quasi-imperial nation-states. We can call this type 'new' centres of state power, which include proto-states. As Cederman points out, states and nations should be seen as 'emergent' actors, and we need 'explicit studies of state formation' in the historical processes after the end of the Cold War.[12] New centres can be formed in a number of different ways. They may arise directly from fragmentation of existing states, so that a previously subordinated layer of power becomes the locus of a bid for statehood. The simplest form is secession of subordinate 'national' entities during the crisis of a quasi-imperial multinational state. Principal examples come from the break-ups of the Soviet Union and Yugoslavia, where 'republics' – already defined in the previous constitution as 'national' in character – have sought to establish themselves as autonomous centres of state.

However, the emergence of new centres is not confined to entities already having a semi-sovereign character as federated republics. Clearly, the transitions in the Soviet Union and Yugoslavia also involved attempts – often supported by newly defederated republics – to create autonomous regions within other republics and to make these secede, in their turn, just as the republics seceded from the previous federation. These were often based partly on 'autonomous' provinces or districts within republics – such as the Armenian-majority enclave of Nagorno-Karabakh within Azerbaijan, or the Albanian-majority province of Kosova within Serbia. New centres have also been based, moreover, on party-defined networks, reinforced by local governments, such as those of the Serbians in Croatia and the Serbians and Croatians in Bosnia. New centres have not necessarily used either regional or local government: the Kosovans, for example, having been expelled from control of both, nevertheless created new parallel statelike institutions. They have always been based on armed force as well as political organization – either by fragmenting existing forces or by building new armed forces or militia.

Thus in both Croatia and Bosnia, Serbian power rested on parts of the Yugoslav National Army, converted into the armies of local

---

[12] Cederman (1995: 5).

Serbian parties, reinforced by local militia. Similarly, Croatian power in Bosnia rested on the Croatian army (itself an essentially new formation) together with local militia. Nascent Albanian power in Kosova depended first on the parallel administration, then on the Kosova Liberation Army. All of these claimed to be and acted as local forms of state, aspiring to recognition as sovereign entities, although they were also clearly in part extensions of larger centres and sought federation with these.

These examples show that state cannot be defined simply in terms of legitimate, internationally recognized centres of 'sovereign' power. As state power fractures and is reconstituted, the line between constitutional authority and arbitrary violence blurs. Serbian and Croatian forces within other Yugoslav republics could claim vestiges of constitutionality even as they violated legitimate republican authority and acted as warlords and genocidists. Despite all their manifest breaches of international as well as republican law, these arbitrary local regimes were recognized by the 'international community' in the Dayton settlement as the bases of new state 'entities'. Hence they gained what many regard as spurious legitimacy, in the context of new internationally legitimate 'unitary' state institutions within existing borders.

In short, warlordism and genocidal power cannot be opposed categorically to state. While statehood always involves aspirations towards legitimacy and rule-making, it is also necessarily rooted in the organization of violence. We may distinguish proto-statehood from gangsterism by its aspirations, but we need also to recognize the commonality of even the most law-regulated state with gangsterism. Both mobilize force and in its exercise, their legitimacy – whether established or aspired to – is brought into question and constantly needs to be reproduced. Even if proto-state centres of power, which have not unequivocally established their claims to authoritative statehood, are often particularly and arbitrarily violent, they are part of the phenomena of state. Established states, even the Western state, despite all their paraphernalia of legitimacy, can be even more violent, and just as arbitrary in relation to many claims of human rights. New centres of state power often present the unacceptable faces of statehood. But they are faces of statehood, none the less.

Other writers have offered threefold categorizations of contemporary statehood which partly overlap with those presented here. According to Robert Cooper, states today are 'modern', 'post-modern' and 'pre-modern'.[13] According to Georg Sørenson, they are 'Westphalian', 'post-modern' and 'post-colonial'.[14] Both these writers recognize that statehood today is not encompassed simply by the 'modern' or 'Westphalian' nation-state. On the one hand, Western 'states', they agree, are 'post-modern' in the sense that they are internationalized and no longer classic centres of war-making. On the other hand, many non-Western 'state' entities have not achieved, or have lapsed from, the levels of authoritative control over territory required for nation-statehood. In both schema, the nation-state remains as a residual category occupied by the major non-Western centres of power.

The problem of both these approaches is that they start from the sovereign state entity, rather than from bordered power centres defined by relations of violence. Their categories, although indicative, are therefore unlocated within these relations, even if the intention is to use them to analyse questions of war and peace. Thus if entities within the West are 'post-modern' in form, this is precisely because state power is increasingly concentrated in a single centre of armed power projection. If the major non-Western states are to be considered 'modern' nation-states, we must understand the quasi-imperial power relations in which they (like the former Western nation-states) are involved. And if weaker non-Western centres (not only in sub-Saharan Africa) fail to match the standards of nation-statehood, this is because of the power dilemmas which face new states and proto-states, not because they are 'pre-modern' or 'post-colonial'.

The global layer of state

I have argued that the world is now divided between three principal types of state power: the Western state, quasi-imperial nation-states, and new and proto-states (although there are other kinds of state entity, such as dependent smaller states and 'quasi-states'). The power relations between states of these three types are crucial to understanding world order. These relations are more important than what are conventionally understood to be the stuff of international relations, namely the relations between states as juridically constituted sovereign entities. This is not because legal sovereignty is unimportant. The idea of legitimate authority is a necessary element of statehood, *one* of its ingredients – although it can be more aspiration than realized fact.

---

[13] Cooper (1996).   [14] Sørenson (1997).

But sovereignty is not a *sufficient* condition for autonomous statehood in a sociological sense, as I shall discuss further later in this chapter.

At the beginning of the twenty-first century we are therefore a long way from a simple singularity of state, in the sense of the complete dominance even of a complex centre, and this will not be realized in the foreseeable future. State is not singular in the sense that all state power is concentrated in one state. Even if the trend towards incorporation of nation-states into the Western state was to accelerate to the point where all major established state entities were included, new centres would still be likely to emerge. Nevertheless, the singularity of state is already partially realized in the dominance of a single set of new norms and institutions, which more or less governs the various state centres, and which constitutes a layer of state power that overlays the different centres. Since this layer of norms and institutions is largely dependent, in turn, on the main Western centre, we may consider the trend towards a single complex of state power to be more powerful than it first appears.

The idea of a common authoritative framework within which distinct centres of state power operate is of course an old one. Within the West it can be traced back to the common order of European Christendom, and its modern form is often said to have originated in the Treaty of Westphalia. In post-1945 international relations thought this understanding has been codified in 'international society' theory.[15] According to this school, international norms condition whether given states can claim to be sovereign, and also constitute a framework within which legitimate behaviour by states is defined.

Even during the Cold War period, there was a profound development of this legitimation framework. The effectiveness of United Nations institutions may have been deeply restricted by East–West rivalry, but they nevertheless grew in significance. As the number of member-states grew with decolonization, and especially with the inclusion of Communist China, the UN was seen as increasingly representative of the political organization of worldwide humanity. As the Helsinki process cast East–West relations within a normative framework, interstate relations became increasingly embedded in a common understanding of individual and collective human rights.

Since the end of the Cold War, the authoritative layer of state has grown as a common framework to the point at which we can regard it

---

[15] For example, Bull (1977), Wight (1977).

as a *global layer* of state power. This has four main elements: global political power and legitimate force; global legal institutions, including means of enforcement; global economic, environmental and social institutions; and a global ideological framework. The development of the global layer, in all these dimensions, is not the simple elaboration of a loose framework of global 'governance', involving a loose 'multilateral' agglomeration of nation-states, international institutions and civil society actors, which we encountered in the literature (see chapter 3). This is partly because of the degree of autonomy which global institutions have achieved from the nation-state entities that comprise them. As Michael Barnett puts it, international organizations (IOs) 'are not simply passive mechanisms and handmaidens of states, rather, they can be creative, energetic, and independent entities that have agentic properties. Studies of an impressive range of international organizations . . . document how IOs have a distinct organizational culture, how IO officials have autonomy, and how IOs can act without the permission of states and in opposition to state interests.'[16]

As Barnett suggests, the key to the 'relative autonomy' of international organizations from national states is resources, especially 'knowledge and material resources'.[17] The paradox of the global layer is that, while it does indeed involve all centres of state power (as well as other organizations) to varying degrees, it is fundamentally dependent upon Western state institutions within it. The Western state is the key source of informational and financial resources, of personnel, and of political leadership. The global layer should be seen as such precisely because of its symbiotic relationship with the consolidation of the Western state as a single dominant centre in world politics and society. Likewise, as we have stressed, the Western state should be seen as more than a single neo-imperial centre because of its complex articulation with the global layer. The autonomy of the global layer is indeed 'relative': it simultaneously depends on and transforms the power of the West.

The first and most important element of the global layer is the institutional framework of legitimate global political power and its enforcement. This element is represented by the United Nations system, with a triple legitimacy deriving from the involvement of: the principal centres of state power (represented in the permanent

---

[16] Barnett (2000).   [17] Barnett (2000).

p of the Security Council of three major Western and two
Western states); virtually all juridically recognized state
̇esented in the General Assembly; and world society, the
̇ ῀οse individual members are partially recognized in the
Universal Declaration of Human Rights and advanced both by UN
agencies and by non-governmental organizations working with and
within the UN system.

Because the UN possesses this broad framework of legitimacy,
major non-Western states (especially Russia and China), smaller state
entities and non-governmental bodies all have some leverage within
it, and in balancing all these interests with the Western state, the UN
bureaucracy itself is finding some autonomous authority. However, it
is clear that the UN depends for both its resources and its political
direction on the West, and that the united West is mostly able to
mobilize the UN system to its own purposes. Despite the deeply
ambiguous relationship between the main component of the West (the
USA) and the UN, it is difficult to conceive of either without the other.
The mutual dependence of Western power and the UN system is
fundamental. Major and minor exercises of Western military power
have been legitimated through the UN; the UN has not authorized or
undertaken any significant actions against Western interests.

The second main element of the global layer is the institutional
framework of world economy and society. From the nineteenth
century onwards, Western states initiated world international institutions in order to provide frameworks for trade and investment.[18]
After 1945, the Bretton Woods system was a new Western framework
of world institutions. Bodies such as the International Monetary Fund
and the World Bank mediated, under UN auspices, between the
Western bloc's financial power and state entities across the world.
Many organizations were, however, like the Organization for
Economic Cooperation and Development and the Group of Seven,
essentially Western-bloc institutions.

In the aftermath of the Cold War, with the formal incorporation of
former Soviet-bloc-states into the world market economy, the world
layer of state economic power has been significantly expanded and
has become global in scope. In particular, the General Agreement on
Tariffs and Trade was 'globalized' as the World Trade Organization.[19]

[18] Murphy (1994).
[19] Haus (1992), Qureshi (1996), Hoeckman and Kostecki (1999).

Although the WTO remains dominated by the West and is partly a forum for resolving intra-Western economic differences, it is now more or less universally accepted as the framework for regulating trade, as China's admission in 1999 (almost as significant a step as its earlier admission to the UN) recognized. Parallel with the development of economic regulation, the emergence of environmental regimes reflected the broad thrust of this dimension of the global layer of state. Although globalization has been seen largely as driven by technology, communication and markets, it would not have been possible without the framework of global state institutions, themselves dependent on the integration of the Western state.

The third element is the developing framework of global legal institutions and means of enforcement. Although it has been true historically that 'international law reflects first and foremost the basic state-oriented character of world politics' and that there is 'no unified system of sanctions',[20] this is beginning to change. The enormous growth of both private and public international law reflects the tremendous expansion of economic and social connections of all kinds across historically discrete jurisdictions, as well as of 'international institutions and the network of rules and regulations that have emerged from them within the last generation'.[21] International law 'has not just expanded horizontally to embrace the new states which have been established . . . it has extended itself to include individuals, groups and international organizations within its scope. It has also moved into new fields covering such issues as international trade, problems of environmental protection and outer space exploration.'[22]

International law, as Malcolm Shaw emphasizes, 'is clearly much more than a simple set of rules. It is a culture in the broadest sense in that it constitutes a method of communicating claims, counter-claims, expectations and anticipations as well as providing a framework for assessing and prioritising such demands.'[23] It is also more than a culture: it is a dense framework of institutions reaching far into 'national' law, through the 'harmonization' of law (criminal as well as commercial) which, as Jarrod Wiener points out, accompanies the integration of the world economy.[24] It also possesses increasingly clear means of enforcement, partly from the parallel harmonization of national policing and extradition arrangements, but also from an

---

[20] M.N. Shaw (1997: 37, 4).   [21] M.N. Shaw (1997: 9).
[22] M.N. Shaw (1997: 38).   [23] M.N. Shaw (1997: 53).   [24] Wiener (1999).

increasing array of global legal institutions. The establishment of the International Criminal Tribunals for former Yugoslavia and Rwanda, and the agreement to establish an International Criminal Court, have taken international law enforcement into areas critical to the prerogatives of separated statehood, judging forms of rule and war-making. Not only are these Western initiatives, but they have depended overwhelmingly on the resources of Western state power.

The final main element of the global layer of state is ideological. Its key expression is the idea of the 'international community'. This ambiguous concept has become the dominant justification of action by the Western state, and extensions of the roles of global state institutions. It draws on conflicting sources of legitimation, and its indeterminacy reflects the tensions between them. On the one hand, it invokes the idea of a worldwide community of states (or international society). It develops this idea from the passive notion of a framework for states' action into the active notion of the community of states as a collective actor. In many ways this is the realization of the original ideal of the 'united nations', stunted during the Cold War. On the other hand, the idea of the international community appeals to the global idea of the commonality of humankind, with common values of human freedom and democracy. This is also legitimated, of course, in the founding documentation of the United Nations system. The ambiguity of the notion of an international community is largely that built into the UN order, although its contradictions take on new salience in the global era.

The substantive, constantly reproduced (if changing) *plurality* of states as power centres is thus complemented by an increasingly developed *singularity* of the multi-dimensional framework of global state power. This development is greatly stimulated by the growth of the Western state as a single, massive and internally highly complex centre. The consolidation of the West's pacified international space, constituted by a large number of juridically autonomous states, means that processes within this state are increasingly law-bound. A giant, increasingly dense, overlapping web of international treaties and institutions regulates this pacified complex of Western state power. The regulatory structure it has generated is not merely an internal affair. From its Western core, the impetus towards international regulation envelops most relations between all states. What some have seen as a series of discrete regimes, others as a loose framework of global governance, is thus rooted in the consolidation of the single core state framework. However, as Barnett emphasizes, the bureaucratic quality of international organization adds its own distinctive quality to global power.[25]

All centres of state power – including quasi-imperial nation-states and new states – are thus enmeshed in an increasingly important common *global layer of state*. The major non-Western states are deeply implicated: Russia and China, after all, are permanent members of the UN Security Council and thus guaranteed a pivotal status in the world legal-political order. Many of the smaller and weaker neo-nation-states, which lack the scope, capacity or will for autonomous military action, have only limited alternatives to integration with the dominant state. Those which feel most vulnerable to major non-Western powers – central and eastern European and smaller east Asian states, for example – actively seek the tightest integration possible. Even those states which are consistently opposed, politically and militarily, to Western state interests – and are thus branded as 'rogue' states – belong to many international institutions. In principle, they accept the legitimacy of these layers of state power and pay lip-service to them (thus Iraq accepted UN inspection; Serbia accepted NATO control in Bosnia and even, reluctantly, UN forces in Kosova). So too do new states, all of which seek recognition and membership within these layers. New entities may survive for periods with support from sponsor-states (for example, Republika Srpska of Bosnia, from Serbia; the Turkish republic of Northern Cyprus from Turkey) but all seek the wider recognition of the Western state and incorporation into formal United Nations institutions. It is understood that without this fuller recognition, long-term survival is problematic.

The development of layers of statehood in which all centres of state power are implicated should not disguise, however, the deeply contested nature of this process. The development of global legal, regulatory and representative institutions engenders deep conflicts of interest even between national and regional centres of the Western state itself. At the level of commercial law, for example, the principle (if not the practice) of harmonization may be relatively uncontroversial: even authoritarian regimes understand the need for stable legal frameworks for investment and trade. But the development of global legal institutions which touch on more central prerogatives of

---

[25] Barnett (2000).

independent states is much more problematic. For authoritarian and semi-authoritarian state elites, the consolidation of international law and especially law enforcement is clearly dangerous. For the elites of the Western state, it is also problematic. So although international tribunals have been established, the West and the UN have been reluctant to support and resource them – failing, for example, to enforce their arrest warrants against prominent indicted war criminals. In the setting up of the International Criminal Court, the United States sided with China – against most of the rest of the West – in blocking a genuinely independent global jurisdiction.

The central contradiction of world order, between 'international society' based on states and a global society based on individual human rights, is especially evident in the contested growth of international legal institutions. All of this underlines that the development of genuinely global layers of state remains highly contradictory, so long as the conflict between state sovereignty and global universality remains at the heart of the constitutive authoritative framework. These common layers of state become one of the arenas in which the rivalries of the major Western entities are expressed. The contradictions in the framework are a major focus of both inter- and intrastate conflict. As we shall explore in the next chapter, they are central to the conflicts of the global revolution with the different kinds of state in the global transition.

State relations and 'intervention' in globality

The emergence of global statehood – in its double senses of a global centre and global layers of state – has been both a result and a cause of changed social relations, in which state power is implicated. It is possible to distinguish two sides of these state relations: the social relations surrounding particular states, and the social relations of interstate warfare. In order to understand their transformation in the global transition, we need first to consider how these two sides developed in early periods. In the early phases of the national and international world order, social relations clustered increasingly around national centres of state power. In the later phases, states were increasingly active organizers of social relations. In the early twentieth-century heyday of rivalry between nation-state-empires, economies and societies became increasingly national rather than local or transnational. This development gave rise to the idea of 'state intervention', in which the state expanded its functions and 'intervened' in social and economic relations hitherto considered 'private'.

From the point of view of economics, this was intervention in the market. From that of sociology, however, it was a far-reaching intervention in social relations. From that of politics, it was statism in the sense of a balance of power tilted in favour of states and against society; in extreme forms, it was 'totalitarian'. All these were facets of the same process of state intervention in social arenas previously outside the scope of the state. All were linked to a great expansion of the institutional forms of state power. But to the extent that society was able to control the state, this too was through national organization. Democracy developed within the nation-state; social movements were primarily national organizations, even if they also linked internationally; likewise revolutions, however internationally conscious, were mainly attempts by national social groups to secure control of state power.

The expansion of the state and its various forms of 'intervention' went hand in hand with expanded organization of states for interstate rivalry and especially war. In this sense, the social organization needed for interstate conflict was often a driving force of greater intervention in general. A greatly expanded, industrialized mode of warfare led the processes of statization in the mode of production and society in general. In this sense, the two sides of state relations, national (or domestic) and international (war), became increasingly linked in their expansions, even as these two spheres became more tightly defined.

This sharper differentiation of the national and international spheres in modernity led, however, to another concept of state 'intervention' in international relations, normally meaning military intervention. This took three principal forms: of one territorially based state in the territory of another, of a third-party state in a conflict of two states, or of one state in a conflict within another state (i.e. a civil war). This concept of intervention has rested, however, on a simple concept of the 'sovereign' state, and as Richard Little has pointed out, 'For specialists in international relations to contribute to this debate about intervention, they will require a much more sophisticated conception of the state than the one usually relied upon.'[26] The starting-point of 'sovereignty' inhibited understanding, because most

---

[26] Little (1987).

analysis failed to recognize that sovereignty is a historical transformed and contested concept.[27]

There was, however, a common meaning in this 'external' international and military concept and the 'internal' concept of socio-economic state intervention. The state was assumed to have a definite field, either social or territorial, any movement beyond which constituted 'intervention'. Paradoxically, the principal social field of the state was understood to be the authoritative control and exercise of violence; this was the base from which states 'intervened' in other areas of social life. However, the artificiality of both boundaries was evident in the fact that it was actually the expanded military organization of states which drove both internal and external intervention. During the high national-international era, both types of intervention became normal. Nation-states expanded their interventions in domestic society just as they intervened in other territories, to expand their empires and wage war.

Even in the Cold War, there was a transformation of these state relations. The ending of war between the major nation-states of the West, even while war between blocs remained a possibility, reduced the role of the nation-state as a military centre within society. At the same time, far-reaching changes in military technology and organization – beginning with nuclear weapons – meant that state-blocs could prepare for war without mobilizing economy and society in the same 'total' manner as previously. The effect of the first change was to internationalize state relations, so that the social relations of state power shifted increasingly to the expanded field of the Western bloc. The effect of the second change was to partially de-link the two sides of state relations, since with high-technology weaponry it was no longer necessary to mobilize society to the same extent. The social relations of Cold War rivalry and of the domestic state became increasingly distinct spheres.

Even these changes, more limited than those of the global era, should lead us to question classic concepts of intervention as a way of representing state relations. The internationalization of the Western bloc-state meant that rather than one nation-state intervening in another, internationalized power became part of the real constitution of each national state apparatus. Although the distinction of domestic and international levels of power was still viable, states were no

---

[27] C. Weber (1992).

longer external to each other in any simple sense. In the early phases of this process, the distinction of bloc rivalry and domestic politics restricted internationalization largely to the former, allowing states considerable autonomy in the latter. Later, the domestic sphere was also increasingly penetrated by internationalizing tendencies, especially in Europe as the regional integration process advanced, but also, if to lesser extents, elsewhere.

Thus the concept of intervention began to lose its core meaning of territorial externality. 'Intervention' by internationalized state organizations in member-states was in an important sense internal, representing an intervention of one layer in another layer, rather than of one state centre in another centre.[28] At the same time, the concept of state intervention in society also began to lose its meaning. The national state's role in the ongoing reproduction of the national economy and society became part of its, as well as their, regular functioning. Expanded state participation in economic and social regulation became normalized; it too became internal to the economic and social spheres and thus difficult to categorize as intervention. This role also became largely dissociated from the state's military function, and hence from particular kinds of national strategic interventions in economy and society.

Hence the perception of the 'retreat of the state'.[29] But this idea was only partially valid. First, national state apparatuses retained important domestic economic functions and capacities.[30] Second, in the bloc-state, international state organizations shared economic and social regulation with national institutions. In the expansion of a liberal world economic space – managed by a range of international institutions – economic intervention also becomes a matter of intervention from one layer of state organization into another, rather than of one state into another. Thus the core meaning of intervention is modified. As the state became more deeply internationalized, so the state's domestic role lost not only its classic interventionary but also its historic national character. This old meaning remained, of course, in relations between distinct centres of state power: for intervention

---

[28] Of course, this was only true to the extent that internationalization was deep and consensual; in the Soviet bloc, real internationalization was weak and so 'bloc' interventions were experienced as imperial.

[29] Strange (1996).

[30] See Weiss (1998), Hirst and Thompson (1996).

by the West in the Soviet bloc, or of Western or Soviet-bloc-state organizations in Third World states and economies.

In the global transition, state relations are being further transformed. The new global dominance of the Western state, no longer challenged by a rival bloc, means that the world institutions which it dominates have increasingly worldwide legitimacy. The development of global layers of state power, accepted – even if problematically – by almost all national states, has the effect of consolidating a common world social space. The elements of a global economy, society and culture are strengthened by – and themselves reinforce – the globalization of the state. Clearly many economic and social relations remain embedded in nation-states, new states and the national levels of the Western state. However, emerging world markets and communications depend on the Western state and the global layers of state power to provide their infrastructure. Hence the economic, social and cultural processes normally held to constitute globalization are mutually constitutive of global state forms. The rapid advances in communications, for example, not only sometimes owe their origins to state activities but depend on a 'worldwide web' of state jurisdictions for their practicality. They also provide the impetus and means for new forms of global state integration and action.

In the global context, therefore, concepts of intervention become ever more problematic. As all states at least pay lip-service to elements of global commonality, some kinds of previously interstate issues become seen in terms akin to traditional domestic relations. This is especially true with the development of international law and the corresponding internationalization of national law and law enforcement. State leaders are becoming accountable in international law (and hence to the national courts of other states) for the conduct of their governments – as the 1999 decision by the highest British court in the case of Augusto Pinochet, the Chilean dictator, has confirmed. Hence many cases are neither purely domestic nor purely international. This old division is broken down, as the international arena is brought within the remit of lawbound statehood, and so is judged in accordance with terms which were previously thought to be specific to the domestic sphere.

In so far as state is globalized, then, society is understood as one, there is a common sphere of overlapping jurisdictions, and common norms apply. From the standpoint of the old nation-state, international legality represents new and maybe dangerous forms of intervention.

In its own terms, however, intervention as previously understood is no longer possible, since there is no simple internal–external division to breach. Intervention becomes that of one layer of state power, or of complementary components of the same layer, in another.

In increasingly globalized state relations, extraterritorial action by juridical state entities is becoming normal. Within the Western state, especially, it is a routine component of the internationalization of the state. The development of the global layer of statehood extends it worldwide. To the extent, however, that it involves action by a distinct centre of state power in the territorial basis of another centre, the old idea of intervention still has some force. The global layer of state power depends heavily on the Western state for its political rationale and effective force. In this sense, the enforcement of global state power takes the character of intervention by the Western state in other states.

The partial breakdown of the internal–external division brings the concept of international intervention closer to that of internal socio-economic intervention. But at the same time this linkage reinforces the question-mark against the continuing viability of the concept of state intervention. The worldwide policing function of global state organization can be seen as analogous to domestic policing. Global state management of the world economy can be seen as analogous to state intervention in the national economy. Global state regulation of world-wide commerce, communications and transportation can be seen as parallel to the state regulation of national infrastructure. The limited global state regulation of health, education and welfare, and its proposed expansion, can be seen as global social action similar to the social policies of national states.

The force of the concept of intervention, in international and domestic contexts, derives from the idea that the kind of state action breaches boundaries, either interstate or between social spheres. To the extent that global state organization and activity are normalized, this is no longer true. Global state action becomes part of the reproduction both of all forms of state power, and indeed of society itself, on a world scale.

Changing conditions of sovereignty

In this book I have defined statehood by the authoritative control of the means of violence. The centres of power which I have defined as states have been those bordered by actual or potential relations of violence with other centres. Thus I have defined as states both a unit which encompasses many conventional, juridically defined states – the Western state – and units which are conventionally seen as lacking in some of the legal requirements of statehood – new and proto-states. I have also argued that there is a global layer of state power which, although closely connected with the Western state, is not reducible to it, and in some senses encompasses more or less all autonomous centres.

There is thus a growing, general gap between the conventional international legal criteria of statehood – recognition by other states, membership of the United Nations – and the real definition of centres of state power. Indeed it is widely recognized that many units which constitute states by traditional criteria are not, in any full sense, autonomous states. Thus for Jackson, many such states, especially in Africa, are 'quasi-states'.[31] For Sørenson, many 'post-colonial' states are not 'Westphalian' in the sense that '[p]ositive sovereignty, the substantial capacity for self-government, is no longer a precondition for negative or formal, juridical sovereignty'.[32] As Clapham points out, 'governments agreed among themselves to pretend in many cases that the criteria for legitimate statehood were met, regardless of how evidently fictitious this pretence may have been'.[33] As in the past, 'zones of statelessness in some parts of the world have coexisted with the maintenance of an international system' in others. Clapham argues, however, that with 'the creation of a global society and especially the spread of global communications', zones of statelessness can 'impose themselves as an issue, not only on the management of the international system, but on the analysis of international relations.'[34]

Thus either because of intrinsic weakness or through effective incorporation in the larger Western state-conglomerate, most internationally recognized entities fail the major test of statehood which I have posed. This failure to accept the conventional centrality of internationally recognized legality should not be read as dismissing the significance of either juridical state units, or legal and authoritative sides of statehood in general. On the contrary, the fact that states are internationally recognized legal and political units is clearly of great importance in the constitution of both new categories of states that I have proposed. However, we cannot do what Wendt does, when as

[31] Jackson (1990).   [32] Sørenson (1997: 260).
[33] Clapham (1996: 15).   [34] Clapham (1996: 274).

Darel Paul points out, he 'explicitly relies upon sovereignty t
states in the world, and in this way sovereignty enters into the
nature of the state itself'.[35]

New states invariably aspire to international recognition as legal
and political entities. Only with such recognition can new states cash
in on the *de facto* control of territory which they achieve by military-
political means. Even if they settle for less over substantial periods,
new states are condemned to a shadowy existence, usually as political
dependencies of larger states, unless they can achieve widespread
international recognition. This is more so today, now that a global
layer of statehood has been created, than even in the recent past, when
a major state such as Communist China could be excluded from full
international recognition. Juridical statehood has thus become a
necessary – but not a sufficient – condition of achieving and sustaining
full statehood. Juridical statehood confers considerable authority and
some real power even on small and weak entities. Thus even the
smallest legally 'independent' jurisdictions have been able to exploit
their status to 'sell' the economic results of sovereignty, to corporations and rich individuals.

Sovereign statehood is only one kind of constitutional condition
which is significant in this way, of course. Some legally dependent
territories, with specific statuses different from those of the sovereign
states of which they are a part, have been similarly able to exploit
their statuses. Component units of sovereign states – regions, provinces and municipalities – are also able to exploit their formal
authoritative conditions. Indeed within the Western state, there is
extensive competition both of national and of regional and local state
units. All kinds of unit use their variable authoritative as well as
financial and other resources to tweak their competitive standing – to
secure inward investment, for example.

The sovereign state is therefore politically, economically and socially
a very significant kind of entity. Although critics of imperialism and
dependency have long dismissed the formal political independence of
post-colonial states as relatively meaningless, this position today is
truly myopic. Many state organizations have used juridical statehood
as a means to achieve substantive, military-political statehood (the
major states of south and south-east Asia, the Middle East and
Africa). Others have used it to forge successful economic and social

---

[35] Paul (1999: 227), emphasis in original.

development (the 'newly industrializing countries' of Asia). More recently, in the break-up of the Soviet bloc and Yugoslavia, some new states (the Baltic republics, Slovenia, Azerbaijan) have used juridical statehood to achieve considerable economic and political advances. In other cases, especially in Africa, Central America and much of the former USSR, much less has been achieved: this is not because sovereignty is necessarily insignificant but because other power relations render it so in these cases.

Moreover, if sovereignty no longer equates with statehood, it is a component of even its most advanced forms. Historically, the Western state came into existence through the agglomeration of previously existing sovereign nation-states. Part of the secret of the Western bloc's evolution into a permanent state-conglomerate, while the Soviet state-bloc eventually fell apart, was the very different role it accorded to sovereignty. Soviet-bloc power largely negated the sovereignty of its components: the re-achievement of the attributes of sovereignty became an aim, stated or unstated, of both national elites and popular movements inside the bloc. The bloc, and even the Soviet state itself, disintegrated into a large number of old and new sovereign units. The Western bloc-state, in contrast, involved a pooling rather than a denial of sovereignty. Certainly, it always involved radically unequal power relations between national capitals, especially in military policy. But Western sovereign units retained, and even enhanced, their real authority in domestic economic and social relations – even as they ceded authority in external military-political relations. They remained the sole, or in the European Union the principal, focus of democratic electoral legitimation. They therefore possessed real, even if unequal, voices in bloc decision-making.

The Western state has grown into a genuine power conglomerate precisely through the the development of authoritative structures from their sovereign bases. It has evolved complex overlapping international institutions, from NATO and other military organizations through a wide range of political and economic bodies. Within Europe, it has developed an unprecedentedly deep economic and political union, with complex institutions, now directly as well as indirectly legitimated. While nation-states remain conceptualized as the sovereign entities, many of the hitherto-ascribed attributes of sovereignty now belong at least partly in the international organizations of the Western state. A vast development of law- and rule-making has accompanied the growth of all these institutions. All of these changes internationalize the national institutions of the West, just as they continually draw on distinctive national contributions.

This development of authoritative power in the West fuels the larger authoritative structures of the global layer of state power. From their nineteenth-century origins, permanent international state organizations have reflected the West's need to regulate a common world-wide infrastructure for the economies of its separate imperial domains. The authoritative framework of contemporary international relations, the prehistory of which can be traced in the evolution of the European state-system, derives from the attempt of the Western victors of 1945 to consolidate their victory in a new world order. It included from the start, of course, the main non-Western victors, the Soviet Union and Nationalist China, as well as most other sovereign states. The tensions involved in proclaiming a liberal world order based on states, many of which were in no sense democratic, was evident from the start.

Although the West has dominated the elaboration of this layer, it is important to emphasize that its global legitimacy rests precisely on its representation of the vastly larger number of juridical states created in the non-Western world since 1945. Most of these entities are, of course, based on former colonial territories of Western empires, swelled in recent years by former republics of the Soviet Union and Yugoslavia. The expansion of the General Assembly of the UN from around fifty to almost two hundred member-states, many of which participate in each of the main international organizations which make up the global layer, has meant a massive, complex amplification of its structures.

The global layer is the principal, although not the only, site of regulatory and authoritative world institutions. Although some of the most powerful organizations are those of the narrower Western state, the most legitimate international institutions are those which are more broadly based. With the completion of European decolonization and the collapse of the Soviet bloc, there are now more organizations, more inclusive and more complexly interlinked within a growing framework of law.

National and international in the global era

These reflections on state forms must lead us necessarily to revisit the question of nationality-internationality. The paradox of the global era is that while, in a fundamental sense, it involves transcending the national and international, it also inescapably requires new forms of both. Far from eliminating nationality-internationality, globality can only be constituted, in important part, through their transformation. This becomes evident once we realize that the infrastructure of the global is not primarily commercial, technological or communicative, but social, cultural and above all political. If globality arises, as I have argued, through political change, including the transformation of state, it simply cannot dispense with the national-international. Equally, however, it cannot leave these categories without fundamental modification.

Our understanding of nationality-internationality has undergone two major transformations in relatively recent times. In its classic, nineteenth-century form, deepened in the era of total war, the dominant idea of nationality was of immutably antagonistic political communities. Internationality was, therefore, an essentially conflictual relation. Of course, there was always a need for cooperative relationships across national boundaries: this was reflected in the growth of interstate international organizations as well as unofficial international linkages. And yet internationalism, the ideal of cooperative internationality, remained largely an oppositional idea at least until the flowering of liberal idealism in the aftermath of the First World War.

Internationalism has gained an enormous new impetus in the second half of the twentieth century, but has been largely shorn of its idealist content. In the ideology of the Cold War Western bloc, internationalism meant alliance – hard-nosed realist cooperation by nation-states in pursuit of common interests. Embedding this kind of cooperation was an important structural change – but it represented a retreat from the more universalist internationalism of 1945. Liberal internationalism was dissociated from radical democracy, and widely compromised by its association with anti-Communist authoritarianism. Although nationality as a defining principle was brought into question by the Second World War, alliance internationalism, the essence of the dominant Western idea, reinstated this principle. It thereby pre-empted the kind of universalism which might grow into globalism.

In global transformation, nationality and internationality are once again reconfigured. National-international forms become, paradoxically, more universal. Almost all 'national' communities claim, and many achieve, either sovereign statehood or at least some advanced form of autonomy. International organizations of all kinds proliferate, societal as well as interstate. Legitimate, world-level state institutions become, as I noted above, ever more inclusive. The idea of the 'international community' dominates. Academic writers see in this the expansion of the 'international society' of states.[36]

It is quite clear, however, that these changes represent more than the extension of classical nationality-internationality. Ideas of worldwide commonality, involving a universalism which refers primarily to people rather than states, are becoming increasingly powerful. Globality is understood as loosening nationality, not simply reinforcing it. Cooperative internationality is understood not as an end in itself, but as a means towards implementing common global values, laws and standards. Internationality is understood not merely as cooperation among nations, but as a convenient form in which the worldwide cooperation of individuals and groups of all kinds can be facilitated. International law, for example, elaborates the common law of worldwide humankind, as well as law across or between nations and state-entities.

Nationality-internationality becomes, therefore, part of the infrastructure of common globality. It is displaced as the self-sufficient, dominant structural principle of worldwide social relations. Part of the widespread confusion of the terms derives from the fact that contemporary internationality is often a surrogate for globality. Legitimate global institutions are international in composition. Even globalism, the politics of globality, manifests itself in international organization – globalist campaigning organizations are, like Amnesty, international. Even the most radical globalism cannot avoid the national-international forms which are the infrastructure of globality.

The significance of the new, global meaning of nationality-internationality is often clouded by the persistence of old forms. International relations retains meaning both as interstate conflict and as interstate cooperation. There are ambiguous relationships between these older meanings and the new, and the contradictions cannot be legislated away. They are embedded in the real, often chaotic and violent politics of the emergent global world, and fought over by the forces of global revolution and counter-revolution. As we shall see in the next chapter, behind the conceptual uncertainty lies the profoundly unfinished quality of globality.

---

[36] Mayall (1990).

8   Contradictions of state power: towards the global state?

The global revolution poses fundamental problems for states of all kinds. Even the most democratic state involves the separation of power from society, and apparatuses with inherited modes of insulating themselves from accountability. Even the most internationalized state is still a particular concentration of power, and comes with the historic baggage of nationality and (usually) empire. The expansion of democracy, individual rights and an autonomous realm of civil society challenge the established modes of power in all state centres. The common, global character of the transformation challenges all states' assumptions about the particularity of their dominions.

The global revolution is rooted in society rather than in states, but its core *process* is a transformation of state relations – the social relations surrounding state institutions – and it necessarily involves major changes in state forms. State elites are not the primary social forces transforming these relations, but they are active participants in the processes. Given the physical, authoritative and infrastructural resources of states, the responses of their elites to movements for change are crucial. States are paradoxically both obstacles to global transformation *and* central means through which change comes about.

The roles of quasi-imperial nation-states, new and proto-states, the Western state and the global layer in these changes are all subject to fundamental contradictions, but of radically different kinds. Nation-states are the centres of state power least transformed in the global revolution so far, and their relatively imperial and authoritarian power structures are most challenged by its further advance. Their problems are the most fundamental and intractable, and their solution is fundamental to prospects of a peaceful transition in global order. As we have seen, the principal threats of war in the global transition are connected with the challenges to these states. Most new states emerge out of the crises of the nation-states, and so their trajectories are closely bound up with them.

The challenge of the global revolution to the Western state is more complex. It is a direct, regional[1] challenge, to develop the internal consolidation of this unprecedented conglomerate of state power in ways which satisfy the demands of society. It is also, however, an indirect, worldwide challenge. As the dominant state centre, the West is challenged to manage the contradictions of non-Western state power. Given the close interdependence of the West and the global layer of state power, it is particularly pressured to resolve these conflicts in line with global principles. The Western state conglomerate comes under contradictory pressures, therefore: from society both within and beyond the West; from non-Western states; and from its own constituent political centres, each of which responds to society in different ways.

Thus although the direct challenge of the global revolution to each type of state is radically different, the challenges are closely inter-linked. There is a worldwide crisis of state power and institutions, of which the localized contradictions of nation-states and new states are often catalysts. In these crises, the characters and roles of the dominant Western state and the global layer of state power are constantly brought into question.

Crises of the quasi-imperial nation-states

In the Western world, its original home, the classical nation-state-empire has been increasingly (if, as we shall see, unevenly) transformed into a post-imperial, internationalized, increasingly democratized component of a larger conglomerate of power. Outside the West, however, as we have seen, the nation-state form has found a new lease of life in the major centres of state power. The major nation-states, in Asia, Latin America, the Middle East and Africa, are only weakly internationalized or democratized, and are mostly quasi-imperial in character.

Both the democratic and global dimensions of world political change are fundamentally challenging not only to non-Western states,

---

[1] In the sense that the West as a whole constitutes a 'region'.

233

but to the analytical consensus on Third World politics. As Remmer points out,

> the global processes of democratization and market-oriented reform . . . began in the late 1970s, just as consensus had been achieved on the undemocratic and statist direction of politics in the Third World. Notwithstanding the survival of islands of theoretical continuity, most notably in the study of the Middle East, where scholars are still examining the roots of the authoritarian state, the predictable outcome was theoretical decay. The analytical consensus that had come to dominate the study of Asian, African, and Latin American politics had been constructed to address the rise of statist and authoritarian modes of governance. None accounted for, much less predicted, the dramatic reversal in global development trends.[2]

However, democratization should be seen not as a simple, especially not as an automatic tendency. On the contrary, democratic change has been highly contested. In some circumstances, struggles around transformation actually *intensify* the authoritarian and imperial character of states.

Although the academic literature conventionally reflected the Cold War division of the world, so that Communist and Third World politics were mostly treated separately, the fundamental problems of state power were similar in the two 'worlds'. This became clearer as the Soviet bloc splintered into nation-states, in most of which rule remained semi-authoritarian and quasi-imperial, despite the general spread of formal democratization. However, because the crises of the old Soviet Union and Yugoslavia were very acute, they have demonstrated most starkly the tensions which the global revolution stirs in quasi-imperial nation-states in general. Both were manifestly multinational and federal states: Soviet and Yugoslav versions of nationality coexisted with older ethnic versions, recognized in the republican layers of state. Although the Soviet Union ruled more or less the same territory as the old Imperial Russia, it was a new kind of imperial polity. The Stalinist state continued the political domination of Russians across eastern Europe and central Asia, but through party rule new local elites shared in power. Their autonomy increased with the normalization of Soviet power after Stalin's death in 1953, and especially under the impact of national revolts in eastern Europe. This was even more true in Yugoslavia, where despite the primacy of

---

[2] Remmer (1997: 42).

Belgrade, national-republican elites always had some autonomy, which increased rapidly after Tito's death in 1981.

The break-up of the Soviet bloc-state was stimulated, as we have seen, by openings to the Western-dominated world economy and society, the winding-down of Cold War, and the beginnings of democratic change. Democratic transformation did not advance far, however, before it was harnessed to the reinvention of authoritarian elite rule. If anything, the demise of the old Soviet state accentuated the imperial character of its residual Russian core. Tensions sharpened between the Russian elite and non-Russian elites and populations. Moscow attempted to reconstruct looser forms of quasi-imperial relationships: formally through the Commonwealth of Independent States and in practice by asserting its superiority over Ukraine in control of the former Soviet nuclear systems and naval forces; by semi-reincorporating Belarus; by using the status of Russian populations as a pretext for intervention in the Baltic republics, Moldova and elsewhere; by tacitly backing separatists within republics like Georgia; and within the Russian Federation itself, by military force, in Chechnya. Within other post-Soviet republics, too, there are semi-imperial relations between political centres in the hands of dominant nationalities and parties and populations of other ethnic groups.

The break-up of Yugoslavia shows the reinvention of the state as an imperial nation-state in even starker terms. Communist Yugoslavia was a multilateral federation with complex checks and balances, which gave some protection to minorities. Here, democratic reform led to an intensification of nationalist politics in all the republics. The responses to these challenges by the leaders of the strongest nationalities – Serbia and Croatia – produced programmes of expansion and domination. In pursuit of the aim of greater Serbia, Slobodan Milosevic launched wars in Slovenia, Croatia, Bosnia-Herzegovina and Kosova, by increasingly genocidal means. With his ambition of a greater Croatia, Franjo Tudjman pursued similar policies in Bosnia and Serbian-populated areas within Croatia.

Many nation-states across the world are more or less imperial in character, and contain potentials for similar crises. In major nation-states on the edge of democratic change, the question of whether tensions with subordinated national groups can be handled without fragmentation of the state is crucial. Democratization is a potent lever for conflict, enabling subordinate groups to express grievances and mobilize for autonomy. Thus groups such as the Chiapas movement in Mexico, the Kurdish guerrilla movement in Turkey, and separatist movements in East Timor, Aceh and Ambon in Indonesia, have emerged into open political struggle as democratization has strengthened in these major nation-states. The democratization of China may raise not only demands for Tibet's autonomy and greater democracy in Hong Kong, but secessionist movements in the Muslim north-west. The democratization of Nigeria, after prolonged military rule, could involve several breakaways.

Central states have pursued repressive policies as well as partial accommodation with insurgents or the populations supporting them. The ultimate balance between democratic reform and war is far from certain in many cases. There will always be the temptation for elites to reinvent authoritarian, imperial rule, and to resort to war as a means of extending or maintaining power. Even in established democracies, the tendency towards fragmentation and war has been manifest. Thus in India, in addition to the longstanding conflict in Kashmir, localized caste-based violence is endemic in several states. In Sri Lanka, there is a long-running war between the state and Tamil insurgents. Of course, even within the West, with more or less stable democratic national entities increasingly incorporated in international networks, the management of these challenges has proved particularly difficult. Belgium and Quebec are testimony to the intractability of these questions, while wars in Northern Ireland and the Basque country have taken decades to subdue. However, it is a striking confirmation of the relatively mature consolidation of democratic politics in the West that these conflicts are now increasingly managed so as to minimize violence. This is all too rarely the case outside the West.

In the world of quasi-imperial nation-states, therefore, global-democratic change can easily turn into its opposite, national and imperial war. Ruling elites often fear democratic reform, and seek to block, limit and manipulate it to prevent the loss of power and territorial control. They also oppose the extension and deepening of the global layer of state power, because it threatens to bring with it surveillance of the local order and its subordination to authoritative global institutions. They likewise suspect the involvement of the Western state, under pressure from Western civil society, for its tendency (however inconsistent) to support global-democratic principles in these struggles.

It would be a great error, of course, either to see the nation-state sectors of the world as homogeneous, or to see them as simply resistant to global-democratic change. Nor are these sectors equivalent to geographical regions: in each region, on the contrary, there are different kinds of state and variable dynamics of change. The surviving major national centres of power are subject to powerful economic, social and cultural, as well as political, global processes. In general, moreover, states have no choice but to engage in reform, because of the mutually reinforcing pressures of democratic and secessionist movements, Western civil society and the Western state, the development of the global layer of state, competitive economic pressures, etc. They have no real alternative but to manage the processes of change, so as to control their impact on the fundamentals of their power. In so doing, however, they risk accentuating conflict.

Dilemmas of new states

New states are formed out of struggle with, or the break-up of, existing states. The formation of a new state often involves, as we have seen, transforming an existing layer of state into a distinct centre of power. To this extent, the character of a new state is partially given by pre-existing relations and forms. However, as state institutions take on the attributes of a separate centre, especially in conflict with other centres, these relations and forms are changed. The processes by which new states are formed determine much of their development. States formed by the relatively peaceful and legal dissolution of larger entities tend to have very different relationships with society, and with other centres of state power, from those formed through war. New states do not really offer new models of development, moreover, but largely adapt the models offered by existing states, tending either towards the classic nation-state model, or towards accommodation with the Western state.

New states established through war often produce exaggerated versions of the social relations and forms of nation-states. Kaldor has described the parasitic economies of 'new wars': para-statal organizations generally do not organize or encourage production, but tax external remittances and international aid.[3] In this sense, many mini- or proto-states are themselves parasitic on larger state organizations. They depend directly on sponsoring states, or indirectly on other states whose resources they are able to siphon off through violent

---

[3] Kaldor (1999), chapter 4.

control of territory. States established in this way often present caricatures of their sponsors' nationalism and authoritarianism. Thus Serbian and Croatian statelets in Bosnia have been even more nationalist and less pluralist than their sponsor-regimes in Serbia and Croatia. Where they are based on genocidal clearances of populations, new state centres are structurally hostile to global-democratic change. Democracy in such states inevitably means little more than competition between rival ethnic-nationalist elites, as elections legitimate genocide and its consequences. Any extensive enforcement of human rights and international law would undermine their very existence, threatening to bring their entire ruling elites into international courts.[4]

The alternative model of development for new states is to seek wider international recognition, usually through as close as possible integration with the Western state and global layer. Like many existing small states and other states with weak autonomous capacity in their regional contexts, new states seek to enter Western-led international organizations as deeply and extensively as possible. The paradox here is that while new states often have strong needs to develop national forms, in order to consolidate domestic legitimacy, they often have an even greater need to internationalize, for external security and survival.

The range of new states thus offers apparently polar extremes – for example, Western-oriented Slovenia almost cheek by jowl with Republika Srpska (the Serbian entity in Bosnia), or the Baltic states and Chechnya, radically different products of Soviet dissolution. What these states have in common is that, whether their nationalism is rampant and ethnicist, or relatively muted, civic and internationalist, their long-term autonomy is generally problematic. During their periods of crisis, these (generally small) centres of state power pose serious problems of order in the state system. In general, crises are resolved through confirmation of dependence in one mode or the other. Where juridical statehood is not confirmed, such dependence – either on one of the larger nation-states (for example, Turkish Northern Cyprus) or on the internationalized Western state (the Kurdish entity in northern Iraq) – is most acute.

---

[4] The Dayton regime in Bosnia has balanced the autonomy of the ethnically defined 'entities' with very limited prosecution of war criminals and enforcement of the right to return; hence it remains an inherently unstable regime.

Evolving structure of the Western state

The contemporary Western state presents a striking contrast to all other centres of state power. It originated, as I have noted, in the Second World War alliance of the United States, the United Kingdom and the British dominions, together with the Free French and other exiled governments of Nazi-occupied Europe. After the breach in this West's wider wartime alliance with the Soviet Union, the transatlantic Western bloc-state developed through conflict in the Cold War. Defeated Japan and Germany (except for the Soviet zone) were incorporated into the bloc. Germany became with Britain the main support of the European side of transatlantic union. Japan became in time the third corner of the larger Western triangle. This was incongruous only if we think of the West in simple geographical or cultural terms. The West was, however, a world bloc of state power which had emerged from the worldwide – Asian-Pacific as well as Euro-Atlantic – struggle of the 1939–45 war. It was consolidated in the equally worldwide rivalry of the Cold War. It aimed at world dominance, in rivalry with a Soviet bloc which had similar ambitions.

Although the Western like the Soviet bloc had regional bases, it was essentially pan-regional in scope (where regions are understood in conventional continental terms). It encompassed previously separated centres in power in North America, western Europe, east Asia and also, if less centrally, Australasia. The core, military links in the bloc were pan-regional: connecting the United States with western Europe, on the one hand, and Japan, on the other. Regionalism was, however, from the beginning an important means of consolidating and integrating the components of the bloc, initially through military alliances such as NATO, SEATO (the South-East-Asia Treaty Organization), etc.

It is important to note that even these 'regional' organizations were not restricted to conventional regional memberships. On the contrary, they integrated local state entities with the core member-states of the Western bloc, so that not only were the United States and Canada members of the European-oriented NATO, but both the USA and United Kingdom were also members of SEATO. Regional organizations, within the political West, were from the start components of the larger bloc structure. As I discuss more fully below, this was as true of the economically centred European organizations as of the military alliances.

From the start, moreover, the West clustered secondary state entities around the core linkages of the major North American, western European and Japanese states. The series of networks through which this was done equally defied the distinction between regional and worldwide power. These networks built on older, pre-1945 worldwide power linkages: notably the European empires, especially those of Britain and France, reborn as the Commonwealth and Union Française respectively, and United States dominance in Latin America, reconstructed in the Organization of American States. Thus was a proliferation of nation-states combined with the bloc organization of the Cold War era. Only the development of loose 'third camp', Third World interstate politics partially contradicted this tendency.

The transitions in the Western state – from the Second World War alliance to the Cold War bloc-state and finally the globalized conglomerate of the twenty-first century – involved the larger form becoming increasingly constitutive of the national entities. Centrally, it involved integrating the nation-state's functions as an organizer of legitimate violence and authoritative rule-maker into the larger bloc structures. The primary loci of these transfers of functions were NATO and the other military institutions of the bloc. However, since state power was expanding its core roles into systematic economic regulation, the development of economic institutions such as the OECD, GATT and later the Group of Seven complemented the core military-political structures. It was extensive economic-political as well as military-political internationalization which increasingly consolidated the West as an integrated state centre.

Western linkages used to be grasped as contingent on the Cold War, and likely to disappear with it. 'It has been argued', Gier Lundestad points out, 'that almost without exception alliances do not survive the disappearance of the threat against which they are developed.'[5] Thus many saw the Western bloc as likely to break up with the dissolution of its Soviet rival. Instead, the post-Cold War period has seen a new deepening of Western (as well as wider world) integration at all levels. Part of the reason is the continuing uncertainty over the future political evolution of Russia: to this extent, 'in modified form the original rationale for NATO still exists'.[6] However, the Western state has not only maintained this role, but has developed many new ones. NATO itself has developed a broader *raison d'être*, as an organization

---

[5] Lundestad (1998: 167).
[6] Lundestad (1998: 167).

to police conflicts throughout Europe,[7] relegating the more broadly based Organization for Security and Cooperation in Europe to a largely civilian and monitoring role. Not only has the military linkage of the USA, western Europe and Japan been maintained, it has intensified, and the core NATO alliance, despite early uncertainties, has been consolidated[8] and (in Kosova) tested in war.

At the same time, the broader Western state has crystallized variously in *ad hoc* coalitions and 'contact groups' as well as through the globally legitimate institutions of the United Nations. In these guises, it has attempted to police the relations of nation-states and new states worldwide, intervening both politically and militarily in regions of crisis ranging from Palestine, Iraq, North Korea and Indonesia to central, north-east and west Africa. Politically, the West's organization is an ever more complex web of national and international organizations. Different national entities of the West have played pivotal roles at different times: while the USA has generally played the leading role, other national capitals have variously attempted to lead, such as the French in Rwanda in 1994, Canada during the Central African crisis of 1996, the UK at some stages of the Kosova crisis, and Australia in East Timor. In other situations, leadership roles have been assigned to non-Western states, such as Nigeria in the West African intervention forces in Liberia and Sierra Leone.

The Western state's economic organization has also seen further consolidation. The transformation of GATT into the World Trade Organization not only developed the infrastructure of free global trade, but strengthened the framework for resolving intra-Western disputes. The depth of economic conflict between the United States, European Union and Japan, taken in earlier periods as indicating the potential for break-up of the West,[9] remains serious and has reached the point of trade sanctions (for example in the US–EU dispute over bananas). However, overriding common interests, both of a military kind and more fundamental economic interests in global market stability, have prevented such conflicts from leading to fundamental disruption of Western unity. The development of the WTO also offers a means of incorporating non-Western centres of power: the accession of China to the organization, agreed in 1999, was widely seen as a

[7] Carr and Ifantis (1997), Gardner (1997), Brenner (1998), Yost (1998).
[8] Kaplan (1994).   [9] Mandel (1974), Kaldor (1979).

fundamental step towards a more stable framework for commercial relations between it and the West.

The West's common interest in world economic stability has also led to the Group of Seven (expanded to eight, with Russia) increasingly taking the role of world economic leadership. The G7 dealt with the immediate challenges to the West's common interest in a stable world market economy posed by the 1997–8 financial crisis in Asia, Russia and Latin America. However, as Jonathan Mitchie points out, these crises 'once again demonstrated that national governments have become increasingly at the mercy of global financial markets; yet little has been done in response to strengthen international economic institutions'.[10] It is clear that the Western state is bound together in its need to control these common economic as well as military problems. Increasingly, governments within the G7 have recognized, in principle, the need for reform of the world currency and financial systems, even it is less clear that in practice they could manage these problems effectively. However, at the beginning of the twenty-first century, a radical shift was taking place in world currency systems. With the development of the euro, there were only three major Western currencies, each of which was tending to spread, formally as well as informally, beyond its borders. (Thus small state entities in the Balkans, and even possibly East Timor, were adopting the euro; Ecuador scrapped its national currency in favour of the US dollar.) This consolidation of currencies will facilitate pan-Western, and therefore global, management of the currency system.

As we saw in chapter 3, in conventional international relations analysis, the military and economic dimensions of Western unity are understood (following the formal, juridical situation) as discrete sets of relations between a range of independent states. International organization has been grasped largely as the creation of a variety of international 'regimes' (in which each issue area is regulated by a distinct interstate agreement and enforcement agency). However, these are not simply the discrete issue areas which pluralist methodology discloses, but a complex structure of institutions through which the *same* set of common interests are organized. The pluralist approach misses the multiple, consistently overlapping as well as comprehensively institutionalized nature of the linkages between Western political centres. The same major national entities are combined in a large

---

[10] Mitchie and Grieve Smith (1999: 5).

range of international organizations. More or less the same set of national political leaders is called upon to make common decisions in a whole series of institutions. These institutions provide a highly regulated context for the common mobilization of both military and economic power. It makes little sense, therefore, to continue to regard these as separate realms. In Mann's term, the variety and plurality of regimes should be seen as the 'polymorphous crystallization'[11] of a common network of Western state power.

Nor can these common interests be conceptualized as those of transnational capital, when the linking structure is actually that of state organizations, *at the level of state*, and framed by military power. Even as we try to understand the complexity of the many different international state institutions, we need to grasp the dynamic, evolving unity of the state-conglomerate which they help comprise. I call the contemporary Western state a conglomerate, rather than a bloc, for several reasons. Bloc primarily indicates (even when used in the term bloc-state which I have employed) an adhesion of initially separate states to each other for military purposes. It is also linked historically to Cold War conditions. The continuing use of this term tends to obscure the further profound development since 1989. The Western state has become a comprehensive structure of economic and political as well as military power, including a complex set of international and national institutions, and it has developed new global roles.

The term conglomerate suggests the messy way in which these institutions combine together in the Western state, and a loose analogy with the way in which conglomerates of capital are formed. It helps to indicate both the aggregation of old national units and the uneven meshing of various layers of international integration and regulation. Conglomerate suggests, too, the lack of any simple unity in the Western state, such as would be indicated by a single formal constitutional structure. Instead, this state is constituted by complex, overlapping political relations. Although the main centre of these relations – in the US state – is clear, they have not been elaborated in a single formal structure. The Western state has evolved out of nation-states which were real, as well as juridical, power centres. This history still has major importance for state relations.

There remain, moreover, fundamental tensions between continuing US definitions of state in 'national' and European definitions in

---

[11] Mann (1993: 80).

'international' terms. Here it is of great importance that the constitutive political doctrine of the Western state, democracy, is still applied almost exclusively at the national level. State power is directly accountable overwhelmingly in these terms. International parliamentary accountability, through the European Parliament and assemblies of national parliamentarians attached to some international organizations, is still limited. In reality, most democratic accountability of the international organization of the Western state occurs through national parliaments and elections. The Western state presents therefore a paradoxical national and international structure: increasingly internationalized in its military and economic organization, but still overwhelmingly national in its politics. The West is a single state with many 'governments'. National leaders cooperate with each other to run common Western institutions and policies, but they account chiefly to separate national parliaments and electoral constituencies. The significance of this contradiction is deepened when we examine the unevenness of internationalization in the Western state, between its main national and regional political centres.

The superpower, the Union and the future of the West

The unified Western centre emerged under the undisputed leadership of the American nation-state. In the aftermath of the Second World War, as we saw in chapter 4, Germany and Japan lay comprehensively defeated and economically devastated. France and most other western European countries were restored as autonomous states by American and British armies. Even Britain was financially and militarily dependent on the United States. The revived Western world depended unprecedentedly on the economic and military might of this one power; the origins of the common state structure lay in American hegemony. The nature of the Cold War, considered as a form of war, reinforced this dominance. Only the United States could outstrip the Soviet Union in military power, maintaining a lead in prime military technologies. Britain and France developed 'independent' nuclear weapons systems – the former increasingly dependent, though, on American technology – but chiefly as political symbols of their continuing great-power status. The West was understood as an American bloc, a fact largely accepted by political leaders in Japan, West Germany and most of Europe and massaged by the 'special relationship' in Britain (but a cause of much unease in the French elite, reflected in de Gaulle's withdrawal from the military side of NATO, which continues to reverberate to this day).

Despite growing calls from European leaders for an autonomous European Union military capability, post-Cold War wars have repeatedly confirmed American leadership of the West. Modest moves towards a common European defence and security policy have not been matched by real autonomy in the exercise of military power. Even in the Yugoslav wars, despite the large numbers of French, British and other west European troops deployed, American political leadership and military power through NATO have proved decisive. Outside Europe, notably in Iraq, US dominance has been even more complete. In the early twenty-first century, the likely expansion of autonomous European military capability will still occur within the transatlantic framework.

Even in military terms, however, the idea of American hegemony is too simple to characterize relations within the Western state. The American state, for all its great military strength, cannot alone project the power necessary to control even the principal wars which the West wishes to manage. Politically, economically and even militarily, the United States needs the consistent support of the other main Western political centres to pursue these projects. Within Europe, this is achieved primarily through NATO; elsewhere, through more *ad hoc* coalitions of more or less the same forces. The projection of Western force under American leadership takes the form of constant coalition-building by US administrations. However, this appearance of *ad hoc* organization belies the underlying integration of forces, policies and institutions, through military-political alliances of over half a century's standing.

The inadequacy of a simple idea of American hegemony is underlined when we consider the balance of economic forces. While in 1945 the United States dominated the world economy, at the beginning of the twenty-first century its economic strength is rivalled by that of the European Union, and Japan's is still greater than any national economy other than the USA. For all the resilience – indeed dynamism – of the American economy, it is clearly no more than first among equals. Although America needs world markets less than do Europe and Japan, it is still interdependent with the rest of the West. It has huge worldwide interests that only a combined West can hope to manage. Economic rivalry also reinforces the USA's need for military cooperation, since (as American leaders have long recognized) unequal military burdens distort economic competition. America is decisively embedded in the wider Western state, and its dominance should be understood within this context.

Nevertheless, the clear superiority of America over all other national units has profound consequences, both for its particular role and for the general international character of the Western state. For most sections of the American power elite, world politics are still primarily understood in terms of its 'national' interest; common Western and global interests are subsumed into it. The 'international community' is seen to a considerable extent as an adjunct of American policy, not the other way round.

Although Clark endorses John Ruggie's claim that American hegemony is associated with multilateralism, transnationalism, and globalization, and that this is a reflection of its national political and economic beliefs,[12] relations between American nationalism and Western internationalism are not simply benign. In American politics, even after more than half a century of world leadership, isolationism remains a strong strand. American leaders retain a preference for bilateral arrangements and *ad hoc* coalition-building in many circumstances, because this enables them, as the strongest unit, to manoeuvre others most effectively behind their politics. This tendency in American policy inhibits the growth of formal international institutions, especially of a representative character. It leads to over-definition of the West through its military institutions, especially NATO, membership of which becomes the ultimate criterion of membership within the transatlantic zone.

Lundestad, in a survey of Euro-American relations over the past half-century, asks the revealing question, 'Why was there not more Atlantic integration?' His answer is essentially that 'there was virtually no interest in the United States in anything that would reduce American sovereignty'. The Atlantic area 'was both too small and too big for integration. On the one hand the United States had global interests and could not give too exclusive a priority to Europe over other parts of the world. On the other hand the USA would not give up any real sovereignty to anyone under any circumstances.'[13] This tendency contrasts increasingly sharply with the development of the European side of the Western state. Europe comprises many historic, still juridically discrete national state entities, and the excesses of

---

[12] Clark (1997: 132).   [13] Lundestad (1998: 148–9).

nation-statism have been seen as a key problem (especially in the case of the largest historic state, Germany). Therefore the development of the European side of the Western state has taken the form of international institution building. From the modest beginnings of the five-nation European Iron and Steel Community of 1955 has developed an institutionally complex and powerful fifteen-nation European Union. In the early twenty-first century, the Union will be expanded to include many more central and southern European members. With the 1999 launch (by eleven states) of a single European currency, the Union has taken over one of the core functions of national states in much of Europe.

Of course, the European side of the Western state is still partially constituted by powerful national entities, even as the latter are increasingly shaped by European state institutions. The paradox of the major European entities is that while on many levels they are increasingly locked into common EU institutions, they still play largely autonomous roles both in wider Western institutions (NATO, G7, etc.) and in bilateral relations with extra-European Western entities (above all the American centre, but also Japan, Australia, etc.), as well as states outside the West.

Although the European Union has emerged through institutions concerned primarily with economic matters within a limited region, we should not see it solely or even principally in economic terms, or as a simple regional development. From its origins, post-Second World War European integration has also been concerned with international institutional development, to bind European states together and prevent further wars. Europe was never simply one region among others, but the pivot of the historic conflicts of the state-system, then the centre of the Cold War. Integration was one mechanism in the consolidation of a transatlantic Western bloc, promoted by the United States as well as European elites.

We should give little credence, therefore, to the Chinese wall which the political-economic and security literatures artificially erect between the two main sides of Western institutional development in Europe. The core EU states were also core NATO members. In the aftermath of the Cold War, the EU has increasingly matured into something like a transnational polity, with the euro, common foreign policy-making, common policing of borders in the Schengen core, and the transformation of the European Parliament into a more substantial instrument of democratic accountability.

At the same time, however, the centrality of NATO and American leadership to European military policy has been reinforced. The failures of the EU in Yugoslavia in 1991–2 did not lead to more viable autonomous European military-political policies and organization, but to the deepened integration with the USA in NATO manifested in the 1999 war with Serbia. The increasingly tight linkages of the EU and NATO can be seen in two developments. First, since 1989 the EU has added more European neutrals – already integrated in the many other international institutions of the Western state – to the one (Ireland) which was already a member. During the Cold War, the European Community's close linkage with NATO was considered a barrier to membership for Sweden, Finland and Austria. In the 1990s all have not only joined, but given increasing tacit support to NATO, signing for example the EU's statement in support of NATO's war over Kosova (1999). The remaining neutrals, including Switzerland, may not be far behind. Only one European NATO member, Norway, has so far declined to join the Union.

Second, NATO and EU expansions in central Europe are closely linked. Poland, the Czech Republic and Hungary, admitted to NATO in 1999, are also prime candidates for Union membership. The wider circles of potential applicants to both key organizations of the Western state largely overlap. NATO, as a military organization, represents a narrower, although still fundamental, commitment for new member-states on the fringes of the West. EU membership, on the other hand, involves very broad economic and institutional integration, including stricter criteria of democratic political organization. The major discrepancy between memberships of the two organizations in the European region, Turkey, is a legacy of the Cold War era when America was less politically discriminating in its allies. NATO membership is a key reason why Turkey may eventually achieve membership of the EU.

The general compatibility of European and transatlantic Western integration does not mean that the tensions between them are unimportant. There are indeed three main types of contradiction. First, the economic interests of the EU and USA diverge. As the Union becomes a more integrated economic unit, European and North American interests become more distinct rivals in each other's and world markets. Second, Europe has distinct geopolitical orientations, arising from its regional location closer to Russia, the Middle East and north Africa, as well as from its historic post-imperial linkages in Asia and sub-Saharan Africa. North America, on the other hand, is much more interested in the Americas and east Asia.

Third, and possibly most important to the future development of the Western state, there are deep political divergences. In part these have to do with the very different traditions of European social democracy, and even conservatism and Christian democracy, compared with American liberalism and conservatism. These are reinforced, however, by different attitudes towards international organization, international law and the use of force. Negative wartime experiences and positive contributions of international organization in the recent development of Europe have contributed to a different kind of political culture, at both elite and popular levels. European elites, and to a lesser extent populations, have a generally supportive attitude to formal internationalization, because this is the internal experience of Union development. Of course, we should not overestimate the high-mindedness of European internationalism. The international culture of European institutions also fosters a sort of self-interested nationalism – different in expression, but similar in inspiration to 'pork-barrel' state and local politics in the USA.

There is however a general contradiction between American and European trajectories. This is highlighted by the way in which internationalization is transforming European society as well as state institutions. European integration involves the increasing development of a common citizenship, albeit based on national citizenship. There is also a culture, spreading (however unevenly) beyond elite social groups, in which the transcendance of national boundaries is celebrated. The transformation of citizenship in Europe is undoing historic national traditions, such as those of universal military service. It is opening up traditional ethnic-national definitions of community, incorporating not only other Europeans but the non-European cultures of many migrants in a new 'multiculturalism'.

In many ways, of course, Europe is only catching up with historic American achievements, not least in developing plural concepts of community and identity. But the changes involve a dynamic of internationalization with ramifications for America, even if its national politics seems so far relatively immune. American society is clearly affected, if only since many US citizens can claim by descent one or other European national citizenship. The Europeanization of these national citizenships will mean that many Americans (and Canadians, Australians, New Zealanders, etc.) will also have citizenship rights across Europe. Indeed the little-investigated phenomenon of dual citizenship is one way in which the internationalized pan-Western state is becoming a reality for individuals.

At the level of high politics, American elites remain ambivalent about internationalization. But at other levels therefore this process is more pervasive. Since the majority of large transnational corporations are American-based, the USA has a profound interest in the internationalization of law, especially commercial law. This involves not merely the development of public international law, but the harmonization of national legislation, legal procedures and law enforcement. These processes are promoted within the European Union, but they also occur throughout the West and indeed worldwide, by the proliferation of international organizations and regimes and (relatively spontaneously) through competitive pressures on jurisdictions to ensure incoming investment. Although much of the drive in the internationalization of law comes from economic relations, it also includes the harmonization of norms relating to criminal law and human rights. As we have seen, the extradition case in 1998–2000 against Augusto Pinochet Ugarte, the former Chilean dictator, shows how national legislation in European jurisdictions provides an institutional sub-stratum for the general internationalization of law within the West and beyond. The dense extradition arrangements within the Union, in particular, are increasing the integration of law enforcement. These European-centred developments are challenges which the American state will find it difficult to avoid, given US interests in other areas of international legal development.

These Euro-American relations are the core axis in the Western state. The European Union is increasingly confirmed as the second centre of power, complementary if still subordinate to the United States. The development of other centres is increasingly refracted through this axis. As Japan's economy grew, it diversified its economic linkages, concentrated on America in the early post-war period, through European investment. As the Japanese elite have sought to consolidate their international political role, this too has led to diversification through increasing connections with Europe. Japan has been precluded even more than Germany, because of the results of the Second World War, from major regional military and political roles. Its prospects of regaining these through simple economic expansion have been checked by the late twentieth-century crisis of the Japanese economy, as well as by the growing challenge of Chinese economic and political power. Hence despite continuing nationalist tendencies in Japanese politics, elites cannot escape an interest in the wider pan-Western internationalization which increasingly emanates from Europe.

For similar reasons, internationalization is a strategic preference for elites in weaker national entities of the West. In order to offset US dominance in the regional context, the Canadian state has always maintained its British, French and wider linkages and has been disproportionately involved in international organizations. Australia and New Zealand have evolved distinctive international roles through complementary linkages to America, Britain and Japan and relatively high-profile involvements in wider international organizations. Among the smaller European entities, the Benelux countries have specialized in providing bases and personnel for the European Union and NATO, while the neutral Scandinavian countries and Switzerland have played this role for worldwide international organizations.

Within the Western state, therefore, some national entities are much more intensively internationalized than others. For all units, however, the 'national' interest is increasingly specified by international commitments. Even for the larger national units, the common Western interest in many issues is far larger than specifically national interests. These more particular interests may develop, however, through the forms of national participation in international action. If the armed forces of a particular state participate in a NATO action, their actions and experiences define a national interest as a variant of the common Western interest. Notoriously, for example, the behaviour of the Dutch battalion during the Srebrenica massacre in 1995 became a *cause célèbre* which created a particular Dutch national interest in the future of the international intervention and international justice in Bosnia.[14]

Towards a global state?

The fundamental questions posed by my analysis are to do with the relationships between the different types of centres of state power. What is the extent of Western dominance? How far do the principal non-Western states pose a limit to this dominance? What sorts of contradictions does the emergence of new states create for the Western state and the global layer? Can the synergy of the West and the global layer be said to be leading towards the consolidation of a

[14] Norbert and Both (1996).

global state? If this process is under way, what contradictions are involved, and how fundamental are they likely to prove?

During the Cold War, the existence of the Soviet bloc, other Communist states and Third World states, which attempted to isolate themselves from the world market economy, limited the effective scope of Western power. The Soviet veto in the United Nations Security Council curtailed the West's ability to utilize the global layer of state institutions. Despite all of these constraints, however, the worldwide power of the Western bloc-state during the Cold War was already extensive, and far greater than that of its Soviet rival. Formal military alliances tied some states into the West; looser formal international organizations such as the Commonwealth maintained the inclusion of Third World state elites in Western-centred networks. Political relationships, often more or less directly corrupt, maintained pro-Western, anti-Communist regimes in many states. These regimes often depended on America and other Western centres to maintain and (through counter-insurgency) defend their power. More specific arrangements, such as the education and training of military and political leaders, were also very important, although the Soviet state also competed in this arena.

These extensive networks of the Western state were in addition to the informal power relations, grasped in the widely diffused ideas of 'neo-colonialism' and 'dependency'. The absolute and relative backwardness of many non-Western societies allowed Western state and commercial interests to exercise deep economic power, tied into parallel power networks of Western-based corporations and banks. Even expatriate Western employees usually maintained extreme economic and social advantages over local populations. The links of Third World elites were often consolidated though their extensive property and financial interests in the West, as well as their desires to import affluent lifestyles – creating rich Western-style enclaves inside generally very poor societies. For these elites, barriers of citizenship had little substance, and they were able to secure Western boltholes in case of rebellions in their home countries. Many peripheral societies had broader social connections to a Western metropolis, of course, through mass immigration, often but not always following former imperial links (south Asia and the Caribbean to Britain, north Africa to France, as well as Turkey and the Balkans to Germany).

Thus despite Cold War competition, the Western bloc was already overwhelmingly the dominant world centre, even if the extent and forms of its dominance varied greatly. Despite the influence of the Soviet Union, and in the 1980s also Communist China, in the Security Council, the United Nations system as a whole reinforced and was reinforced by Western power. The UN system was largely designed, financed and staffed by Western state elites. Its institutions were physically based in North America and western Europe and used the major Western languages. Agencies which developed global economic policies, notably the IMF and World Bank, were clearly Western institutions. Certainly others – including at times the Council and General Assembly – could sometimes be mobilized by non-Western majorities. The USA and UK actually withdrew from UNESCO in the 1980s. But overall there was a large measure of congruence between the development of the Western state and of global layer of state institutions.

Two major developments have enhanced the dependence of the global layer on the West, although there are also contradictions in and limitations to this process. With the disappearance of the alternative Soviet bloc, the influence of Western state institutions (as well as of corporate power) has been greatly broadened, deepened and generalized. There is only one major 'pole' or state centre in world politics, and the attraction of it to state elites across the world, especially in smaller states, has been greatly extended. Third World elites no longer have the options of playing off Soviet and Western blocs, although they may still exploit the economic rivalries of state entities and corporations within the West. The continuing instability of the major nation-states, and their military potential, worry many smaller national elites and populations. The possibilities of attracting investment and achieving international recognition, as well as of enrichment and Western lifestyles, attract state elites.

Similarly, many non-Western populations are attracted by the protective power of the West, by its democratic ideas, and by its lifestyle. Migration to all sectors of the West is massive, and would be much larger were it not for 'fortress' policies in Europe, America and Japan. With the collapse of the Soviet Union, and China's adaptation to Western-dominated world markets, neither national elites nor their societies any longer have alternative models of social or political development. To the extent that there are variants on the dominant model, these are those of different centres and political tendencies within the West.

In the global era, the Western state operates to a considerable extent as a closed economy of wealth, power and citizenship. The West marks the boundaries of a large, relatively pacified, prosperous, democratic and law-bound social universe. These are widely acknowledged, both within and beyond its borders, as the major lines of economic and social as well as political division in the contemporary world. In a world which has seen the end of Communism, and in which 'Third World' barely remains a meaningful category,[15] the division between West and non-West is one of the most important indicators of political, social and economic inequality. This situation poses deep problems of legitimacy for Western power. However, it does not lead to simple delegitimation. The Western state has ever greater worldwide influence, resting fundamentally on the unrivalled economic, military and infrastructural power which it can mobilize. It reflects the combined economic weight of the economy within the Western sphere, and its centrality to the world economy as a whole. It reflects the more advanced technologies and higher productivity of the Western economy, and the latter's continuing centrality to the world economy. It reflects the world centrality of Western cultural and communications systems.

The West's political dominance utilizes all these advantages of Western power more generally, but it also reflects the specific ways in which they have been constructed in state institutions. Thus Western power is based upon the much more developed infrastructural capacity of the state, with sophisticated abilities to mobilize economic, technical and cultural resources for political and military power projection. It reflects the West's relatively advanced democratic political institutions, and the relations between state and society which they represent. It reflects the ideological power of Western values and ideas, with their ambiguous appeals to both elites and populations as ways of managing market economies and achieving their benefits. The West's power reflects, indeed, the relatively successful transformation of the state into post-imperial, internationalized and democratized forms, and the active processes of transformation which Western elites have undertaken. Much of this has been accomplished under the

---

[15] To the extent that 'Third World' remains meaningful it no longer indicates a specific space defined by geopolitical exclusion from First and Second Worlds. Rather, the Third World today represents the socio-economic groups and areas of socio-economic exclusion from Western-centred prosperity. The border is social rather than geopolitical and runs through the former Second and even First Worlds, as well as within the former Third World.

pressure of demands from society, both within the West and in the post-colonial and former Soviet areas of the world, as I shall discuss below. The changes have many inadequacies, but Western elites have both transformed their own internal state structures and developed ways of influencing post-colonial and post-Communist states and their elites.

The emergent global state is constituted, therefore, by the complex articulation of the globalized Western state with the global layer of state power. Neither is conceivable without the other. Although the West is able to project power worldwide, and is accepted as a dominant centre of power, with a considerable measure of legitimacy in its own right, this is also highly contested – by nation-state elites and large sections of their populations, by elites and societies which are (or during the Cold War were) engaged in national struggles against pro-Western states, and by dissident Western intellectuals. The Western state can only be a global centre through its increased ability to harness the global layer of state. The latter, in turn, is fundamentally dependent on the West and is incapable of constituting a global centre in its own right, without the West.

Limits and contradictions of global state power

Both the expanded power of the West, and its articulation with the global layer, have definite limits and involve extensive contradictions. In direct authoritative and coercive terms, the Western state is less powerful than the old formal European empires. It has greater difficulty than the old empires even in managing problems of order in relatively small, weak states, such as those of state breakdown in African countries like Somalia. It has found it very difficult to subdue 'rogue' states, such as Libya, Iraq, North Korea and Serbia, despite the considerable use or threat of military force. It cannot seriously pretend to project military power into the territories of the major non-Western states, such as Russia, China and India. Hence the contrast between intervention in Kosova and non-intervention in Chechnya, in the wars of 1999.

The relationship of the West to the global layer exacerbates the problems of Western power. Although the West is relatively united on the principle of developing global economic institutions, their practical development often brings to the fore the contradictory interests of the main Western entities. When it comes to political and legal institutions, the West is even more divided. American institutions project extremely ambivalent attitudes: although US administrations recognize in a general way the need for the legitimation which the United Nations provides, they adopt highly instrumental stances towards it, habitually withholding financial contributions and bypassing its Security Council whenever it seems unlikely to deliver the desired result. The West's divided support for the UN thus combines with the defensive stances of many non-Western states and bureaucratic inertia in the UN itself, to limit the development of the global layer.

These contradictions in Western-global power are highlighted by repeated crises in major and minor non-Western states, by each upsurge of global-democratic revolution, and by the new states which they throw up. On the one hand, these crises provoke serious divisions within the West and the UN. These in turn have led to abject failures, even in the face of relatively minor local enemies such as the warlord Aideed in Mogadishu, the *interahamwe* militia in Rwanda, and the Bosnian-Serbian army at Srebrenica. On the other hand, however, these crises are precisely what make the West *aware* of its common interests and its need for the global layer. The problems posed by unstable authoritarian, quasi-imperial nation-states, in major centres such as Russia and China as well as smaller centres, are central reasons why not only Europe and Japan but even the USA cannot afford to allow either the West or the global layer to fall apart. The ways in which even relatively small non-Western crises affect Western civil society, through television and other media, reinforce the pressure on Western state power to maintain and develop the global layer.

Theoretically it is clearly possible that the Western-global state will fracture, as other large-scale state structures have done before, most recently the Soviet bloc and before that the European world empires. Complex conflicts of interests between component national, regional and international entities will certainly provide many occasions of crisis. Nothing guarantees that these will be managed successfully, and there are many reasons for thinking Western elites seriously ill-prepared for them. However, at the same time, the emerging global structure of power cannot be judged simply according to the historical precedents. It is a novel form, not merely because of its global character, and the extensive internationalization and democratization which it involves, but also because of the relations of worldwide society which it includes.

Part IV
Conclusion

9   Politics of the unfinished revolution

If politics are about social relations in the broadest sense, as we have increasingly come to understand, they are also about power, and especially about state power. The key questions of all politics are whether, and how, the power and organization of state can be brought into harmony with the needs of society – of people in their social relations.

Classic modern answers to this question have hinged on how malleable state power in general, or in its particular forms, has been taken to be. For anarchists, the very character of the state as a distinct centre of power prevents it being useful to society. Liberals and socialists, in contrast, while often agreeing with anarchists that the concentration of power in the state is problematic, have seen it as more adaptable to social needs. They have argued instead (as in the classic socialist debate about reform and revolution) about the suitability of particular forms of state for meeting social needs or furthering social transformation.

These arguments have been about two aspects of the social relations of state institutions: how far given forms of state are necessarily linked to certain social interests, and whether they are inescapably repressive or bureaucratic. Although the location of politics within an international framework has clearly been recognized, in the modern era politics has generally been defined or understood primarily within a national context. Politics has been about how power is or could be exercised within nation-states, even if national power has been grasped as internationally linked.

In the global transition, these classic debates do not disappear, but they are necessarily redefined. If power is understood in global terms, clearly the function of the nation-state is altered, at least partially. For liberal and free-market globalizers, the perceived undermining of national state power has generally been not only inescapable, but a good thing. For radical and socialist critics of globalization, it has been fundamentally problematic. For them, globalization is primarily a phenomenon of transnational corporate power, and thus to be 're-sisted'. In this view, the undermining of national state power is a danger, notably since it leaves non-Western peoples unprotected against global or Western capital, and because it weakens the demo-cratic, welfare side of national states in the West itself. In this view, the integrated power of what I have called the Western state is barely distinguished from Cold War American 'hegemony' and 'neo-imperialism'. In a current which was still gathering momentum as the twentieth century ended, globalism was coming to be defined as an enemy of socially responsible politics.

Many recognize, of course, that these simpler negations of globalism are inadequate, and as a response to the dominant global political economy propose alternative forms of global governance. This is an altogether more progressive politics, but it still fails to address concretely how state power and political struggle are implicated in current transformations. It fails to recognize both the sharpness of the global democratic revolutionary upsurge against authoritarian state power, and the contradictory roles of Western and global state power in current conflicts. In this sense, it is an inadequate basis for a 'global' politics. An adequate politics will need, therefore, to grasp the 'unfinished' character of the democratic revolution of globality and its connection to the trajectory of the Western-global state.

Old politics and new

People's ideas are formed over periods of time and are reshaped only slowly by changing historical experiences. As Marx so cogently phrased it, 'the ideas of all the dead generations weigh like a night-mare on the brain of the living'.[1] The theoretical and political traditions of the national-international era live on, too little trans-formed by global consciousness, so that in the public debate many fall back on old ways of thought. A whole generation has not let go of mindsets, forged in the Cold War period, which are deeply problem-atic in the new situation.

---

[1] Marx (1967).

This is especially serious among those who claim to advance progressive politics. A most fundamental aspect of this is a residual Third Worldist ideology, according to which Western, especially American, 'imperialism' is the touchstone for all world politics. This approach recognizes neither the quasi-imperial character of many non-Western states nor the transformation of Western state power. Even in a situation such as that in Kosova in 1998–9, where the Serbian state was carrying out genocidal clearing of the majority population, it was the West's intervention (seen as American power) that was often identified as the main problem. Thus Edward Said's conclusion from Kosova was the rhetorical demand: 'When will the smaller, lesser, weaker peoples realize that this America is to be resisted at all costs, not pandered to or given in to naively?'[2] Whatever the real criticisms to be made of American and NATO policies in Kosova, a systematic blindness lay behind the twin beliefs that America was the principal threat and that there was no need for international action against genocide.[3]

From this viewpoint, however, non-Western states (however repressive) remain potential sites of resistance, organizers of 'underdeveloped political economies'[4] which can contest the dominant form. While sovereignty in general may be regarded as a political form of capitalist social relations,[5] the sovereignty of non-Western states must be defended from Western power. Yet to support Serbian-Yugoslav sovereignty over Kosova, or Chinese over Tibet, gives sustenance to forms of imperial domination deeply mired in blood. Critics find themselves in an inversion of the double standard of which they accuse the West: if it is right to support Timorese self-determination against Indonesian claims to sovereignty, how can the same right be denied to the Kosovans or Tibetans?[6] In these arguments, there are

---

[2] Said (1999: 75).

[3] There are of course imperial (and neo-colonial) echoes in the new globalism; but it is limiting to ascribe these to continuing American, rather than broader pan-Western, dominance, and even more to ignore the new, partial congruence between Western state interests and worldwide democratic movements.

[4] This term is used by MacLean (1999: 192–3).   [5] Rosenberg (1994).

[6] Even from a narrow juridical viewpoint it is questionable whether the Kosova case can be regarded as substantially different from that of East Timor. First, Kosova's incorporation in Serbia earlier in the century had doubtful legitimacy. Second, international decisions to recognize constituent republics of the former Yugoslavia as legitimate bases for independent states and to exclude Kosova (an autonomous province with its own representative in the federal presidency) appear arbitrary.

echoes of the intellectual left's ambiguous attitudes to Communism itself. A residual affinity for post-Communist states made NATO's attack on Serbia, and its sidelining of Russia, particularly shocking.[7] There was also a rather pious attitude to the United Nations, seen as requiring a consensus of the world's major states to act as a legitimate world centre. Thus criticisms of NATO's failure to seek UN authorization over Kosova were often disingenuous – ignoring the Russian and Chinese determination to veto action against Serbia, in the light of their own imperial repression in Chechnya, Tibet, etc.

These elements are linked to the generalized pacifism of anti-Cold War politics. In Kosova, objections to the use of airpower were compounded by complaints about 'the fastidiousness articulated about the loss of American lives', which Said was not alone in finding revolting.[8] Nevertheless, this concern too often remains at the level of abstract criticism, and fails to specify the kinds of alternative power-projection that might address the dire situations of people such as the Kosovans or Timorese. A simple pacifism was only partially viable during the Cold War (even then there were demands for 'alternative defence policies'). It does little to address the realities of global politics, in which a relatively modest use of military power may protect a threatened civilian population. Louise Arbour, then Chief Prosecutor of the International Criminal Tribunal for the Former Yugoslavia, provided a terse comment on the changing politics of peace: 'Since the creation of this Tribunal, the Rwanda Tribunal, the Rome statute . . . there is now a much more ambitious agenda: the one of peace with justice, where no one can hijack the concept of state sovereignty and use it to guarantee his own impunity. These are yesterday's visions of a peaceful world.'[9]

These changed realities have been partially recognized in the literature of academic international relations. Recent scholarship has increasingly prioritized individual human rights against the claims of

---

Third, the abuse of 'sovereignty' and constitutional order by the Serbian-Yugoslav state machine, in flagrant violation of international agreements and principles to which it had subscribed, can be held to invalidate its claims to authority.

[7] Yugoslavia held, of course, a special place in 'third camp' left-wing affections as a state between East and West which had long developed its own more market- and worker-control-oriented model of socialism. Left-wing critics ignored the way in which the unstable and self-serving character of the Russian government's position made it an unreliable partner. See for example Ali (1999).

[8] Said (1999: 75).   [9] Arbour (1999).

states, and has argued for cosmopolitan frameworks for political community.[10] In these contexts, as Ken Booth has argued, states should be seen more as the source of 'human wrongs' than of order.[11] However, this perspective, while highlighting the fundamental problems of the older statist international politics, often fails to recognize the extent to which state power must be seen as part of the solution as well as the problem.

International relationists have been, for the most part, international anarchists. They have believed not only that the world is, but also that it must necessarily remain divided between 'sovereign' political communities. Whatever their other differences, they have tended towards 'anarchophilia', agreeing that world order can only be constructed on this basis.[12] Thus answers to the problems of state violence are often sought in bypassing the state, in a position which opposes classical anarchism to its international realist mutation. For Booth, for example, 'No central government deserves much trust . . . Even decent governments are not necessarily mindful of the interests and diversity of all their citizens.' World government is dismissed as an almost totalitarian nightmare: 'The idea of centralising all power on a world scale is a fearful prospect, and not likely to work.' Security will be created, he proposes, through 'an anarchical, global "community of communities"'.[13]

Hence anarchism proves to be even more deep-rooted in international relations than first appears. Indeed a similar trend is evident in the Gramscian literature on social movements and civil society. Thus Robert Cox argues for a 'two track' strategy:

> first, continued participation in electoral politics and industrial action as a means of defensive resistance against the further onslaught of globalisation; and secondly, but ultimately more importantly, pursuit of the primary goal of resurrecting a spirit of association in civil society together with a continuing effort by organic intellectuals of social forces to think through and act towards an alternative social order at local, regional and global levels.[14]

[10] Notably Linklater (1998).
[11] Booth (1995: 103–26). For critical reflection inspired by Booth's ideas, see the essays in Dunne and Wheeler (1999).
[12] The phrase 'anarchophilia' is coined by Buzan and Little (2000).
[13] Booth (1991: 540). No contemporary proposals for world government actually propose the kind of centralization which Booth appears to envisage.
[14] Cox (1999: 28).

The mistakes in this passage are also twofold. First, the myth of globalization as threat or onslaught – which can only be resisted – is combined with the myth of the weakening of the state.[15] Second, hopes for 'an alternative social order' are vested in the 'resurrection' of civil society; but Cox himself identifies a fundamental difficulty with this scenario, 'the still small development of civil society'.[16] The expansion of civil society is indeed crucial to the long-term consolidation of a worldwide democratic order. But civil society is not only too weak to take the full weight of global transformation, it is also still too national in form.[17] Moreover, it is theoretically and practically inconceivable that we can advance emancipation without simultaneously transforming state power.[18]

While Booth explicitly rejects world government, Cox largely avoids the role of internationalized state organizations. As we saw in chapter 3, for him nation-states play 'the role of agencies of the global economy':[19] there is little understanding of the global transformations of state power, nor does he envisage a constructive role for them. Thus, critical international theorists have dug themselves into a hole. In committing themselves to 'globalization from below', as Richard Falk calls it,[20] they are tending to miss the crucial political battles over contemporary state power. Falk is certainly moving towards a new position when he writes: 'An immediate goal of those disparate social forces that constitute globalization-from-below is to *reinstrumentalize the state* to the extent that it redefines its role as mediating between the logic of capital and the priorities of its peoples, including their short-term and longer-term goals.'[21] But this tortuous language is hardly necessary, since people's movements have been attempting to make both national and international state organizations more responsive and accountable, throughout the past few decades. The real question is how could this question ever have been marginalized in any serious radical project?

It often seems that critical international theorists have left the state –

---

[15] For critiques, see Hirst and Thompson (1996) and Held et al. (1999).
[16] Cox (1999: 13).   [17] Shaw (1996: 30–70, 175–8).
[18] It is a theoretical curiosity that new 'Gramscian' thought should have been caught in the political economy/civil society trap. Gramsci's own work was clearly all too aware of the state as the ultimately defining context of political change. For a parallel argument see Germain and Kenny (1998).
[19] Cox (1999: 12).   [20] Falk (1999).
[21] Falk (1999: 150–1), emphasis added.

and war – aside.[22] Critics evacuate the harsher edges of world politics for the soft 'non-realist' territory of political economy, gender and civil society. As we have seen, no such refuge is possible. Economic and gender inequalities will not be solved so long as the repressive state is untamed. A new global social science will have to formulate its response to the continuing role of organized violence in the world order. However, while Booth is obviously correct in stating that all government is imperfect, the differences between 'relatively decent' and tyrannical government, both nationally and globally, are absolutely critical. Without addressing the nature of contemporary global state networks, and a serious discussion of the ways in which they could be developed into an adequate global authority framework sustained by and sustaining local democracies, we have hardly begun to fashion a new agenda.

Completing the global revolution

The new politics of global state power require us, therefore, to go beyond the semi-anarchist traditions of the academic discipline as well as the old anti-imperialism of the intellectual left. We need to recognize three fundamental truths. First, in the early twenty-first century people will be struggling for democratic liberties across the non-Western world, on a huge scale. Second, the old international thinking in which democratic movements are seen as purely internal to states no longer carries conviction – despite the lingering nostalgia for it on both the American right and the anti-American left. The idea that global principles can and should be enforced worldwide is firmly established in the minds of hundreds of millions of people. This consciousness will be a powerful force in the coming decades. Third, global state formation is a fact. International institutions are being extended, and they have a symbiotic relation with the major centre of state power, the increasingly internationalized Western conglomerate. The success of the global-democratic revolutionary wave depends first on how well it is consolidated in each national context – but second, on how thoroughly it is embedded in international networks of power, at the centre of which, inescapably, is the West.

---

[22] In effect, they have abandoned the state to realism – a serious mistake because realists have never had more than a superficial understanding of these problems. I have developed this argument more fully in Shaw (2000b).

From these political fundamentals, strategic propositions can be derived. First, democratic movements cannot regard non-governmental organizations and civil society as ends in themselves. They must aim to civilize local states, render them open, accountable and pluralistic, and curtail the arbitrary and violent exercise of power. These considerations are obvious to people within authoritarian and semi-authoritarian states, but are often underemphasized by civil society thinkers and activists in the West. Attacking world inequalities of social and economic power, in which Western corporations and state agencies are involved, cannot be an alternative to democratic change. On the contrary, democratic political transformation is an essential precondition of social change. Only if democratic rights are established and upheld can people struggle effectively to transform their social conditions. Of course, social struggles also reinforce democratic demands – there are no mechanical stages in transformation. A broadly social democratic agenda, far more radical than that envisaged even by globalist Western social democrats, will be required to complete the consolidation of any global democratic change.[23]

Second, democratizing local state structures is not a separate task from integrating them into Western-centred global and regional state networks. Reproducing isolated local centres of power carries with it classic dangers that new states will become centres of war, and war is the fundamental enemy of social, economic and political progress in any region. Embedding global norms and integrating new state centres with global institutional frameworks are essential to the control of violence. To put this another way, the proliferation of purely national democracies is not a recipe for peace.[24] Where national-democratic projects are dominated by self-sufficient nationalism, they lead towards war with other state centres. The choice of war as a strategic option, even if war is successful, is at least highly damaging to social progress, and at worst catastrophic. The misery of war-

---

[23] See for example Giddens (1998), where the global agenda is an add-on to an essentially national programme. I have developed this point further in Shaw (2001).

[24] Thus the key error in the argument that Western 'democracies' don't fight each other is that it ignores the effect of Western international integration which occurs for complex reasons, among which the democratic character of key states is only a part. For new states, democracy may be a necessary condition of peace, but only with integration into internationalized power networks can it become sufficient.

stricken regions in the Balkans, Caucasus and central, west and northeast Africa is testimony to this.

Third, while the global-democratic revolution cannot do without the West and the UN, neither can it rely on them at all unconditionally. We need these power networks, but we need to tame them, too, to make their messy leadership structures and bureaucracies a great deal more accountable and responsive to the needs of society worldwide. In the internationalized state apparatuses of the West, political leadership is still primarily national (but in Europe, also regional). Responses to global political crises are necessarily mediated through the national, ultimately often electoral interests of state leaders, as well as the bureaucratic politics of international organizations.

The dominance of the USA means that the responses of Western-global state power to global political crises are often inordinately dependent on 'domestic' US politics. The pull of isolationist nationalism and the self-protective instincts of US military leaders, even on an administration ideologically disposed towards global responsibility, was profound during the crises of the 1990s. Moreover, the learned political timidity of European leaders, the complexities of European Union politics and the institutionalized inertia of UN bureaucracies have all combined with US semi-detachment to make global networks of power impotent more often than they have proved effective.

The greater determination of local authoritarian centres of power, often enjoying the overt or covert support of larger centres such as Russia and China, has meant that they were often capable of prevailing against the Western-global state. The genocidal massacre at Srebrenica in 1995 is only the most prominent of the resulting failures of Western-global power.[25] Both the US President and the UN Secretary-General have apologized in Kigali for a disaster with much larger consequences, the failure of the 'international community' to prevent the Rwandan genocide. But apologies counted for little, without reforms that guaranteed the failings would not be repeated. Western leaders often seemed stronger on rhetoric than on the substance of power.

Even where Western-global power has actually been mobilized to protect civilians, its forms have reflected the political priorities of the West and the UN bureaucracy. It was often too late; thus the UN

[25] See Norbert and Both (1996).

intervention in East Timor in 1999 was not merely the conclusion of a quarter of a century of genocidal repression, but it came only after a new wave of violence by Indonesian paramilitaries had already claimed many victims. The military intervention in Kosova earlier in the same year was carried out (as Said pointed out) in a manner which protected the lives of American and other Western military personnel (to the point that there was not a single direct casualty during the campaign) but put large numbers of Albanian as well as Serb civilians at risk.

These examples underline the fundamental contradictions surrounding Western-global state power at the beginning of the twenty-first century. An increasingly integrated West finds itself in a position of inescapable dominance, and hence leadership. It is irrevocably implicated in the development of a global layer of state institutions, which both entrench but also extend Western dominance. Although an ideology of globalism has increasingly developed among Western leaders, they are uncertain and divided about the extent to which their interests lie in extending the global layer and integrating world-wide state power through it. They lack the confidence to develop (still less apply) their hesitant globalism consistently in practice. They face, moreover, other state centres, whose leaders see themselves as essentially autonomous, and who only partially recognize the necessity of integration into global institutions. Both the West and other major states face the challenge of global-democratic movements, with more consistent demands for democratic change, and of new centres of power, formed out of the struggle of democratic movements and anti-globalist counterrevolution.

Despite the widespread new rhetoric of anti-globalism, it is actually the globalist and democratic movements that have the strongest interests in consolidating global state institutions. For state institutions, even those of the West and the UN, war and genocide, oppression and poverty may be unfortunate realities, but in and of themselves they do not threaten their interests. Only for peoples threatened by violence, and those in civil society in the West who identify with them, are the prevention of war and the conquering of misery *overriding* values. The paradox is that consolidating global-democratic networks of state institutions is a necessary means through which these social interests can be defended. Only by elaborating a single, complex global structure of political authority, meshing national democracy with international integration, is there any realistic possibility of constraining large-scale violence and sustaining peaceful social development. It is the political conflict of global democracy versus anti-globalist nationalism that has already stimulated the development of those global state institutions which most reflect global principles – international policing, law and humanitarian action.

There is no certainty that the outcome of the turbulence of the early twenty-first century will be the consolidation of a stable global state framework. Theoretically it is possible that the Western state could collapse under the strain of its external pressures and internal differences. It is possible that the expansion of the global layer of state power could be halted or reversed. For reasons discussed earlier, both of these prospects seem unlikely. More probable is that there will be a sustained period of instability, in which Western-global state structures continue to develop, but without any decisive shifts in the character of the world situation. The series of crises and conflicts that began at the end of the twentieth century will continue, accompanied by extensive violence, and large numbers of people will be forced to endure great misery.

The tragedy is that it will almost certainly require such a lengthy period of struggle to complete the global revolution. By 'completion' I do not mean the realization of simple world harmony or total abolition of war, desirable as these may be. I mean that global authority networks would have been developed to the extent that they incorporated all or most major centres of power, in the kind of densely integrated structures that would strongly inhibit war. I mean that aggrieved groups in society, and ambitious proto-state organizations, would see their interests served by political mobilization within global-democratic forms, rather than by violent reconstruction of the state, and that if they did resort to violence they would usually face a real risk of effective global policing. I mean, therefore, that the present shifts towards democracy and global principles would have been more or less effectively consolidated on a world scale.

If the global-democratic revolution could be sustained towards these ends, then the historic transformations of state power in late modernity would have come to some sort of interim conclusion. These huge changes, which began in the mid-twentieth century with the exhaustion of the classic nation-state-empires, and continued at the end of the century with the ending of inter-bloc struggles, can lead towards a single, if complex and messy, agglomeration of power. State power could be far more responsive to society within this framework than in any previous state formations. This sort of power framework could begin to meet the needs of an ever more globally integrated society for a common set of political institutions. Given the available technologies of destruction, society cannot afford to return to the violent competition of separated state centres which has been normal in history.

One of the new writers of the old international relations has written that 'anarchy is what states make it'.[26] In contrast it can truly be said that globality, and the suppression of the old anarchy of national-international relations, are what *we*, the people as well as the statesmen of the world, make it. As political intellectuals we need to raise our eyes to this horizon. We need to grasp the historic drama that is transforming worldwide relationships between people and state, as well as between state and state. We need to think about how the turbulence of the global revolution can be consolidated in democratic, pluralist, international networks of both social relations and state authority. We cannot be simply optimistic about this prospect. Sadly, it will require, as I have argued, repeated violent political crises to push Western and other governments through the required reformations of world institutions.[27] This is a huge challenge; but the alternative is to see the global revolution splutter into defeat, degenerate into new genocidal wars, perhaps even nuclear conflicts. The practical challenge for all concerned citizens, and the theoretical and analytical challenges for students of society, are intertwined.

[26] Wendt (1992).
[27] One of the most troubling aspects of the West's handling of Kosova during the 1990s was the failure to respond to peaceful movements for reform, and in contrast the success of the Kosova Liberation Army in helping to provoke Western military and political intervention. This was a negative lesson for the new century, after the unprecedentedly peaceful revolutions of 1989.

References

Addison, P. (1975) *The Road to 1945*. London: Quartet.

Adorno, T. (1984) *Aesthetic Theory*. London: Routledge.

Albrow, M. (1996) *The Global Age*. Cambridge: Polity.

Ali, T. (1999) 'Springtime for NATO', *New Left Review* 234: 62–72.

Anderson, B. (1983) *Imagined Communities: Reflections on the Origin and Spread of Nationalism*. London: Verso.

Anderson, P. (1976) *Considerations on Western Marxism*. London: Verso.

(1998) *The Origins of Postmodernity*. London: Verso.

Arbour, L. (1999) Comments, *Tribunal Update*, 128 (9 June) http://www.iwpr.net.

Aron, R. (1958) *War and Industrial Society*. Oxford: Oxford University Press.

(1979) 'War and industrial society: a reappraisal', *Millennium* 7: 5–14.

Asad, T. (ed.) (1971) *Anthropology and the Colonial Encounter*. London: Ithaca.

Ash, T.G. (1983) *The Polish Revolution: Solidarity, 1980–82*. London: Cape.

(1990) *We the People: the Revolution of '89 Witnessed in Warsaw, Budapest, Berlin and Prague*. Oxford: Granta.

Barnett, M. (2000) 'Historical sociology and constructivism: an estranged past, a federated future?' in S. Hobden and J. Hobson (eds.) *Bringing Historical Sociologies into International Relations*. Cambridge: Cambridge University Press.

Baum, R. (ed.) (1991) *Reform and Reaction in Post-Mao China: the Road Through Tiananmen*. New York: Routledge.

Bauman, Z. (1990) *Modernity and the Holocaust*. Cambridge: Polity.

(1992) *Intimations of Postmodernity*. London: Routledge.

Baylis, J. and Smith, S. (1997) *The Globalization of World Politics*. Oxford: Oxford University Press.

Benjamin, W. (1970) *Illuminations*. London: Cape.

Bhaskar, R. (1978) *A Realist Theory of Science*. Hassocks: Harvester.

Bloomfield, J. (1979) *Passive Revolution: Politics and the Czechoslovak Working Class, 1945–1968*. London: Allison & Busby.

Booth, K. (1991) 'Security in anarchy: utopian realism in theory and practice', *International Affairs* 67(3): 527–46.

(1995) 'Human wrongs and international relations', *International Affairs* 71: 103–26.

(1997) 'A reply to Wallace', *Review of International Studies* 23: 371–7.

Brenner, M. (1998) *NATO and Collective Security.* London: Macmillan.

Bryson, V. (1992) *Feminist Political Theory: an Introduction.* Basingstoke: Macmillan.

Bukharin, N. (1972) *Imperialism and World Economy.* London: Merlin.

Bull, H. (1977) *The Anarchical Society.* London: Macmillan.

(1990) *Hugo Grotius and International Relations.* Oxford: Clarendon.

Burke, V. (1997) *The Clash of Civilizations: War-making and State Formation in Europe.* Cambridge: Polity.

Buzan, B. (1991) *People, States and Fear: an Agenda for International Security Studies in the Post-Cold War Era.* Hemel Hempstead: Harvester-Wheatsheaf.

Buzan, B. and Little, R. (2000) 'International systems in world history: remaking the study of international relations' in S. Hobden and J. Hobson (eds.) *Bringing Historical Sociologies into International Relations.* Cambridge: Cambridge University Press.

Buzan, B. and Wæver, O. (1993) *Identity, Migration and the New Security Agenda in Europe.* London: Pinter.

Calhoun, C. (ed.) (1994) *Social Theory and the Politics of Identity.* Oxford: Blackwell.

Carr, E. (1939) *The Twenty Years' Crisis, 1919–1939: an Introduction to the Study of International Relations.* London: Macmillan.

Carr, F. and Ifantis, K. (eds.) (1997) *NATO in the New European Order.* London: Macmillan.

Cederman, L.-E. (1995) *Emergent Actors in World Politics: How States and Nations Develop and Dissolve.* Princeton: Princeton University Press.

Cerny, P. (1990) *The Changing Architecture of Politics: Structure, Agency and the Future of the State.* London: Sage.

(1996) 'What next for the state?' in E. Kofman and G. Youngs (eds.) *Globalization: Theory and Practice.* London: Pinter, pp. 122–36.

Checkoff, J. (1994) *Ideas and International Political Change: Soviet/Russian Behavior and the End of the Cold War.* New Haven: Yale University Press.

Cheng, C. (1990) *Behind the Tiananmen Massacre: Social, Political and Economic Ferment in China.* Boulder: Westview.

Chomsky, N. (1999) *On Humanitarian War.* London: Pluto.

Clapham, C. (1996) *Africa and the International System: the Politics of State Survival.* Cambridge: Cambridge University Press.

Clark, I. (1997) *Globalization and Fragmentation: International Relations in the Twentieth Century.* Oxford: Oxford University Press.

(1999) *Globalization and International Theory.* Oxford: Oxford University Press.

Clausewitz, K. von (1976) *On War.* Princeton: Princeton University Press.

Colley, L. (1992) *Britons: Forging the Nation 1707–1837.* London: Pimlico.

Commission on Global Governance (1995) *Our Global Neighborhood*. Oxford: Oxford University Press.

Cooper, R. (1996) *The Post-modern State and the World Order*. London: Demos.

Cox, M. (ed.) (1998a) *Rethinking the Soviet Collapse: Sovietology, the Death of Communism and the New Russia*. London: Pinter.

Cox, M. (1998b) 'The end of the Cold War and why we failed to predict it' in A. Hunter (ed.) *Rethinking the Cold War*. Philadelphia: Temple University Press, pp. 157–74.

Cox, R.W. (1987) *Production, Power and World Order: Social Forces in the Making of History*. New York: Columbia University Press.

(ed.) (1997) *The New Realism: Perspectives on Multilateralism and World Order*. London: Macmillan.

(1999) 'Civil society at the turn of the millennium: prospects for an alternative world order', *Review of International Studies* 25(1): 3–28.

Cumings, B. (1981) *The Origins of the Korean War, Volume I: Liberation and the Origins of Separate Regimes, 1945–47*. Princeton: Princeton University Press.

(1990) *The Origins of the Korean War, Volume II: the Roaring of the Cataract, 1947–1950*. Princeton: Princeton University Press.

(1998) 'Warfare, security and democracy in East Asia', conference paper, Minneapolis: University of Minnesota.

Dalby, S. (1996) 'Crossing disciplinary boundaries: political geography and international relations after the Cold War' in E. Kofman and G. Youngs (eds.) *Globalization: Theory and Practice*. London: Pinter, pp. 29–42.

Davidowicz, L. (1985) *The War Against the Jews*. Harmondsworth: Penguin.

Deacon, B., with Hulse, M. and Stubbs, P. (1997) *Global Social Policy: International Organizations and the Future of Welfare*. London: Sage.

Debray, R. (1967) *Revolution in the Revolution: Armed Struggle and Political Struggle in Latin America*. New York: Monthly Review Press.

Derrida, J. (1997) reply to a question from M. Shaw at an open meeting at Sussex University. The global site, http://www.sussex.ac.uk/Users/hafa3/derrida.htm.

Desmond, C. (1983) *Persecution, East and West: Human Rights, Political Prisoners and Amnesty*. Harmondsworth: Penguin.

Deutscher, I. (1967) *The Prophet Armed: Trotsky 1917–21*. New York: Vintage.

Dicken, P. (1998) *Global Shift: Transforming the World Economy*, 3rd edn. New York: Guildford.

Doyle, M. (1986) *Empires*. London: Cornell University Press.

Doyle, M.W., Johnstone, I. and Orr, R.C. (eds.) (1997) *Keeping the Peace: Multinational UN Operations in Cambodia and El Salvador*. Cambridge: Cambridge University Press.

Dunne, T. and Wheeler, N.J. (eds.) (1999) *Human Rights in Global Politics*. Cambridge: Cambridge University Press.

Durkheim, E. (1962) *Socialism and Saint-Simon*. London: Collier-Macmillan.

Edles, L. (1998) *Symbol and Ritual in the New Spain: the Transition to Democracy After Franco*. Cambridge: Cambridge University Press.

Evans, G. and Rowley, K. (1990) *Red Brotherhood at War: Vietnam, Cambodia and Laos Since 1975*. London: Verso.

Evans, P. (1997) 'The eclipse of the state? Reflections on stateness in an era of globalization', *World Politics* 50(1): 62–87.

Evans, P., Rueschemeyer, D. and Skocpol, T. (1985) *Bringing the State Back In*. Cambridge: Cambridge University Press.

Falk, R. (1995) *On Humane Governance: Towards a New Global Politics*. Cambridge: Polity.

(1997) 'State of siege: will globalization win out?', *International Affairs*, 73(1): 123–36.

(1999) *Predatory Globalization*. Cambridge: Polity.

Fardon, R. (1995) *Counterworks: Managing the Diversity of Knowledge*. London: Routledge.

Featherstone, M. (ed.) (1990) *Global Culture: Nationalism, Globalization and Modernity*. London: Sage.

Fields, R. (1976) *The Portuguese Revolution and the Armed Forces Movement*. Westport: Praeger.

Fisera, V.-C. (ed.) (1978) *Writing on the Wall: May 1968, A Documentary Anthology*. London: Allison & Busby.

Foucault, M. (1972) *The Archaeology of Knowledge*. London: Tavistock.

(1977) *Discipline and Punish: the Birth of the Prison*. London: Allen Lane.

Frank, A.G. and Gills, B. (1993) *The World System: Five Hundred Years Or Five Thousand?* London: Routledge.

Freedman, L. (ed.) (1990) *Europe Transformed: Documents on the End of the Cold War*. London: Tri-Service Press.

Friedman, H. (1998) 'Warsaw Pact socialism: detente and the disintegration of the Soviet bloc' in A. Hunter (ed.) *Rethinking the Cold War*. Philadelphia: Temple University Press, pp. 213–32.

Friedman, J. (1994) *Cultural Identity and Global Process*. London: Sage.

Fukuyama, F. (1992) *The End of History and the Last Man*. London: Penguin.

Gaddis, J.L. (1987) *The Long Peace: Inquiries into the History of the Cold War*. New York: Oxford University Press.

(1992) *The United States and the End of the Cold War: Implications, Reconsiderations, Provocations*. New York: Oxford University Press.

Galeotti, M. (1997) *Gorbachev and his Revolution*. London: Macmillan.

Gamble, A. and Payne, T. (eds.) (1996) *Regionalism and World Order*. London: Macmillan.

Gardner, H. (1997) *Dangerous Crossroads: Europe, Russia, and the Future of NATO*. Westport: Praeger.

Garthoff, R. (1994) *The Great Transition: American-Soviet Relations and the End of the Cold War*. Washington, DC: Brookings.

Germain, R. and Kenny, M. (1998) 'The new Gramscians', *Review of International Studies* 24(1): 3–28.

Gerth, H. and Mills, C.W. (eds.) (1978) *From Max Weber: Essays in Sociology*. New York: Oxford University Press.

Giddens, A. (1972) *Politics and Sociology in the Thought of Max Weber*. London: Macmillan.

(1981) *A Contemporary Critique of Historical Materialism*. London: Macmillan.

(1985) *The Nation-state and Violence*. Cambridge: Polity.

(1990) *The Consequences of Modernity*. Cambridge: Polity.

(1991) *Modernity and Self-identity*. Cambridge: Polity.

(1998) *The Third Way*. Cambridge: Polity.

Gilbert, F. (ed.) (1975) *The Historical Essays of Otto Hintze*. Oxford: Oxford University Press.

Gill, S. (1990) *American Hegemony and the Trilateral Commission*. Cambridge: Cambridge University Press.

Gill, S. and Laws, D. (1988) *The Global Political Economy: Perspectives, Problems and Policies*. Hemel Hempstead: Harvester-Wheatsheaf.

Ginifer, J. (ed.) (1997) *Beyond the Emergency: Development Within UN Peace Missions*. London: Cass.

Goldmann, L. (1968) *The Human Sciences and Philosophy*. London: Cape.

Goode, P. (ed.) (1983) *Karl Kautsky: Selected Political Writings*. London: Macmillan.

Gough, I. (1984) *The Political Economy of the Welfare State*. London: Macmillan.

Guttman, R. and Rieff, D. (eds.) (1999) *Crimes of War*. New York: Norton.

Halliday, F. (1982) *The Second Cold War*. London: Verso.

(1990) 'The ends of cold war', *New Left Review* 180: 5–24.

(1999) *Revolution in World Politics*. London: Macmillan.

Hannerz, U. (1996) *Transcultural Connections: Culture, People, Places*. London: Routledge.

Harman, C. (1988) *The Fire Last Time: 1968 and After*. London: Bookmarks.

Hathaway, R. (1981) *Ambiguous Partnership: Britain and America, 1944–1947*. New York: Columbia University Press.

Haus, L. (1992) *Globalizing the GATT: the Soviet Union's Successor States, Eastern Europe and the International Trading System*. Washington, DC: Brookings.

Havel, V. et al. (1985) *The Power of the Powerless: Citizens Against the State in Central-Eastern Europe*. London: Hutchinson.

Held, D. (1989) *Political Theory and the Modern State: Essays on State, Power and Democracy*. Cambridge: Polity.

(1995) *Democracy and Global Order*, Cambridge: Polity.

Held, D. and McGrew, A. (1998) 'The end of the old order? Globalization and the prospects for world order', *Review of International Studies*, 24 (Special Issue): 219–44.

Held, D., McGrew, A., Goldblatt, D. and Perraton, J. (1999) *Global Transformations*. Cambridge: Polity.

Herman, E.S. and McChessney, R.W. (1997) *The Global Media: The New Missionaries of Corporate Capitalism*. London: Cassell.

Hewson, M. and Sinclair, T. (1999) *Approaches to Global Governance Theory*. New York: SUNY Press.

Hilferding, R. (1981) *Finance Capital: a Study of the Latest Phase of Capitalist Development*. London: Routledge.

Hirst, P.Q. (1997) 'The international origins of national sovereignty' in P.Q. Hirst (ed) *From Statism to Pluralism: Democracy, Civil Society and Global Politics*. London: UCL Press.

Hirst, P.Q. and Thompson, G. (1996) *Globalization in Question*. Cambridge: Polity.

Hoare, Q. and Smith, G.N. (eds.) (1971) *Selections from the Prison Notebooks of Antonio Gramsci*. London: Lawrence & Wishart.

Hobden, S. and Hobson, J. (eds.) (2000) *Bringing Historical Sociologies into International Relations*. Cambridge: Cambridge University Press.

Hobsbawm, E. (1968) *The Age of Revolution*. London: Weidenfeld & Nicolson.

(1990) *Nations and Nationalism since 1780: Programme, Myth, Reality*. Cambridge: Cambridge University Press.

(1994) *Age of Extremes: the Short Twentieth Century 1914–89*. London: Michael Joseph.

Hobsbawm, E.J. and Ranger, T. (1983) *The Invention of Tradition*. Cambridge: Cambridge University Press.

Hobson, J. (1998) 'The historical sociology of the state and the state of historical sociology in international relations', *Review of International Political Economy* 5(2): 284–320.

Hoeckman, B. and Kostecki, M. (1999) *The Political Economy of the World Trading System: From GATT to WTO*. Oxford: Oxford University Press.

Hogan, M. (1987) *The Marshall Plan: America, Britain and the Reconstruction of Western Europe, 1947–52*. Cambridge: Cambridge University Press.

(1992) *The End of the Cold War: Its Meaning and Implications*. Cambridge: Cambridge University Press.

Holden, G. (1989) *The Warsaw Pact: Soviet Security and Bloc Politics*. Oxford: Blackwell.

Hollis, M. and Smith, S. (1991) 'Beware of gurus: structure and action in international relations', *Review of International Studies* 17(4): 393–410.

(1994) 'Two stories about agency and structure', *Review of International Studies* 20(3): 214–51.

Holm, H. and Sørenson, G. (eds.) (1995) *Whose World Order?: Uneven Globalization and the End of the Cold War*. Boulder: Westview.

Horkheimer, M. and Adorno, T. (1973) *Dialectic of Enlightenment*. London: Allen Lane.

Horowitz, D. (1967) *From Yalta to Vietnam: American Foreign Policy in the Cold War*. Harmondsworth: Penguin.

Howard, M. (1980) *Clausewitz*. Oxford: Oxford University Press.

Huntington, S.P. (1996) *The Clash of Civilizations*. New York: Simon & Schuster.

Hurrell, A. (1993) 'International society and the study of regimes: a reflective approach' in V. Rittberger (ed.) *Regime Theory and International Relations*. Oxford: Clarendon, pp. 49–72.

Inayatullah, N. and Blaney, D.L. (1997) 'Knowing encounters: beyond parochialism in international relations theory' in Y. Lapid and F. Krachtowil (eds.) *The Return of Culture and Identity in International Relations*. London: Lynne Reiner, pp. 65–84.

International Institute for Strategic Studies (1998) *The Military Balance, 1998–99*. London: IISS.

Jackson, R. (1990) *Quasi-states: Sovereignty, International Relations and the Third World*. Cambridge: Cambridge University Press.

Jameson, F. (1998) *The Cultural Turn: Selected Writings on the Postmodern, 1983–1998*. London: Verso.

Jessop, B. (1989) 'Capitalism, nation-states and surveillance' in D. Held and J.B. Thompson (eds.) *Social Theory of Modern Societies: Anthony Giddens and his Critics*. Cambridge: Cambridge University Press, pp. 103–126.

Kahn, J. (1995) *Culture, Multiculture, Postculture*. London: Sage.

Kaldor, M. (1979) *The Disintegrating West*. Harmondsworth: Penguin.

(1982) 'Warfare and capitalism' in *New Left Review* (ed.), *Exterminism and Cold War*. London: Verso, pp. 261–88.

(1990) *The Imaginary War*. Oxford: Blackwell.

(ed.) (1991) *Europe from Below*. London: Verso.

(1997) 'Introduction' in M. Kaldor and B. Vashee (eds.) *New Wars*. London: Cassell, pp. 1–10.

(1998) 'Nations and blocs: towards a theory of the political economy of the interstate model in Europe' in A. Hunter (ed.) *Rethinking the Cold War*. Philadelphia: Temple University Press, pp. 193–212.

(1999) *New and Old Wars: Organized Warfare in the Global Era*. Cambridge: Polity.

Kaltefleiter, W. and Pfalzgraff, R. (eds.) (1985) *The Peace Movements in Europe and the United States*. London: Croom Helm.

Kaminski, B. (1991) *The Collapse of State Socialism: the Case of Poland*. Princeton: Princeton University Press.

Kaplan, L. (1994) *NATO and the United States: the Enduring Alliance*. New York: Twayne.

Kavan, Z. (1999) 'Civil society and anti-politics in east-central Europe' in M. Shaw (ed.) *Politics and Globalisation*. London: Routledge, pp. 113–26.

Keane, J. (1995) *Tom Paine*. London: Bloomsbury.

Keithly, D. (1992) *The Collapse of East German Communism: the Year the Wall Came Down, 1989*. Westport: Praeger.

Keohane, R.O. and Milner, H. (1993) *The Internationalization of Domestic Politics*. Cambridge: Cambridge University Press.

Keohane, R.O. and Nye, J.S. (1977) *Power and Interdependence: World Politics in Transition*. Boston: Little.

Kidron, M. (1968) *Western Capitalism Since the War*. London: Wiedenfeld & Nicolson.

Kiernan, V.G. (1998) *Colonial Empires and Armies, 1815–1960*. Stroud: Sutton.

Kilminster, R. (1998) 'Globalization as an emergent concept' in A. Scott (ed.) *The Limits of Globalization*. London: Routledge, pp. 257–83.

References

King, A.D. (ed.) (1990) *Culture, Globalization and the World-system*. London: Macmillan.

Kodama, K. and Vesa, U. (eds.) (1990) *Towards a Comparative Analysis of Peace Movements*. Aldershot: Dartmouth.

Korey, W. (1993) *The Promises We Keep: Human Rights, the Helsinki Process and American Foreign Policy*. New York: St. Martin's Press.

Lapid, Y. (1997) 'Culture's ship: returns and departures in international relations theory' in Y. Lapid and F. Kratochwil (eds.) *The Return of Culture and Identity in International Relations*. London: Lynne Reiner, pp. 3–20.

Lapid, Y. and Kratochwil, F. (eds.) (1997) *The Return of Culture and Identity in International Relations*. London: Lynne Reiner.

Larson, D. (1997) *Anatomy of Mistrust: US–Soviet Relations During the Cold War*. Ithaca: Cornell University Press.

Lenin, V.I. (1964) *Collected Works*. Moscow: Foreign Languages Publishing House.

(1967) *State and Revolution*. Moscow: Foreign Languages Publishing House.

(1973) *Imperialism: Highest Stage of Capitalism*. Moscow: Foreign Languages Publishing House.

Levinson, C. (1978) *Vodka Cola*. London: Gordon.

Lightbody, B. (1999) *The Cold War*. London: Routledge.

Linklater, A. (1998) *The Transformation of Political Community: Ethical Foundations of the Post-Westphalian Era*. Cambridge: Polity.

Little, R. (1987) 'Revisiting intervention: a survey of recent developments', *Review of International Studies* 13: 47–60.

Lomax, B. (1976) *Hungary 1956*. London: Allison & Busby.

Luckham, R. and White, G. (eds.) (1996a) *Democratization and the South: the Jagged Wave*. Manchester: Manchester University Press.

(1996b) 'Democratizing the South' in R. Luckham and G. White (eds.) *Democratization and the South: the Jagged Wave*, Manchester: Manchester University Press, pp. 1–10.

Lukács, G. (1971) *History and Class Consciousness*. London: Merlin.

Lundestad, G. (1998) *'Empire' By Integration*. Oxford: Oxford University Press.

Luxemburg, R. (1963) *The Accumulation of Capital*. London: Routledge & Kegan Paul.

MacFarlane, S. (1985) *Superpower Rivalry and Third World Radicalism: the Idea of National Liberation*. London: Croom Helm.

McGrew, A. (ed.) (1997) *Globalization and Territorial Democracy*. Cambridge: Polity.

McGrew, A. and Lewis, P.G. (eds.) (1992) *Global Politics: Globalization and the Nation-state*. Cambridge: Polity.

MacKenzie, J. (1984) *Propaganda and Empire: the Manipulation of British Public Opinion, 1880–1960*. Manchester: Manchester University Press.

MacLean, J. (1999) 'Towards a political economy of agency in contemporary international relations' in M. Shaw (ed.) *Politics and Globalisation*. London: Routledge, pp. 174–201.

MacNeill, W. (1982) *The Pursuit of Power*. Oxford: Blackwell.

Machiavelli, N. (1999) *The Prince*. Harmondsworth: Penguin.

Macpherson, C.B. (1962) *The Political Theory of Possessive Individualism*. Cambridge: Cambridge University Press.

Mandel, E. (1970) *Marxist Economic Theory*. London: Merlin.

(1974) *Europe Versus America*. London: Verso.

Mann, M. (1984) 'Capitalism and militarism' in M. Shaw (ed.) *War, State and Society*. London: Macmillan, pp. 25–46.

(1986) *The Sources of Social Power*, Volume I. Cambridge: Cambridge University Press.

(1987) 'War and social theory: into battle with classes, nations and states' in M. Shaw and C. Creighton (eds.) *The Sociology of War and Peace*. London: Macmillan, pp. 54–72.

(1988) *States, War and Capitalism*. Oxford: Blackwell.

(1993) *The Sources of Social Power*, Volume II. Cambridge: Cambridge University Press.

(1996) 'Authoritarian and liberal militarism: a contribution from historical sociology' in S. Smith, K. Booth and M. Zalewski (eds.) *International Theory: Positivism and Beyond*. Cambridge: Cambridge University Press, pp. 221–39.

(1998) 'Is there a society called Euro?' in R. Axtmann (ed.) *Globalization and Europe*. London: Pinter, pp. 184–207.

(1999) 'The dark side of democracy: the modern tradition of ethnic and political cleansing', *New Left Review* 232.

(2000) 'The polymorphous state and ethnic cleansing' in S. Hobden and J. Hobson (eds.) *Bringing Historical Sociologies into International Relations*. Cambridge: Cambridge University Press.

Marcuse, H. (1964) *One Dimensional Man: Studies in the Ideology of Advanced Industrial Society*. London: Routledge.

(1968) *Reason and Revolution*. London: Routledge & Kegan Paul.

Marwick, A. (1968) *Britain in the Century of Total War: War, Peace and Social Change 1900–67*. London: Bodley Head.

(1974) *War and Social Change in the Twentieth Century*. London: Macmillan.

(ed.) (1989) *Total War and Social Change*. London: Macmillan.

Marx, K. (1962a) *Capital*, Volume I. London: Lawrence & Wishart.

(1962b) *Capital*, Volume III. London: Lawrence & Wishart.

(1963) 'Critique of Hegel's Philosophy of Right' in T. Bottomore (ed.) *Early Writings of Karl Marx*. London: Watts.

(1965) 'Theses on Feuerbach' in K. Marx and F. Engels, *The German Ideology*. London: Lawrence & Wishart, pp. 645–7.

(1967) 'The Eighteenth Brumaire of Louis Bonaparte' in *Marx-Engels Selected Works*. Moscow: Foreign Languages Publishing House.

(1971) 'Preface' in K. Marx (ed.) *A Contribution to the Critique of Political Economy*. London: Lawrence & Wishart, pp. 19–26.

Marx, K. and Engels, F. (1965) *The German Ideology*. London: Lawrence & Wishart.

References

(1998) *The Communist Manifesto*. London: Verso.

Mastny, V. (ed.) (1992) *The Helsinki Process and the Reintegration of Europe 1986–1991: Analysis and Documentation*. London: Pinter.

Mayall, J. (1990) *Nationalism and International Society.* Cambridge: Cambridge University Press.

(ed.) (1996) *New Interventionism 1991–1994: United Nations Experience in Cambodia, Former Yugoslavia and Somalia.* Cambridge: Cambridge University Press.

Meyer, M. and Prugl, E. (eds.) (1999) *Gender Politics in Global Governance.* Lanham: Rowman & Littlefield.

Meyer, P., Rittberger, V. and Zürn, M. (1993) 'Regime theory: state of the art and perspectives' in V. Rittberger (ed.) *Regime Theory and International Relations.* Oxford: Clarendon, pp. 391–430.

Miersheimer, J. (1991) 'Back to the future: instability in Europe after the Cold War', *International Security* 15(1): 5–56.

Miliband, R. (1965) 'Marx and the State' in R. Miliband and J. Saville (eds.) *The Socialist Register 1965.* London: Merlin, pp. 278–96.

Mills, C.W. (1956) *The Power Elite.* New York: Oxford University Press.

(1958) *The Causes of World War Three.* New York: Simon & Schuster.

(1959) *The Sociological Imagination.* Harmondsworth: Penguin.

Milner, H.V. (1988) *Resisting Protectionism: Global Industries and the Politics of International Trade.* Princeton: Princeton University Press.

Mitchie, J. and Grieve Smith, J. (1999) *The Global Economy.* London: Routledge.

Morgan, E.S. (1988) *Inventing the People: the Rise of Popular Sovereignty in England and America.* New York: Norton.

Morgenthau, H.J. and Thompson, K. (1985) *Politics Among Nations: the Struggle for Power and Peace.* New York: Knopf.

Mukherjee, R. (ed.) (1993) *The Penguin Gandhi Reader.* New Delhi: Penguin.

Murphy, C.N. (1994) *International Organization and Industrial Change: Global Governance Since 1850.* Cambridge: Polity.

New Left Review (1999) 234, *The Imperialism of Human Rights*.

Nisbet, R. (1967) *The Sociological Tradition.* London: Heinemann.

Norbert, W. and Both, H. (1996) *Srebrenica: Anatomy of a War Crime.* Harmondsworth: Penguin.

O'Neill, O. (1991) 'Transnational justice' in D. Held (ed.) *Political Theory Today.* Cambridge: Polity, pp. 276–304.

(1992) 'Justice, gender and boundaries' in R. Attfield and B. Wilkins (eds.) *International Justice and the Third World.* London: Routledge, pp. 50–76.

O'Tuathail, G. (1996) *Critical Geopolitics: the Politics of Writing Global Space.* London: Routledge.

Offe, C. (1996) *Varieties of Transition: the East European and East German Experience.* Cambridge: Polity.

Ohmae, K. (1990) *The Borderless World.* London: Collins.

(1993) *The End of the Nation State.* New York: Free Press.

Owen-Vandersluis, S. (ed.) (2000) *State and Identity Construction in International Relations.* London: Macmillan.

Palan, R. (1998) 'Having your cake while eating it: how and why the state system has created offshore', *International Studies Quarterly* 42(4): 625–44.

Palan, R. and Abbott, J. (1996) *State Strategies in the Global Political Economy.* London: Pinter.

Palmier, L. (1973) *Communists in Indonesia.* London: Weidenfeld & Nicolson.

Paolini, A., Jervis, A.P. and Reus-Smit, C. (eds.) (1998) *Between Sovereignty and Global Governance: the United Nations, the State and Civil Society.* Basingstoke: Macmillan.

Parekh, B. (1989) *Colonialism, Tradition and Reform: an Analysis of Gandhi's Political Discourse.* New Delhi: Sage.

Parker, W. (1982) *Mackinder: Geography as an Aid to Statecraft.* Oxford: Clarendon.

Parkin, F. (1968) *Middle Class Radicalism.* Manchester: Manchester University Press.

Parsons, T. (1949) *The Structure of Social Action: a Study in Social Theory with Special Reference to a Group of Recent European Writers.* Glencoe, Illinois: Free Press.

(1972) *The Social System.* London: Tavistock.

Paul, D.E. (1999) 'Sovereignty, survival and the Westphalian blind alley in international relations', *Review of International Studies* 25(2): 217–32.

Pearton, M. (1982) *The Knowledgeable State.* London: Burnett Books.

Pietersee, J.N. (1988) 'A critique of world system theory', *International Sociology* 3: 251–66.

Pilger, J. (1999) 'Revealed: the amazing NATO plan, tabled at Rambouillet, to occupy Yugoslavia', *New Statesman*, 17 May: 17.

Potter, D., Goldbatt, D. and Kiloh, M. (eds.) (1996) *Democratization.* Cambridge: Polity.

Qureshi, A. (1996) *The World Trade Organisation: Implementing International Trade Norms.* Manchester: Manchester University Press.

Raina, P. (1991) *Independent Social Movements in Poland.* London: LSE.

Reinecke, W.H. (1998) *Global Public Policy: Governing Without Government?.* Washington, DC: Brookings.

Reiss, H. (ed.) (1990) *Kant's Political Writings.* Cambridge: Cambridge University Press.

Remmer, K.L. (1997) 'Theoretical decay and theoretical development: the resurgence of institutional analysis', *World Politics* 50(1): 34–61.

Rittberger, V. (ed.) (1993) *Regime Theory and International Relations.* Oxford: Clarendon.

Robertson, R. (1990) *Globalization: Social and Cultural Theory.* London: Sage.

Robinson, W.I. (1996) *Promoting Polyarchy: Globalization, USA Hegemony and Democracy.* Cambridge: Cambridge University Press.

Rosecrance, R. (1984) *The Rise of the Trading State.* New York: Basic Books.

Rosenau, J.N. (1990) *Turbulence in World Politics.* Princeton: Princeton University Press.

(1997) *Along the Domestic-Foreign Frontier.* Cambridge: Cambridge University Press.

References

Rosenau, J.N. and Czempiel, E.-O. (eds.) (1991) *Governance Without Government*. Cambridge: Cambridge University Press.

Rosenau, J.N. and Dufee, M. (1995) *Thinking Theory Thoroughly: Coherent Approaches to an Incoherent World*. Oxford: Westview.

Rosenberg, J. (1990) 'A non-realist theory of sovereignty? Giddens' *The Nation-state and Violence'*, *Millennium* 17(2): 249–60.

(1994) *The Empire of Civil Society: a Critique of the Realist Theory of International Relations*. London: Verso.

Rowbotham, S. (1992) *Women in Movement: Feminism and Social Action*. New York: Routledge.

Rowbotham, S., Segal, L. and Waininght, H. (1979) *Beyond the Fragments: Feminism and the Making of Socialism*. London: Merlin.

Ruggie, J.G. (1998) *Building the World Polity: Essays on International Institutionalization*. London: Routledge.

Said, E. (1999) 'Protecting the Kosovars?', *New Left Review* (234): 73–81.

Salvatori, M. (1979) *Karl Kautsky*. London: New Left Books.

Scholte, J.A. (1999) 'Globalisation: prospects for a paradigm shift' in M. Shaw (ed.) *Politics and Globalisation*, London: Routledge, pp. 9–22.

(2000) *Globalisation*. London: Macmillan.

Schrecker, E. (1994) *The Age of McCarthyism: a Brief History with Documents*. New York: St. Martin's Press.

Scott, A. (1990) *Ideology and the New Social Movements*. London: Unwin Hyman.

(ed.) (1998) *The Limits of Globalization*. London: Routledge.

Selm, B. (1997) *The Economics of Soviet Break-up*. London: Routledge.

Shaw, M. (1972) 'The theory of the state and politics: a central paradox of Marxism', *Economy and Society* 3(4): 429–50.

(1984) 'War, imperialism and the state system: a critique of orthodox Marxism for the 1980s' in M. Shaw (ed.) *War, State and Society*. London: Macmillan, pp. 47–70.

(1987) 'The rise and fall of the military-democratic state, 1945–85' in M. Shaw and C. Creighton (eds.) *The Sociology of War and Peace*. London: Macmillan, pp. 143–158.

(1988) *Dialectics of War: an Essay in the Social Theory of Total War and Peace*. London: Pluto.

(1989) 'War and the nation-state' in D. Held and J.B. Thompson (eds.) *The Social Theory of Modern Societies: Anthony Giddens and his Critics*. Cambridge: Cambridge University Press, pp. 129–46.

(1991) *Post-Military Society: Demilitarization, Militarism and War at the End of the Twentieth Century*. Cambridge: Polity.

(1994) *The Global State and the Politics of Intervention*. London: LSE Centre for the Study of Global Governance.

(1996) *Civil Society and Media in Global Crises: Representing Distant Violence*. London: Pinter.

(1997) 'The state of globalization: towards a theory of state transformation', *Review of International Political Economy* 4(3): 497–513.

(ed.) (1999) *Politics and Globalisation: Knowledge, Ethics, Agency.* London: Routledge.

(2000a) 'Media and public opinion in international relations' in B. Nacos and R. Shapiro (eds.) *Decision-Making in a Glass House: Media, Public Opinion and American and European Foreign Policy.* Boulder: Rowman & Littlefield.

(2000b) 'The state of international relations' in S. Owen-Vandersluit (ed.) *State and Identity Construction in International Relations,* London: Macmillan, pp. 7–30.

(2000c) 'The unfinished global revolution: intellectuals and the new politics of international relations'. The global site, http://www.sussex.ac.uk/Users/hafa3/unfinished.pdf.

(2001) 'Social democracy in the unfinished global revolution' in L. Martell (ed.) *The Future of Social Democracy.* London: Macmillan.

Shaw, M.N. (1997) *International Law.* Cambridge: Cambridge University Press.

Sklair, L. (1991) *Sociology of the Global System.* Hemel Hempstead: Harvester-Wheatsheaf.

Skocpol, T. (1979) *States and Social Revolutions.* Cambridge: Cambridge University Press.

Smart, B. (1993) *Postmodernity.* London: Routledge.

Smith, A.D. (1986) *The Ethnic Origins of Nations.* Oxford: Blackwell.

(1990) 'Towards a global culture?' in M. Featherstone (ed.) *Global Culture: Nationalism, Globalization and Modernity.* London: Sage, pp. 171–91.

(1991) *Nationalism and National Identity.* Harmondsworth: Penguin.

(1995) *Nations and Nationalism in a Global Era.* Cambridge: Polity.

Smith, P.M. and Warr, K. (eds.) (1991) *Global Environmental Issues.* London: Hodder & Stoughton.

Smith, S. (1995) 'The self-images of a discipline: a genealogy of international relations theory' in K. Booth and S. Smith (eds.) *International Relations Theory Today.* Cambridge: Polity, pp. 1–37.

Sørenson, G. (1997) 'An analysis of contemporary statehood: consequences for conflict and cooperation', *Review of International Studies* 23: 253–70.

Stonor Saunders, F. (1999) *Who Paid the Piper? The CIA and the Cultural Cold War.* Oxford: Granta.

Strange, S. (1996) *The Retreat of the State: the Diffusion of Power in the Contemporary World Economy.* Cambridge: Cambridge University Press.

Sweezy, P.M. (1967) *The Theory of Capitalist Development.* New York: Monthly Review.

Taggart, P. (1999) 'Comparison, cleavages and cycles: politics and the European Union' in M. Shaw (ed.) *Politics and Globalisation.* London: Routledge, pp. 89–98.

Taylor, P.I. (1996) 'Embedded statism and the social sciences: opening up to new spaces', *Environment and Planning A* 28: 1917–28.

Tehranian, M. (1999) *Global Communication and World Politics.* London: Lynne Reiner.

Therborn, G. (1977) 'The rule of capital and the rise of democracy', *New Left Review* 103: 3–42.

Thompson, E.P. (1967) *The Making of the English Working Class*. London: Gollancz.

—— (1981) *Beyond the Cold War*. London: European Nuclear Disarmament.

—— (1982) 'Notes on exterminism, the highest stage of civilization' in *New Left Review* (ed.) *Exterminism and Cold War*, London: Verso.

—— (1991) 'Ends and histories' in M. Kaldor (ed.) *Europe from Below*. London: Verso, pp. 7–26.

Thucydides (1972) *History of the Peloponnesian War*. Harmondsworth: Penguin.

Thurston, A. (1988) *Enemies of the People: the Ordeal of the Intellectuals in China's Great Cultural Revolution*. Cambridge, Mass.: Harvard University Press.

Tismaneanu, V. (1990) *In Search of Civil Society: Independent Peace Movements in the Soviet Bloc*. New York: Routledge.

Tomlinson, J. (1990) *Cultural Imperialism: a Critical Introduction*. London: Pinter.

Tonneson, S. (1991) *The Vietnamese Revolution of 1945: Roosevelt, Ho Chi Minh and De Gaulle in a World at War*. London: Sage.

Touraine, A. (1971) *The May Movement: Revolt and Reform*. New York: Random House.

—— (1983) *Solidarity: the Analysis of a Social Movement*. Cambridge: Cambridge University Press.

Trotsky, L. (1960) *Literature and Revolution*. Ann Arbor: University of Michigan Press.

—— (1965a) *History of the Russian Revolution*. London: Gollancz.

—— (1965b) *The Revolution Betrayed*. New York: Pathfinder.

Underhill, G. (1994) 'Introduction: conceptualizing the changing global order' in R. Stubbs and G. Underhill (eds.) *Political Economy and the Changing Global Order*. London: Macmillan, pp. 17–44.

Van Creveld, M. (1991) *The Transformation of War*. New York: Free Press.

—— (1999) *The Rise and Decline of the State*. Cambridge: Cambridge University Press.

Van der Pijl, K. (1984) *The Making of a Transatlantic Ruling Class*. London: Verso.

—— (1998) *Transnational Class Formation*. London: Routledge.

Von Laue, T. (1994) 'Globalism and counter-globalism: present trends and the future' in A. Clesse (ed.) *The International System after the Collapse of the East–West Order*. Dordrecht.

Wæver, O. (1993) 'Societal security' in B. Buzan and O. Wæver (eds.) *Identity, Migration and the New Security Agenda in Europe*. London: Pinter, pp. 17–58.

Walker, M. (1986) *The Waking Giant: the Soviet Union under Gorbachev*. London: Michael Joseph.

Walker, R.B.J. (1993) *Inside-Outside*. Cambridge: Cambridge University Press.

Walker, T. (ed.) (1991) *Revolution and Counterrevolution in Nicaragua*. Boulder: Westview.

Wallace, W. (1996) 'Truth and power, monks and technocrats: theory and practice in international relations', *Review of International Studies* 22: 301–21.

Wallace, W. and Clarke, R. (1986) *Comecon, Trade and the West*. London: Pinter.

Wallerstein, I. (1979) *The Capitalist World Economy: Studies in Modern Capitalism*. Cambridge: Cambridge University Press.

(1991) *Unthinking Social Science: the Limits of Nineteenth Century Paradigms*. Cambridge: Cambridge University Press.

Waltz, K.N. (1979) *Theory of International Politics*. Reading, Mass.: Addison-Wesley.

Weber, C. (1992) 'Reconsidering statehood: examining the sovereignty-intervention boundary', *Review of International Studies* 18: 213–16.

Weber, M. (1965) *The Sociology of Religion*. London: Methuen.

(1978) *Economy and Society*. Berkeley: University of California Press.

Weiss, L. (1998) *The Myth of the Powerless State*. Cambridge: Polity.

Weiss, T. and Gordenker, L. (eds.) (1996) *NGOs, the UN and Global Governance*. Boulder: Lynne Reiner.

Wendt, A. (1987) 'The agent-structure problem in international relations theory', *International Organization* 41(3): 335–70.

(1992) 'Anarchy is what states make of it: the social construction of power politics', *International Organization* 46: 391–425.

(1997) 'Identity and change in international politics' in Y. Lapid and F. Krachtowil (eds.) *The Return of Culture and Identity in International Relations*. London: Lynne Reiner, pp. 47–64.

(1999) *Social Theory of International Politics*. Cambridge: Cambridge University Press.

Westergaard, J. and Resler, H. (1975) *Class in a Capitalist Society: a Study of Contemporary Britain*. London: Heinemann.

Wheaton, B. and Kavan, Z. (1992) *The Velvet Revolution: Czechoslovakia 1988–91*. Boulder: Westview.

White, L. (1993) *The Policies of Chaos: the Organizational Causes of Violence in China's Cultural Revolution*. Princeton: Princeton University Press.

Whitehead, L. (1996) 'Concerning international support for democracy in the South' in R. Luckham and G. White (eds.) *Democratization and the South: the Jagged Wave*. Manchester: Manchester University Press, pp. 243–73.

Whitfield, S. (1996) *The Culture of the Cold War*. Baltimore: The Johns Hopkins University Press.

Wiener, J. (1999) *Globalization and the Harmonization of Law*. London: Pinter.

Wight, M. (1977) *Systems of States*. Leicester: Leicester University Press.

Williams, R. (1958) *Culture and Society 1780–1950*. Harmondsworth: Penguin.

(1961) *The Long Revolution*. Harmondsworth: Penguin.

Wollstonecraft, M. (1982) *A Vindication of the Rights of Women*. Harmondsworth: Penguin.

Worsley, P. (1967) *The Third World*. London: Weidenfeld & Nicolson.

References

Wylie, G. (1999) 'Social movements and international change: the case of "detente from below"', *International Journal of Peace Studies* 4(2): 61–82.

Yost, D. (1998) *NATO Transformed: the Alliance's New Roles in International Security.* Washington, DC: United States Institute of Peace.

Young, O. (ed.) (1997) *Global Governance: Drawing Insights from the Environmental Experience.* Cambridge, Mass.: MIT Press.

Index

Index

Burma 164
Buzan, B. 91–2

Cambodia 111, 115, 141–2, 161–2
Canada 239, 241, 251
Capital (Marx) 37
capital, capitalism 34–42, 44–5, 84–90, 117, 125–6, 182–4, 243
Carr, E.H. 54
Castro, F. 111
categories, social 173
Ceaușescu, N. 154–5
Cederman, L. 211
Central Africa 241
Cerny, P. 125–6
change 1–9
Charter 77: 149, 150
Chechnya 157–8, 235, 238
Chiapas 235
Chile 162, 224, 250
China 142, 157, 161, 164, 208, 209, 214, 217, 227, 236, 241, 253, 256, 261, 267
Chinese revolution, Communism 16, 110, 111, 115, 117
Christian democracy 114, 249
citizenship, internationalized 249–50, 252
Civic Forum 155
civil society 40, 144, 196, 263
civil war 62–6, 79, 169
Clapham, C. 226
Clark, I. 95, 101, 104–5, 122, 126, 130, 133, 166, 192n, 246
'clash of civilizations' 56, 168
class, classes 28, 35, 38, 45–6, 54
Clausewitz, K. von 59–61, 62, 106
coalitions 242
Cold War, Cold War system 52, 53, 58, 76, 116, 118–20, 124–33, 239, 244
 and European integration 247
 democratic revolution and 133–43
 end of 76, 145–51, 214
 ideologies 123
 mindsets 260
 see also bloc; Second Cold War
commonality 25–6, 50, 69, 121–3, 124, 169, 231
Commonwealth 240, 252
Commonwealth of Independent States 235
communications studies 75–6
Communism, Communist parties 64, 66, 96, 110–15, 120, 123, 126, 130, 134–5, 136–7, 140, 147, 154, 156–7, 161, 196, 261
 see also Stalinism
comparative method 69–70, 72–3

Comte, A. 58, 106
conglomerate 243
Congo 113, 163
conservatism 249
constitutive theory 78
constructivism (international relations) 56–7, 78
contact groups 242
Cooper, R. 212–13
corporations 55, 187, 250
cosmopolitan nation 202
cosmopolitanism 34, 72
Cox, M. 129, 131, 151, 152–3
Cox, R. 84–5, 87, 93, 263–4
Crefeld, Martin van 83
Croatia, Croatians 79, 158–60, 211–12, 235, 238
counterrevolution 17, 64, 157–8
critical international theory 89
critique 20
Cuba 111, 123, 145, 161
cultural Revolution 140
cultural studies 76
culture 47–51, 174–9
 and international relations 55–6
 in globality 174–9
Cumings, B. 164
Cyprus 113
Cyprus, Northern 238
Czech Republic 155
Czechoslovakia 66, 134, 138, 149, 154, 155
Czempiel, E.-O. 88

Dalby, S. 75
Debray, R. 141
Declaration of Independence 31
Declaration of Rights of Man 31
democracy, democracies 38, 72, 112–13, 123, 135, 166–7, 266
democratic revolution 133–7, 142–3, 146–7, 160–70
democratization 120, 132–3, 162, 166–7, 234–6
dependency 198, 252
Derrida, J. 4
détente 5, 53, 82
deterrence 119
Deutscher, I. 63
development studies 75
Dicken, P. 126
divisions, in human society 26
Doyle, M. 203
Durkheim, E. 58
Dutch battalion (Srebrenica) 251
Dutch empire 113

CAMBRIDGE STUDIES IN INTERNATIONAL RELATIONS